The Practical Guide to Sales & Marketing Management

GENE GAROFALO

PRENTICE HALL

Library of Congress Cataloging-in-Publication Data

Garofalo, Gene.
    The practical guide to sales and marketing management / by Gene
Garofalo.
      p. cm.
    Includes index.
    ISBN 0-13-775867-7 (cloth)
    1. Sales management. 2. Marketing—Management. I. Title.
HF5438.4.G368   1998   98-26482
658.8—dc21   CIP

Printed in the United States of America

10 9 8 7 6 5 4 3 2 1

ISBN 0-13-775867-7

90000

9 780137 758678

ATTENTION: CORPORATIONS AND SCHOOLS

Prentice Hall books are available at quantity discounts with bulk purchase for educational,
business, or sales promotional use. For information, please write to: Prentice Hall Special Sales,
240 Frisch Court, Paramus, New Jersey 07652. Please supply: title of book, ISBN number,
quantity, how the book will be used, date needed.

PRENTICE HALL
Paramus, NJ 07652

A Simon & Schuster Company

On the World Wide Web at http://www.phdirect.com

Prentice Hall International (UK) Limited, *London*
Prentice Hall of Australia Pty. Limited, *Sydney*
Prentice Hall Canada Inc., *Toronto*
Prentice Hall Hispanoamericana, S.A., *Mexico*
Prentice Hall of India Private Limited, *New Delhi*
Prentice Hall of Japan, Inc., *Tokyo*
Simon & Schuster Asia Pte. Ltd., *Singapore*
Editora Prentice Hall do Brasil, Ltda., *Rio de Janeiro*

CONTENTS

Chapter Two
The Role of Advertising   29

Chapter Three
Promotion and Public Relations   71

Chapter Four
Product Development   86

Chapter Five
Price and Profit   112

Chapter Six
Direct Marketing   138

Chapter Seven
Marketing and the Competition   152

Chapter Eight
Fingers in the Wind: Market Research   170

Chapter Nine
Market Share Strategies   190

PART TWO: THE MISSION OF SALES

Chapter Ten
The Sales Process Explained   207

Chapter Eleven
What Goes On in the Sales Department   220

Chapter Twelve
What Goes On in Outside Sales   246

Chapter Thirteen
What Goes On in Inside Sales   269

Chapter Fourteen
Compensation Plans Explained   282

Chapter Fifteen
Sales Meetings, Training, and Trade Shows   293

Chapter Sixteen
The Care and Feeding of Customers   306

Chapter Seventeen
Selling to Major Accounts
and Government Agencies   318

Chapter Eighteen
How to Sell   336

Bonus Section
Start-Up Sales and Marketing:
A Primer for Entrepreneurs   349

Index   375

PREFACE

Sales and marketing are partners in a perpetual tango. Like all dance partners, their performances depend upon one another. A virtuoso performer may make a mediocre partner look better for a time, but seasoned observers (such as senior management) always can tell which one is being "carried." Yet most of the available material on sales and marketing treat each discipline as if it were a separate and distinct entity, unrelated, except in a casual way, to its dance partner. The purpose of this book is not only to explore the intimate relationship between sales and marketing, but to offer down-to-earth advice on how managers with the responsibility for these departments can become better partners and work together to improve their performance.

This is a practical guide for hands-on managers. Marketing strategy and sales tactics are explained simply and in detail. We also concentrate on the nitty-gritty, time-consuming mountain of detail that takes up most of a manager's time. We tackle the headaches that keep managers working late. These are the problems which aren't covered in business-school marketing classes or offered in sales-management training courses.

In dance, one partner leads. That role is marketing's responsibility. Our first chapter explains how marketing plans are developed and implemented; describes various marketing, positioning, and pricing strategies; reviews the importance of test marketing; and even "walks" the marketing manager through the concept of "value added" and the critical task of budget preparation. The follow-up chapters cover advertising, promotion and public relations, product development, market share strategies, market research, and others. This section provides solid, practical advice on the thousand duties that are part of every marketing manager's responsibility.

Sales follows marketing's lead, but is far from a robotlike partner. The sales manager's role is not only to bring in the requisite number of orders, but to deliver them at a profit. This is far from a simple assignment. The sales manager's important mission requires hiring, managing, and training a sales force; assigning quotas; developing compensation plans; monitoring activity; motivating personnel; preparing proposals; gathering intelligence on the competition; personally handling important customers; keeping a lid on expenses; putting out brush fires; and much more.

There's never enough time to accomplish all these tasks. Many sales managers find themselves overwhelmed by the paperwork requirements of their jobs. We offer tested ideas, helpful tips, and suggestions that will allow sales managers to spend more time in the field in front of customers and less time at a desk shuffling papers.

Our bonus section on start-up marketing and sales provides advice on how new business owners can take simple steps to get their enterprises off to a quick start. Our included worksheets encourage would-be entrepreneurs to analyze their chances for acquiring customers, and hence their chances for success, before opening the doors for business.

This comprehensive material is designed so that sales and marketing can better understand one another and are dancing to the same rhythms. It will be useful for new and experienced marketing and sales managers who find that their positions require a hurry-up, self-taught (or self-inflicted) on-the-job training course. Veteran managers will find the material useful as a reference and a refresher, or to color in gray areas. For the one-person show, the business run out of a home, and the person who wears both the sales manager's and the marketing manager's hat, this book is invaluable.

Introduction

ALLIES AND ADVERSARIES: THE DIFFERENCES BETWEEN SALES AND MARKETING

Sales and marketing are like the fictional Corsican Brothers who felt one another's pains and pleasures even when physically separated. These two departments are locked together through triumphs and defeats. If psychiatrists analyzed business organizations they might even view sales and marketing as classical "codependents" who feed upon and sometimes resent one another. It is this mutual dependency for the success of their respective missions that in some organizations leads to synergy of purpose and effort and in others degenerates into back-room squabbles.

Sales and marketing have different but related charters. Marketing's responsibilities are to chart the course for the company's success, set the policies, develop the systems and programs, and plot the strategies. In other words, marketing does the planning.

Marketing managers worry about market share, national rollouts, sales channels, profit margins, and product mix. If there is a single question that occupies every marketing manager's mind, it is "Where will tomorrow's customers come from?"

If marketing is about strategy, then sales is about tactics. Sales managers are "hands-on" operational people. They are the managers in charge of the troops out on the front line. Theory is okay, but it takes second chair to the realities of the marketplace.

The sales manager's responsibility is to accomplish what marketing proposes. The sales manager has to make those darn marketing plans work.

Sales managers worry about sales volume, making quotas, acquiring and retaining big customers, and keeping the sales force in line. If there is a single question that occupies every sales manager's mind, it is "Where will today's orders come from?"

In most organizations, the director of marketing is a shade higher in the corporate pecking order than the director of sales. As planners rather than executors, their duties are considered more cerebral, and this often gives them more access to the corporate boardroom. Often, the sales manager reports to the director of marketing. The reason for this structure is to make certain that marketing's plans are carried out. Sales is considered a marketing function like any other.

When things go well and the company is achieving its goals, the relationship between the two departments is honey sweet. Success stimulates camaraderie. When things go badly, as when goals are not being met, the relationship often sours. Sales blames marketing for the plan. Marketing blames sales for the implementation. Failure stimulates recriminations. Of course when sales reports to marketing, there is no question of who wins the argument.*

In the best companies, sales and marketing cooperate through good times and bad. They share success and failure. When things go well they share credit. When things go badly, they jointly go to work to fix what is wrong. One of the ways this cooperation can be achieved is through a thorough understanding of the functions of both entities, what they are trying to accomplish, and the obstacles they face. This book offers that insight.

---

*Harvard Business School's excellent MBA program teaches that when a marketing plan does not produce expected results, the reason is usually poor implementation. In other words, the plan is never wrong. Of course Harvard teaches the planners and not the implementers, so it's no surprise which side they would choose.

Part One

THE MISSION
OF MARKETING

Chapter One

WHAT THE DIRECTOR
OF MARKETING DOES

PLANNING AND STRATEGY

"When a man does not know what harbor he is making for, no wind is
the right wind."

Seneca (4 B.C.-A.D. 65)

All marketing begins with the question, "Where will the customers
come from?" The director of marketing's job is to find the answers to that
question. That's a simplistic explanation to what the director of marketing
does, but it's accurate. Marketing is nothing more than figuring out where
the customers will come from and then making it attractive for them to come
to you. The second part, making customers come to you, is very difficult.
Thinking of ways to attract customers, both for today and tomorrow,
naturally leads to market planning and strategy.

Planning means pointing the organization in a particular direction and
then drawing a map that highlights the route that will get the company
there. Like all long-distance journeys, there will be stopovers, detours,
unexpected obstacles, and a few fortuitous shortcuts.

To begin planning, the marketer has a laundry list of deceptively
simple questions that help determine where the customers will come from.
These questions are:

1. What products will we offer?
2. What kinds of companies or individuals buy these kinds of products?

3

3. What do these prospects have in common?
4. Where can these prospects be found?
5. What do they want?
6. Who sells to them now?
7. What could we do to encourage them to buy from us?

These questions are simple, but the answers are complicated. The very identity of the company is determined by how it answers these questions.

Let's begin with the question at the top of the list: What products will we offer? Most companies are born because the founder, what we call an "entrepreneur," has an idea for a product or service. An opportunity is seen and exploited. Often, this idea is in the form of a perceived marketing advantage.

Here's a simple example of how this process works in real life: A man in need of having his pants cleaned and pressed walks four city blocks before he can find a dry cleaner. He recognizes an opportunity in the form of an empty storefront midway in his return journey. The man rents the store and opens a dry-cleaning shop.

What our entrepreneur has done is basic market research. His methods, observation and a shoe-leather survey, may not be sophisticated but they can be effective. His product, a dry-cleaning service, has been determined by the results of the survey. He's identified a need. He hasn't done enough planning, but it is a beginning.

Our dry cleaner has made the assumption that his customers will come from the immediate surrounding area. That is a reasonable assumption. His marketing strategy is proximity of the shop to nearby customers. That's not bad strategy either. Convenience is a powerful marketing tool. F.W. Woolworth, a legendary marketer, said, "I'm the world's worst salesman so I must make it easy for my customers to buy." One of the marketing manager's important tasks is to make it easy for customers to buy.

Customers won't continue to come to the dry cleaner, or any other business, if that business doesn't offer value in addition to proximity. Providing value and retaining customers, however, are separate issues, and we'll review these marketing problems later.

The cleaner has decided on a product and location and now should try to identify his prospect base. He could do a demographic study to determine the age, income level, and education of the residents in the area—maybe even including the kind of cars they drive—but in this instance that isn't necessary. Customer identification for our entrepreneur is simple. His prospect base is everyone in the area who needs dry cleaning. Most prospects will be found within walking distance of the shop. What the prospects have in common is locality and soiled clothes.

From this point on, the marketing questions get harder. What do the prospects want from a local dry cleaner? Sure, they want their clothes cleaned, but that's not all. Different preferences begin to emerge.

Some prospects will want the job done for the lowest price possible.

Some prefer a dry cleaner that is open for long hours so they can drop off clothes before and after work.

Some prospects prefer a dry cleaner that handles tailoring and minor sewing repairs.

Some want personalized services such as home pickup, delivery, and fast turnaround.

Some want high-quality work and custom cleaning services on designer gowns, delicate fabrics, wedding dresses, expensive draperies, and so forth.

Each type of customer has a different requirement, or a different desire, which is really the same thing. These requirements can be separated into marketing segments or "targets."

Determining which of these services to provide are marketing decisions that will eventually define the company and identify the customers who will patronize it. The dry cleaner who offers cut-rate prices on pressing men's pants is not likely to be patronized by the society woman who needs her Dior gown cleaned and blocked for a night at the opera.

Our entrepreneur can also make the assumption that his prospects are currently taking their business to other dry cleaners. There may be several competitors in the vicinity, though our entrepreneur may not have noticed them. What do those competitors offer that has made them successful? What can our dry cleaner offer that the competitors do not? Evaluating the competition and determining how to beat it is another marketing task.

Even if he has the local "exclusive franchise," people in the area have been taking their clothes elsewhere for years. Now, our entrepreneur faces a typical marketing problem: getting people to make a change. Inertia is a powerful force. People keep doing what they are doing simply because they are used to doing it. What, other than convenience, could induce local dry-cleaning customers to change their habits? We, all of us, need a good reason to change. What could induce prospects to patronize our dry cleaner? Finding reasons for people to change is yet another marketing challenge.

One of the most common responses to competitive pressure is offering a lower price. This is particularly true in industries where many competitors offer similar products or services. It is up to the marketing managers to set competitive prices. When doing so they must ensure that these prices allow sufficient profit margins to sustain and grow the business. Some marketers set prices very low to discourage competition. Setting prices just right is one of the most difficult marketing challenges.

For our dry cleaner, the first step to attract customers is to make prospects aware of the business and of the services it offers. This phase of marketing is called *advertising*. There are many definitions of advertising. The one we like best was offered by Fairfax Cone. He said, "Advertising is what you do when you can't go see somebody." Our dry cleaner can't visit every prospect in the area so he has to use some other method to let them know about his business.

In its broadest sense, advertising includes everything from a sign in the window to a one-minute television spot during the Super Bowl. The marketing manager must decide which method will be most effective for the product or service that is being offered. He or she must also decide how much money can be spent on the advertising campaign. The advertising must also be appropriate for the business and it must be cost-effective.

Our dry cleaner might decide on handbills distributed in the local area. They are simple and inexpensive, and they are appropriate in this instance because they get the news out directly to potential customers.

The dry cleaner also wants to make it easy for customers to distinguish his shop from all other dry cleaners. He may attempt to do so by using a distinctive business name, a catchy slogan, an attractive logo, a bright sign, an unusual interior store design, a service not offered by others, a particular attitude, or some such. This kind of marketing effort is called *building an image*.

To encourage prospects to try his shop, the dry cleaner might offer an opening-week special. For example, he might offer to clean two garments for the price of one for any customer who brings in the handbill. This is called a *sales promotion*. Promotions are often used to bring the public's attention to a new business or product or to increase sales volumes for limited periods. Requiring customers to bring in the handbill to take advantage of the offer also tests the effectiveness of the advertising. Testing programs are important to make sure that advertising dollars are well spent.

If the dry cleaner had elected to give something away to each new customer, say a traveling sewing kit, this is called *offering a sales premium*. Premiums are intended to give the impression of something for nothing. They are another form of advertising.

The dry cleaner may elect to offer his services to all the tuxedo rental shops in the area. If successful, the dry cleaner has found another *sales channel* for his services. Choosing appropriate sales channels is another of the marketing manager's many responsibilities.

To establish himself in the community, the dry cleaner may offer to clean the uniforms of the local high-school cheerleading team at no charge. He's establishing *goodwill* and engaging in public relations. Too often, new entrepreneurs will ignore this important marketing function. A positive local image may be even more important to a small company than to a corporate behemoth.

How much dry-cleaning equipment should the entrepreneur buy? The answer, of course, depends upon how many customers will patronize his shop and how much work comes through the door. Determining how much business will come through the door is called *forecasting*. It is another important marketing responsibility. The production end of any business depends upon accurate forecasting. Forecasting is particularly difficult for new companies that have no history on which to base business estimates.

The dry cleaner may not have a firm handle on the number of customers who will patronize his shop, but he can set goals. *Establishing targets*, and then making sure those targets are reached, is a basic marketing function.

In our example the entrepreneur dry cleaner wears all the marketing hats. He's the one responsible for the basic market research, for the product line decisions, for identifying potential customers, for investigating and outsmarting the competition, for selecting the advertising, for working out the advertising budget, for building a company image, for setting goals, for forecasting the amount of business that will come through the door, and for doing all the other things that directors of marketing do. Every small business person who hopes for success must pay attention to these functions. They are only a few of any marketer's myriad responsibilities. He or she has many more.

In larger companies these tasks take up enough time so that they are handled by a staff of personnel who report to the director of marketing. A very large corporation may not only have an advertising manager, but a complete department filled with people who devote all their time to the company's advertising. A multiproduct company may employ many managers, each of whom are responsible for the care and feeding of a single product category. These people are called product managers. They all report to the director of marketing, who supervises their activities. In many organizations the sales manager, and thus the entire sales team, also reports to the director of marketing. In others, the reporting structure is reversed.

The director of marketing of any organization, from a dry cleaner to a Fortune 1000 company, has a full plate indeed. Marketers really determine the destiny of the company. In small and large companies alike, lack of marketing vision can be fatal. Market strategy must continually change. Marketing is one of the most important jobs in any organization. That's the overview—now, let's get down to the details.

Market-directed versus product-directed planning: The first critical decision

There are two basic marketing philosophies. The first takes the stance, "Let's provide a product or service we're good at providing and then go out and show the marketplace why they need it." The director of marketing is given the product and told to find customers who need it.

This approach is called *product-directed planning*—build it and they will come. It offers many advantages: production is less expensive and more efficient because it is planned far in advance; scheduling is easier; arrangements and negotiations with suppliers are more definite; profit margins can be calculated to four places after the decimal point. In fact, with a product-directed planning system everyone in the organization has an easier job—except the director of marketing. He or she must convince the marketplace that this product is absolutely indispensable.

The problem with product-directed planning is that it sometimes ignores the realities of the marketplace. When the marketplace does not embrace the product, or loses enchantment with it, the product begins to stack up in the warehouse. There is no fall-back plan. When the warehouse is filled to the rafters, the product is sold at a deep discount and there go those profit margins.

Product-directed planning also seems to foster a rigid mentality. Production managers run the show. The production line is geared toward building a certain configuration, and design changes are not only expensive, but, according to the production boss, they are quite impossible to even contemplate, much less incorporate: "What? You want it in white? We'll have to shut down the production line for a month just to gear up!"

Product-directed planning works best with commodity-type products for which the need is always apparent. There's no problem finding potential customers. These products, however, always attract the most competitors.

In true commodities it is difficult to distinguish one product from another. The petroleum companies spend tens of millions telling consumers why their product is superior, but 89 octane gasoline is 89 octane gasoline is 89 octane gasoline.

HOW TO SUCCEED IN COMMODITY PRODUCT MARKETING

The keys to succeeding in commodity product marketing are to capture dominant market share and to become the low-cost producer. These two things work in tandem. The market-share leader dictates the rules of the marketplace, and the low-cost producer sets the product price. The volume is needed to lower costs. Lower costs are necessary to reduce prices and increase volume.

The product-directed marketer says, "I have what you need and I can tell you why you need it." The *market-directed* marketer has a different philosophy. He or she says, "Tell me what you want and I'll get it for you" That's a different attitude. It relies on the marketplace to determine the direction of the product line.

Market-directed planning starts with the question, "What does the market want, both today and tomorrow?" Then the marketer goes about providing those products.

Market-directed marketing brings its own set of problems. Building products on demand taxes the management skills of any organization. It requires more corporate agility, a different mind-set, more research, more ability to predict the future, and more daring. That means greater risk. It also means greater opportunity.

Deciding which method to adopt is the first critical marketing crossroad. We can't help you out by recommending one method over the other. They both have their advantages and handicaps. Today, neither method is seldom found in a pure form—the purists are all out of jobs. Both methods require modification. Companies can't be completely rigid, nor can they risk everything on untested products. In fact, marketers frequently borrow the best traits of each into a blend that works for their organizations. That is a recommendation we can make.

How marketing plans are developed

Market plans are maps showing the way to the future. In most companies they are a combination of stocktaking, of past performance, of reasonable expectations for the future, and wishful thinking. They're necessary because planning gives a company its direction. Planning sets the course and establishes the objectives.

Twenty questions that help a marketer plan

Remember the popular parlor game, Twenty Questions? Here's a list of twenty marketing questions every marketer should ask at the beginning of every planning period. They are broad-brush questions, but the details necessary for a successful marketing plan can't be developed until the marketer understands these fundamental things about the business.

1. What business are we in?
2. What industry are we in?
3. What products or services do we offer?
4. Who uses these products or services?
5. What other kinds of customers could be using these products or services?
6. How could we reach these new customers?
7. How do we sell our products?
8. What other methods or sales channels could we use to sell our products?
9. What competition do we have?
10. How do our products or services differ from our competitors'?
11. How could we make the distinction between us and our competitors even stronger?
12. How much business did we do last year?
13. How much business shall we plan to do next year?
14. What resources must we allocate to make this plan happen?
15. What products will take us to our goal?
16. What new products must we develop to reach our goal?
17. Which customers will help us reach our goal?

18. How can we reach new customers?
19. What are we doing now that is not working?*
20. What are we doing now that should be expanded?*

The answers to these questions set the marketer in the right direction. They bring marketing's problems, and opportunities, into sharp focus.

Let's see how the marketer can use the answers to the twenty questions to develop a marketing plan. To questions 8 and 16, the marketer of a clothing manufacturer who sells to high-fashion department stores might decide to develop a separate, low-cost line of clothes to be sold through mass-merchants. Not a bad strategy. This new channel might help increase total sales volume. Question 14 now becomes critical. What resources is the company prepared to allocate to make this plan work?

HOW MARKETING PLANS ARE COMMUNICATED

In many organizations, marketing makes the promises and other departments deliver on them. That frequently puts marketing on an adversarial basis with every other department in the company. One way to reduce this friction is to share objectives. Marketing plans are not meant to be locked in the company safe. They are most effective when they are communicated to others in the organization. The more honest communication about the plan, the better chance it will have at success. What form that communication takes may differ according to the level of management. Not everyone in the company is interested in the same things. For example, when communicating with senior-level management, the marketer might offer the following:

- Overall goals of the marketing plan.
- A summary of the complete plan.
- Requested details. (Only on request: The more detail offered, the more likely the people upstairs will micromanage the plan.)
- The budget needed to make the plan work.

---

*Questions 19 and 20 aren't asked often enough by market planners. Plans must be reviewed periodically and corrections made when necessary. Sometimes that correction involves an expansion of a successful program.

To peers in the management organization who provide needed support, the marketing manager might reveal:

- Details of the plan that require the peer's cooperation.
- Changes that affect the peer's operation.
- The reasons why these changes are being made.

To staff members and support personnel who report to the marketing manager, the marketer might reveal:

- Overall goals.
- Specific objectives each staff member is expected to achieve.
- The staff member's role in making the plan work.

The marketing manager has communicated to each group what they need to know and what they want to know. The latter part is important to ensure cooperation. Share objectives and goals with everyone in the organization who is interested.

HOW MARKETING PLANS ARE IMPLEMENTED: A SEVEN-STEP PROCESS

The devil is in the details. Marketing plans don't work on paper. They must be implemented. The following is a seven-step implementation program.

1. In most companies, implementation begins with getting budget approval for the marketing plan from senior management. Even if the business is a one-person operation, that one person must decide if the plan makes economic sense.

2. After budget approval, publish the plan's objectives to everyone in the marketing organization. Let the troops know where the company is headed.

3. Review what needs to get done. See what steps can be taken out of the process to get the plan into action more quickly. In other words, take short cuts.

4. Sweep the micromanagers and bean-counters out of the way— under the rug if possible. Sure, fiscal responsibility must be exercised, but put the planners, not the naysayers in control.

5. To hit the ground running, do things simultaneously. Don't wait for one project to be completed before going on to another.

6. Let department heads and supervisors run with their responsibilities under the plan. To those managers who don't want micromanagement from above, don't micromanage those who are below.

7. Develop contingency plans. Things don't always work out in practice as they were drawn up on paper. Have benchmarks that put the contingency plans into operation.

FIVE DISTINCT MARKETING STRATEGIES

"Marketing strategy" is an intimidating phrase that can mean anything and everything from where advertising dollars will be spent to where national warehouses will be located to get products to customers faster. In this segment, we have it mean the various sales vehicles through which companies reach their customers.

One of the vital questions faced by every business organization is how to market its products. The product itself may dictate the marketing approach, though suppliers have marketing options with most items. The following are five distinct marketing strategies with their advantages and disadvantages.

1. *Direct selling to potential customers*. The direct sales force are salaried, or commissioned employees, or both who call on end-user prospects. This method offers the company the most control over the marketing effort. Prospects are reached and the company's story is told. It is also a costly method because of the expense of maintaining a direct sales team.

2. *Retailers*. Many consumer products are sold through retailers such as department stores, drug stores, clothing shops, and so forth. The producer's sales force calls on the retailer, but must also create a demand for the product through advertising and promotion. If the product won't move off the shelves, the retailer won't carry it.

3. *Mail order and telemarketing*. Some companies have ignored both direct sales forces and retailers to sell their products directly to consumers via direct mail and telephone. They rely on heavy advertising in newspapers and magazines, or through the distribution of catalogs to potential customers. The phone-book-size all-purpose catalogs put out by companies such Sears, Wards, and J.C. Penney have lost their luster, but smaller, specialty, or high-fashion catalogs are flourishing.

4. *Distributors.* Distributors traditionally stock products in quantity and sell them in smaller batches to other resellers and end users. They normally serve a specific geographic area. The advantage for the manufacturer in using a distributor is that selling costs are low because only a few companies need to be called on. Orders from the distributor are placed in bulk, meaning lower handling costs and fewer credit problems for the manufacturer. The disadvantage is that the distributor seldom creates need for a product; rather, it simply responds to need that already exists.

5. *Manufacturer's and independent agents.* Manufacturer's reps are not employed directly by the company, but work on a straight commission basis and are paid only when successful in moving product. They sell to end users and resellers depending on the product. Often, the independent rep will carry several products. Using these kinds of reps is a good choice for small companies that want national coverage at a low cost. The disadvantage to these arrangements is that the independent rep is just that— independent. The amount of time he or she chooses to spend on the company's product is totally up to the agent. Some areas of the country will get good marketing coverage and other areas will be neglected.

Many companies employ a mixture of these strategies. For example, a company may employ direct salespeople in major metropolitan areas and rely on independent reps to handle smaller communities. Companies may market directly to major retailers, but use distributors to handle smaller accounts.

Which method is best for your company? It depends on the product. As a rule of thumb, in industrial marketing the emphasis is on personal contact and service, which means people on the payroll out there calling on customers. With consumer products the emphasis is on advertising. Selling a national brand door-to-door just wouldn't work. The best strategy is the one that works.

HOW TO CREATE A MARKETING PLAN
FOR ANY ORGANIZATION

Want to ensure failure? Start a company without a written marketing plan— if you can. (It's quite difficult to arrange start-up financing without a marketing plan.) Detailed marketing plans depend upon the product, the industry, and the company history. That allows for countless variations in marketing plans, but they all share several things in common:

1. They detail sales goals, likely prospects, methods for reaching those prospects, time frames, and so forth.
2. They contain a budget of how much the plan will cost.
3. They detail product costs, pricing to customers, and profit margins.
4. They describe the sales channels that will be used.
5. They acknowledge the competitive factors that must be overcome.
6. They're simple to understand. It shouldn't take a marketing genius to follow the plan.
7. They're based on reasonable expectations. In their first year of operation the start-up company shouldn't project to do more business than General Motors. (The all-time record for sales volume by a start-up company in their first year of operation is $100 million by Compaq Computer. That's a figure you entrepreneurs can shoot at.)

Check out your marketing plan. Does it contain all these features? If not, go back and work on the hard parts.

A marketing plan outline

Here's a generic marketing plan outline that will work for any product line and any industry. Just fill in the blanks.

Sales goals

Near-term goals _____ (next quarter, next six months, next year)
Long-term goals _____ (two years, three years, five years)

Profit goals

Near-term profit goals _____
Long-term profit goals _____

Markets

Who are the customers? _____
Where are the customers? _____
Best way to reach the customers? _____
What will influence customers to buy? _____

Products

Product lineup _____
Product contributions to sales _____
Planned product promotions _____
Product pricing _____
Products' contribution to profit _____

Implementation

Who is responsible for what _____
Schedule of events _____
Budget for the plan _____

When that outline has been completed, there is still the work of providing the details and the even harder work of making the plan come true.

EIGHT IDEAS TO DEFINE TARGET MARKETS

The company has a great idea for a new gizmo. It is different from anything else they have ever produced. How does this company identify the target markets that could use or, better yet, absolutely can't do without this gizmo? Here are some ways to go about it:

1. Investigate companies who have a similar product available. Who are they selling to? There's your target market.

2. Check out the obvious. If the company has developed a new automobile fuel pump, the obvious suspects might be auto-parts stores.

3. Look to markets that are similar, but not identical to the ones you now service. For example, if your product is being sold to high-fashion department stores, perhaps a lower-cost item might be sold to discounters.

4. Attend trade shows where similar products are sold. The attendees are your target market. The companies with the booths could be competitors or maybe even distributors for your product.

5. Send out a crack salesperson and tell him or her to investigate target markets. Give a bonus for the first order that comes through the door.

6. Subscribe to relevant trade publications. Look at the advertising to see where it is aimed. Set your sights in the same direction.

7. Look at any orders that the sales crew got by accident. Do they show a pattern?

8. Show the gizmo to everyone you meet. Ask them who could use a device such as this.

How to develop a marketing budget

A marketing budget is the total amount of money that is allocated to move a product; that is, how much money will be spent to get the job done. This is an important planning step. Marketing budgets normally include such factors as the following:

- Direct selling costs.
- Advertising costs.
- Promotional costs.
- Costs for product literature.
- Support and administrative costs.

One simple way to calculate a budget is as a percentage of sales: "We project that we'll do $10,000,000 in sales next year. With a ten-percent marketing budget, that gives us $1,000,000 to spend." One attractive feature about this kind of budget is that the budget can be increased or decreased according to the actual sales figures.

Another simple approach is to take last year's budget and add to it or delete from it based on this year's expectations. This kind of budget can also be adjusted based on actual results.

Zero-based budgets are still another method. They take nothing for granted, but calculate this year's costs based on need. The advantage to this kind of budget is that obsolete programs don't get renewed automatically.

Marketing budgets face an obstacle. That obstacle is the expected rate of return on the money to be invested. If this rate is not compatible with the company's overall profit margin, back to the drawing board. Some managers are more tolerant of new, revolutionary products that offer long-term potential or are prepared to pay an "admission fee" for entry into a new market. In most cases, however, management wants a good rate of return on money spent.

New product budgets

For new products without a track record it's a good idea to provide several budget "scenarios" based on different outcomes. Plug in more money if the product proves to be a roaring success. Turn off the spigot if the product disappoints.

TEST MARKETING: MONITORING RESULTS

New products have a high failure rate. Just ask Ford Motor Company about the Edsel. Customers don't always see the same advantages in that new gizmo that the manufacturer did when it was launched. That's why new products are often test-marketed before "national rollouts." McDonald's, for example, will often test a new sandwich in a small geographic area before putting it on their menu nationwide.

A test market allows companies to get customer reactions to a new product before making a total commitment to the product. Sometimes the test reveals how the product can be changed to make it more acceptable to the public.

In addition to the product itself, various pricing strategies can be tested and advertising and sales channels can be reviewed for their effectiveness. For consumer-oriented products, package designs and counter displays can also be evaluated. All these tests are designed to reduce expensive mistakes. They can never be eliminated.

Problems with test marketing

Test marketing is not a panacea. There are problems with the approach. For one thing, test marketing has become expensive. Good results cost money. Spending $2,000,000 for a reliable test is becoming common.

Test markets also telegraph the company's intentions to the competition. That small, clandestine test in Toledo won't remain a secret from the competition—count on it. In some instances, the competition may even attempt to skew the results so that the company doing the test marketing reaches an incorrect conclusion.

The biggest single negative is that test marketing delays the national introduction of a product. Uncertain marketers often use test markets as an excuse not to pull the trigger on a national campaign. Delay too long, and the caravan passes by.

THE CONCEPT OF "VALUE ADDED"

Value-added is what a company does to a product to increase its worth. For example, a computer supplier may buy components from various manufacturers and assemble them into a complete computer package, including software. The finished package is worth more than the sum total of the components. Selecting the right components, assembling them into a package and installing the software is the supplier's value-added. That value-added represents the supplier's greatest opportunity to make a profit.

Even suppliers, such as wholesalers, who add nothing to a product, but simply pass it along to the next buyer offer a value-added. In their instance it is the warehousing of the product, offering rapid delivery to customers, and maybe even easy terms to small-volume buyers. Those who add no value to products, however, necessarily work on smaller profit margins.

Another interpretation of value-added is to add extra features to a product or service to make it worth more to the customer. For example, that same computer supplier might, at no extra charge, add a toll-free "hotline" that customers with systems problems could call for advice. This additional service might encourage more customers to buy.

Just about every marketing expert in the universe advises putting as much value as possible into a product. Adding value is definitely the way to greater profits.

POSITION MARKETING

Positioning simply means making a product or service stand out from the competition in the minds of potential customers. For example, when thinking of corn flakes, the first brand that comes to most people's mind is Kellogg's. That customer reaction didn't happen all by itself. It is the result of years of work by Kellogg's marketers.

Most marketers try to make their products different than competitive offerings to distinguish them from the others. This is particularly important when the competition is the market leader. Gain entry into the market by going after a market segment that has been ignored. When Toshiba entered the computer marketplace, they decided not to compete head-to-head with IBM, Compaq, Apple, and the others who were well established. Instead, they set a place at the table for themselves by concentrating on what was then a small market segment, laptops. Later, Toshiba used the reputation they established in laptops to back into the desktop market.

Many companies position their products into various market segments via different pricing strategies. For example, they will offer one product version at a premium price through a "high tone" channel, another version at a lower price through traditional retailers, and still another "budget" version through discounters. Often, the main difference in the products offered to these various channels is in their packaging.

Positioning also permits concentration of effort. It is difficult to be all things to all people—just look at the demise of the all-purpose mail-order catalog. By concentrating on specific market segments the company is better able to identify with customers and customers are better able to identify with the company. Reaching the mind of the customer is what positioning is all about.

A razor blade is a razor blade is a razor blade, so what makes a particular product a "lady's razor?" The answer is a razor with a pink handle that comes in a package with pretty flowers on it. By identifying one of their razors as the "Lady Schick," and using "feminine" packaging, the company's marketers are aiming at the female segment of the market. Admittedly, this segment represents half the population, but Schick's marketers are still endeavoring to establish position.

Our dry cleaner who set up a shop in area with few other dry cleaners was establishing physical position. He was hoping to draw customers through offering them convenience. Remember when we wrote about the various kinds of service our dry cleaner might offer? He could get a clue as to the services that might be most effective from the other retail shops in the area. If he were located in a strip mall filled with discounters, he might decide to offer budget dry-cleaning services because price is a major factor to the customers who make up mall traffic. In an upscale area he might decide to specialize in cleaning designer clothes. This is called *business compatibility*.

Another positioning strategy used by retailers is to open a retail business near a cluster of like enterprises. An old, but still valid marketing bromide is that "the best place to open a hat store is on a street filled with hat stores." Customers who are shopping for the item will come to that location because they know they'll be able to choose among many options. This is the concept behind the "restaurant rows" found in many towns. Diners frequent the area because there are many restaurants among which to choose.

THE TEN FACTORS THAT DETERMINE HOW PRICES ARE SET

After determining which products to offer, the most difficult marketing decision is determining how to price those products. In the best of all possible worlds, one simply calculates all the costs associated with providing a product or service, plugs in the desired profit margin, and *voilà!* the magical price appears. Unfortunately, the marketplace, the customer, and those nasty competitors intrude on this paradise. The best product in the world cannot be successful if potential buyers perceive that the price is too high related to the product's value.*

Price is part of the product offer, just as important as product features, its desired position in the marketplace, the package, the name, and everything else associated with the product. Positioning a product involves setting certain price points for different market segments. The factors that influence price include:

1. *The supplier's cost for the product.* Obviously, this is the first number that is plugged into the equation when setting the product's price.

2. *The cost to market the product.* This cost includes all advertising, the packaging and distribution costs, sales expenses, and so forth.

3. *Other company overhead.* What is the "burden" in running the organization?

4. *The value of the product to the end user.* Pricing a product beyond its value to the customer is a recipe for disaster.

5. *Profit margins.* Without adequate profit the rationale for any business disappears.

---

*When a salesperson makes the excuse that a sale was lost because the prospect complained the product's price was too high, the experienced sales manager replies, "You didn't explain its value."

6. *Competitive factors.* Why doesn't General Motors charge $75,000 for their basic, entry-level cars? Because they wouldn't sell any. Ford and Chrysler and the Japanese car companies would take all their business in this market segment. Why don't they leave this segment alone? If GM doesn't sell any entry-level cars, then they won't establish customer loyalty and step-up buyers.

7. *The profit margins needed by resellers.* Certain reseller channels, such as department stores, need specific profit margin levels to continue their operations. Smart suppliers tailor their products and their prices to fit the profit-margin needs of these resellers.

8. *Desired sales volume.* Marketers are able to forecast sales volume depending upon specific price points. They can jack up the volume by cutting price, but then profit margins are often reduced, unless, of course, increasing sales volume lowers production costs. This dilemma of increasing sales at the cost of lowering margins is the classic problem faced by every marketing manager.

9. *Supply and demand, the standard economic classic price adjuster.* The supply of a product is one of the strongest influences on that product's price. The more there is of something, the lower the price of that something will be. Demand declines as prices rise. With products that are considered "necessities," demand doesn't stop entirely no matter how high the price is set.*

10. *How the marketer intends to position the product.* Sometimes the price should be set high. The high-fashion, designer dress will not be well accepted by society women if it is priced too low.

ELEVEN POPULAR PRICING STRATEGIES

How much should we ask for our product? That is one of the most difficult questions the marketing manager must answer. There are many possible approaches. Pricing to beat the competition doesn't always mean lowering the asking price for a product. Sometimes just the opposite is true. The following are eleven popular pricing strategies. There are many others.

---

*High margins for a product influence more suppliers to jump into a market, thus increasing supply and lowering prices.

1. *Pricing high.* In the consumer's mind, price is directly related to quality. The woman shopping at an upscale store expects to get not only a high-fashion dress and personalized service, but a better-made dress with more expensive fabric and superior construction. Some marketers use this expectation when developing pricing strategies. They set the price of their products higher than competitors' pricing to give the impression of high-quality merchandise. The appeal is to conspicuous consumers who want to brag to their friends about spending four figures for that "little black dress."

2. *Pricing according to location.* Setting and location also play a role in product pricing. The shops on New York City's Fifth Avenue and Beverly Hills' Rodeo Drive charge more for their merchandise because of where they are located. The additional markup isn't entirely due to the high rent they pay, but to establish a certain panache. Customers entering one of these shops are treated to deference, plush appointments, a hushed, almost reverent atmosphere, and fawning sales clerks. The display of merchandise is often sparse and behind glass to reinforce the impression that what is offered here is precious and exclusive indeed.

3. *Pricing low and establishing a low-price environment.* Some discounters will use the exact opposite strategy in merchandise display. They maintain a "studied," slightly unkempt store in a low-rent district, stock boxes to the ceiling, use in-store signs blaring bargains, cram products in every corner, and generally appear to be in disarray. They're trying to give the impression of a low-cost, bare-bones, cut-rate operation that is charging the lowest prices possible. The store may appear sloppy and unkempt, but the marketing strategy is just as carefully crafted as the one used by the high-tone shop on Rodeo Drive.

4. *Pricing low to discourage competition.* Low pricing is often used to discourage competition from entering a market. Lower prices also sometimes will cause a marginal competitor to quit the arena. When suppliers keep prices low, would-be competitors realize they must pay a higher price to gain entry, or to remain, into that market. Low prices give competitors lots to think about. Their break-even point is higher, their volumes must be larger, and their chances for success are lower. Some companies who "own" a market will react to any competitive pressure by temporarily reducing their prices even further to knock out that competitor before a toehold can be gained. That's why many companies will not compete with market-share leaders head on, but rather position their products into an ignored niche.

5. *Introductory pricing.* "Introductory" or "trial" pricing is often used by marketers to call attention to and build excitement for a new product and to acquaint customers with it. These prices are usually lower than regular prices and available only for a limited period of time.

6. *Raising prices, then putting the product on sale.* When forced to increase prices because of increased costs or the need for improved margins, some marketers will raise the list price of an item, but then immediately offer that item "for sale" at the old price. So what changes? This "sale" price is only available for a limited period of time. This strategy, almost the direct reverse of introductory low pricing, is meant to get customers accustomed to a new, higher price.

7. *Setting product prices low and supply prices high.* Another popular pricing strategy is to set low prices for the main product, then charge higher prices for peripheral products, supplies, and services. Cellular phones are an example of this pricing technique. Cellular phone suppliers are literally giving away the phones to entice customers to sign up for the very lucrative communication service.

Supplies and service are generally priced at higher margins by most companies. The philosophy is that the customer has the product and must buy the supplies for it and have it serviced. "Captive customers," those committed for some reason to do business with an enterprise, are usually subjected to higher prices. The patron of a remote ski lodge set high in the mountains can't really go anywhere else for breakfast. There's no point in the lodge restaurant offering a $1.99 cheese omelet special. There's every point in that restaurant charging $5.00 for a bowl of corn flakes.

8. *Lowering prices even though margins are reduced.* Some companies, to increase market share, will simply lower prices and hope that greater sales volume will make up for smaller profit margins. The problem with this approach is that lower costs alone do not promote customer loyalty. Those flighty customers who were attracted by the "bargains" are off somewhere else when a new competitor tries the same strategy. The lesson is that pricing can be used to attract customers, but it doesn't work forever in keeping them.

9. *Setting prices on novelty items high.* Pricing of a novelty or fad product is often set high because the supplier realizes that maximum profit must be made in a short period of time. Successful novelties and fads are like Scandinavian summers. Their time on earth is short and sweet. Bask in the sun while there is sun to bask in. Good marketers recognize when a novelty or fad item has just about run its course. They lower the price on existing inventory and cut production.

10. *Pricing a product according to the value it provides.* Some products are priced according to the value they provide the end-user/customer. This pricing strategy is not related to the cost incurred by the product's supplier. Some system-related products that save companies money through reorganization of the work are often priced in this manner. If a new system saves a company one million dollars, it's worth half a million to that company even though it may have cost the system supplier only a few thousand.

11. *Pricing to consumer "resistance points."* Smart marketers know that consumers react to certain price "thresholds." They rush to buy when products drop below that threshold and resist purchasing when they rise above it. For example, computer manufacturers believe there is a vast untapped market of computer buyers for the first company that can deliver a complete user-friendly system for about $500. That's why there's a rush to develop such a device.

Everything you need to know about packaging

The first thing to learn about packaging is that the box the product comes in is just as important as what's inside that box. The identity of the product begins with its outer "skin," and it affects consumer reaction to the product. The outer shell of an automobile, the sleek metal that is shaped to suggest speed or luxury, or both, is an example of package design that has a profound influence on potential buyers. Most of us buy a car because of the way it looks and how we think we will look riding in it. We're buying dreams as much as we are buying transportation.

The package is the promise for what is contained inside. Through the marketer's efforts, the package suggests to the consumer elegance, or romance, or sex, or thrift, or a tasty treat, or efficiency, or honesty, or good times, or dozens of other desirable things.

In some instances, packaging costs may even exceed the product's costs. The fancy designer perfume bottle may cost more than the scent

inside. A jewelry box may cost more than the cheap pin it houses. Often, the only real distinguishing feature between two competing products is the package.

Marketers know that eye-appeal is an important factor in the consumer's decision to buy. That consumer is exposed to over a thousand different product offerings in just a single minute of supermarket shopping. With these overwhelming choices, the buyer is going to pick the product that appeals to a desire.

Package design is part art, part science, part side-show pitch, and part hunch. With the recent advances in plastic, package design is limited only by the imagination. Hot sauce could be delivered in a container shaped like a chili pepper. Still, marketers must be careful. A mistake, conveying the wrong message via the package design, can cost the supplier millions of dollars—and market share. The package that looks too expensive will be passed up by thrifty buyers.

When redesigning familiar product packages, the marketer must be cautious not to make the change too dramatic. People remember, and are fond, of old favorites.

The other role of packaging is to deliver the product safely from the supplier to the end user. If you want to lose a customer for life, simply deliver a broken product in an unopened package. That's why packaging must be sturdy, snug enough to prevent rattling and shaking and hardy enough to withstand occasional drops and kicks from clumsy freight handlers.

Packaging as a marketing tool

Product manufacturers now develop packaging to meet the needs of specific sales channels. The blister pack which displays a product under a covering of clear plastic is an example of such packaging. Mass merchants wanted a simple way to display the product the package contained, yet keep it safe from dust, protect it from handling by customers, and secure it from would-be shoplifters. The blister pack accomplishes all these objectives.

Blister packs are also easier to inventory. Space needed to store the product has "shrunk" along with the size of the package.

Stereo equipment, office machines, and other types of electronic equipment are delivered in boxes which, when stacked on the selling floors of electronic hardware retailers, become in-store displays. The products' features are listed on the box along with a picture of the device. Sometimes one box is opened so the customer can see an actual example

of the product. The customer simply takes a box from the stack and carries it to a cashier.

POINT-OF-PURCHASE DISPLAYS AND IMPULSE BUYING

It's up to the director of marketing to develop attractive point-of-purchase (POP) displays to attract customers to the company's products. These displays attempt to capture the shopper's attention at the place where buying decisions are made. They include colorful posters, retail racks stacked with products, cardboard cut-out figures of famous personalities, bins overflowing with merchandise, and stacked boxes filled with products. Even in-store demonstrations by people brought in for the purpose are considered a point-of-purchase marketing strategy. That last sample of sharp Cheddar cheese you took from the tray of an in-store salesperson is an example. Retailers use point-of-purchase displays to trigger impulse purchases on the part of their customers. They will often display high-profit, impulse items near the entry doors of the store so that they are the first thing shoppers see when they walk into a store. Racks of candy bars, magazines, gum, and snack items are placed near the cash register so the kids can pester Mommy and the yummie stuff can be tossed directly on the counter as the shopper checks out.

The entire layout of supermarkets and other consumer-oriented stores are strategically designed to encourage impulse buying. The things shoppers routinely need such as bread, milk, meat, and other staples are usually located at the back of the store, or in another out-of-the-way location. To reach these items the shopper must navigate through a "minefield" of attractive, mouth-watering, high-profit goodies that seem to magically fly into shopping carts.

Product suppliers usually create point of purchase displays to enhance their sale of their items. They give these displays to the retailer, and "detailers" working for the suppliers sometimes set them up in the stores. The retailer has approval over the displays and dictates the amount of time they will be "on stage."

THE BATTLE FOR SHELF SPACE

You have just developed a recipe for the best-tasting, tangiest barbecue sauce in the world. You have bottled it, designed an attractive label, priced it right, and are now ready to bring your product to the attention of smear-faced brisket lovers and rib eaters everywhere. Get ready to do battle. The biggest problem you will face is getting supermarket chains to allocate any shelf space for your product. Delicious taste alone isn't nearly enough to persuade the supermarkets to accept your product.

The battle over shelf space is ferocious. Supermarket chains control the space and they exact a high price from suppliers who want a share of it for their products. Space is so precious that suppliers pay chains hundreds of thousands of dollars for the privilege of stacking up their cereal or catsup or baked beans or fried okra on those shelves.

The shelves must also produce a certain profit per square foot. That puts new-product entries at a double disadvantage. Not only must the product's supplier pay a hefty entry fee just to gain exposure, that supplier must convince the chain's buyers that the product will contribute to the store's profits. That means proving to the chain that the supplier has a complete marketing program including advertising, promotions, in-store displays, tie-ins, perhaps discount coupons, and so forth to promote the barbecue sauce to customers.

Chapter Two

THE ROLE
OF ADVERTISING

WHAT IS ADVERTISING?

The purpose of advertising is to encourage somebody to buy something. Many marketing professionals may quarrel with this definition as too simplistic, but when it comes to crunch time they'll reluctantly acknowledge that companies shell out money for advertising because they hope to influence a consumer's buying decision. In most companies advertising is used in conjunction with other marketing techniques. It's another weapon—a very powerful one—in the marketing manager's arsenal.

When should advertising be used? Fairfax Cone's famous answer to that question is, "Advertising is what you do when you can't go see somebody." Mr. Cone meant that advertising is a substitute for a face-to-face meeting with a potential customer. It isn't as effective as person-to-person contact, but no company that hopes to grow can personally contact all its potential customers. Advertising provides a volume solution. A television ad for mouthwash may be seen by thirty or forty million viewers with bad breath. A flyer distributed by hand in a local neighborhood by a dry cleaner may be read by several thousand people with dirty clothes.

Advertising doesn't always complete the selling job and, despite the warnings about its insidious effects, advertising certainly can't force people to buy things they don't want to buy. What advertising can do is to influence through suggestion, through pointing out the benefits, through polishing the apple.

FIVE THINGS ADVERTISING DOES WELL

Advertising fills many roles. The following are five things that advertising does well:

1. *Advertising educates.* Advertising can't force people to brush their teeth, but it can point out the advantages of the procedure. In the process it helps sell the advertiser's toothpaste, but that's a fair trade-off for fewer cavities and healthier gums.

2. *Advertising motivates.* Advertising encourages people to take immediate action. Why does the sensational sale offer end Saturday exactly at midnight? To motivate people to run down to the store *now*, before it's too late.

3. *Advertises introduces.* Have you just unveiled a new product, or has an infant company just been born? The best way to let the public know about the existence of a new commercial baby is to advertise.

4. *Advertising builds credibility.* Check out any shelf at the local supermarket or drug store. You'll find an overwhelming array of brands for each product category. Which one to choose? Most people pick a brand that they've used before or one that is familiar to them through advertising.

5. *Advertising helps maintain product loyalty.* Continued advertising helps maintain a customer's comfort level in a product.

FIVE WAYS TO USE ADVERTISING

Advertising is used in many different ways. The following five are among the most popular:

1. *Direct selling.* Direct-selling advertising solicits the prospect for an order. Every merchandise catalog with an order form on the back page, every newspaper ad for product suggesting that buyers call in their orders, every television "infomercial," every telephone solicitation, every bulk-mail offering is an attempt at direct selling. The ads say, "Here's what we've got, here's how much we want for it and, if you're smart, you'll buy some before we run out." This type of advertising is most effective with:

- Familiar products, though not necessarily familiar brands, whose benefits are easily recognized by the consumer.
- Products that seem to be offered for lower prices than usually available through regular retail sources. For example, the success of such computer mail-order firms as Dell and Gateway is because buyers believe they are purchasing computer systems at lower prices than those charged at computer retail stores.
- Products that are not generally available through retail stores. Examples include the mail-order catalogs offering merchandise from exotic or remote places, say pure llama-wool sweaters hand-knitted in the mountains of Peru.

2. *Generating leads for a direct sales force.* Lead-generation advertising doesn't attempt to close the sale—perhaps the product is too complicated for an easy close—but rather to encourage the prospect to call and request more information. A salesperson delivers this information and a dialogue begins. This dialogue sets the stage for an eventual sale.

3. *Informing prospects and customers about product features and benefits.* Those automobile ads bragging about car models that go from "zero to sixty in eight seconds" are examples of advertising designed to inform potential customers about a specific feature or group of features that might encourage them to buy. The car manufacturer marketers don't expect prospects to buy a car because of the ad, but they hope it will tempt them into a dealer showroom.

4. *Keeping the company's name in front of the public.* This is often called "institutional advertising." It is meant not so much to sell anything today, but rather to polish and maintain the company's image. Large companies, such as General Electric, use this kind of advertising more frequently than small ones because they can afford to wait longer for a payoff.

5. *Establishing the company as a reliable, trusted supplier.* Name identification is important. Have you ever heard the boss ask, "Why did we give that order to Kropnick Industries? I've never heard of that outfit!" People, and companies, don't like to do business with unknown entities. Advertising provides credibility.

WHAT ADVERTISING CAN'T DO

Advertising is not a panacea; it has limitations. For many products it will bring the horse to water, but it can't make him drink. In other words, for many product categories advertising can arouse the prospect's interest, but it can't close the sale. The company prospect interested in a sophisticated telecommunications system may be attracted to a particular product through effective advertising, but that system must still be sold through a series of face-to-face meetings and a comprehensive proposal.

Advertising can't overcome the problems of a poorly conceived product. If the product doesn't offer consumers genuine value, the consumers will eventually find this out. Advertising may tempt consumers to try a product for the first time, but if the product has flaws, *advertising can't get repeat orders.* (When the product doesn't offer genuine value, the market is limited to those customers who don't know any better. While it is possible to sell to the ignorant, I don't recommend it for companies seeking growth.)

DEMOGRAPHICS EXPLAINED

Demographics is a word that advertising managers and space salespeople bandy about like a shuttlecock: "Our demographic studies show . . ."

Let's begin with a definition. Demographics are *vital statistics*, that is the race, the age, the education level, the income, and so forth of an area, a prospect list, a customer base, a population, a listening audience, or whatever. For example, the demographics of a Texas border town may show that the population is largely Hispanic. The readership of *Sports Illustrated* is likely to be adult male, active, and middle income. The readership of *Working Mother* is likely to be female and politically aware. (Their space salespeople can tell potential advertisers exactly what their readership is.) The residents of Winnetka, Illinois, a high-tone suburb on Chicago's north shore, are likely to have greater yearly income than the residents of South Central Los Angeles.

The audience for *Beavis and Butthead* will be different than the audience for *Discovery*. So demographics is about numbers.

DEMOGRAPHICS USED

Marketers use these statistics to help target their campaigns toward specific audiences. Demographics allow the marketing manager to use a rifle rather than a shotgun when trying to reach potential buyers. An ad for a jazzy, high-performance car is likely to reach more potential buyers in *Sports Illustrated* than it would in *Working Mother.*

Remember our entrepreneurial dry cleaner? If he had researched the average income of the neighborhood's population, he might make more informed decisions on the kind of services to offer. For example, if demographics showed his store was located in a low-income area, the dry cleaner might concentrate on budget-type cleaning. In an area where the Mercedes and Cadillacs outnumbered the pedestrians, he might do better to specialize in high-quality, personalized services.

Demographics explains why certain types of ads appear in different sections of the daily newspaper. Newspapers offer something for everyone, but few people read the paper in its entirety. People pick and choose sections that interest them. Smart advertisers recognize this. Computer resellers know that men make most computer purchases. They also know that men read the newspaper sports and business sections. That's why most sales ads for personal computers appear in these sections. Ads for jewelry and women's high-fashion clothes are more likely to appear in the society section.

A radio station will develop an audience following depending upon the kind of programming it chooses to offer. A station playing classical music will attract a different audience than a station playing hard rock. Advertisers can select the station to deliver their message depending upon the audience they wish to reach.

Demographics then is a statistical tool that provides marketing managers with more efficiency in reaching potential buyers.

THREE DISTINCT ADVERTISING STRATEGIES

1. *Blitzing.* Blitzing comes from *blitzkrieg,* the German word for all-out, lightning-fast war. It means to run many ads in several different media over a short period of time. Turn on the radio, there's an ad for the product. Pick up a magazine or newspaper and you'll see more ads for the same product. When driving, look up toward a billboard and there's yet another ad, this one twelve feet high. Flick on the TV and a big film star tells the audience how the product has changed her life. Open up the mail box and a direct mail piece pops out containing a color picture of the product. The idea is to overwhelm potential buyers with so much exposure to the product that they must become aware of it.

Many marketing experts believe that repetition is the key to a successful advertising campaign and blitzing carries this theory to an extreme. Blitzing is often used when a product is introduced and in conjunction with national rollouts. It is also a popular advertising technique for products with short lifespans, such as blockbuster movies.

There's no question that blitzing works, but it is so expensive that this type of advertising can only be maintained for a short period. Do consumers retain the information about the product when the campaign has run its course? Memory retention is another issue.

2. *Programmed advertising.* This type of advertising buys space or time in various media selections far in advance and runs regularly scheduled ads throughout an entire year. The ads are spaced so the products or services are exposed to the public at intervals. Promotions, sales, holiday offers, and so forth are also planned far in advance.

The advantage of this technique is that advertising costs are reduced because media space and time charges are lower when purchased on a long-term contract basis. The company's advertising is never "shut out" from a publication or broadcasting medium during popular advertising periods. The buying public is exposed to the company's product at regular intervals. It's easier to project a certain company image.

The disadvantage is that the company's entire advertising budget is often committed far in advance. There's nothing left over for targets of opportunity. Even when there are contingency funds available, there is often reluctance to deviate from the program.

3. *Piecemeal advertising.* The piecemeal advertiser has no long-range program, but simply schedules space and time in various media to meet specific short-term goals. When having a sale, they'll run a few ads. When the prospect list gets a bit thin, they'll run a few more. When a persuasive time or space salesperson stops by, they buy a quarter page or a few spots.

The problem with this approach is that there are no objectives other than to sell more product in the short term. The people who operate in this manner are usually not persuaded that advertising actually works.

ALL ABOUT ADVERTISING AGENCIES

Ad agencies design ads, complete advertising campaigns for their clients, and help them select the media through which these ads will be run. They provide many services such as graphic design, photography, copywriting, and demographic studies that small and even medium-sized companies would have difficulty doing in-house.

Agencies come in all sizes, from one-person, freelance outfits to the very large, prestigious companies with offices in major cities. Agencies take projects for their clients and handle them from beginning to end. The good ones are masters at motivating the buying public, and their services are priced accordingly.

The bigger agencies can't afford to take small jobs, such as brochure design, because of their overhead. Most will, however, take on minor projects for major prospects to showcase their work.

The first question to ask when thinking about hiring an advertising agency is, *do you really need one?* There are many circumstances in which a full-service advertising agency is an unnecessary expense.

Three situations when an ad agency isn't useful

1. If what the company calls "marketing" consists of putting out product brochures and occasionally sending out a few direct-mail letters to prospects, you don't need an agency—and you probably couldn't get one to take on the job because the advertising dollars spent wouldn't make it worth their while.

2. If the company knows who the prospects are and the industry knows about the company, or if the market for the product is contained, an agency may not be of use.

3. If the company doesn't have the money to spend on an advertising agency, say a minimum budget of $75,000, you might as well adopt the attitude that you don't need one because you're going to get one. In fact, ten times that amount isn't enough to attract a major agency.

In general, the company must have a big enough advertising budget to make it a worthwhile customer for an agency, and the product line must be one that would benefit from an agency's efforts.

Four circumstances in which using an advertising agency makes sense

The following are the circumstances in which companies benefit from using the services of an ad agency:

1. If the company is placing many ads in magazines, newspapers, radio, or television, using professionals to design these ads and select the best place and time to run them could be useful.

2. If the company is "market-driven," that is, if it intends to react quickly to the perceived needs of the marketplace, an advertising agency can help "drive" it in the right direction.

3. If your company markets through several different channels and niches, or to a very broad consumer marketplace, an advertising agency is almost indispensable.

4. If your company has no experience or expertise in advertising and wants to mount an ad campaign or develop a comprehensive advertising program, you *definitely* need an agency.

How agencies are paid

Ad agencies are paid a percentage of the ads they book for the company. For example, if the agency books a $100,000 ad for your company that will run in the *Wall Street Journal*, the agency will receive 15 percent of that cost, or $15,000 for their services in designing and placing the ad.

With compensation structured in this manner, it's easy to understand why the agencies have a vested interest in keeping the meter running. Be careful about selecting agencies that suggest expensive campaigns merely because the media costs will increase their fees.

Six steps to select the right advertising agency for your company

1. Like most business functions, the first step in choosing an agency is *planning*. What are your company's goals and how much money can be spent to get you there? Make these decisions before meeting with agencies.

2. *Budget* is an important factor in agency selection. As a rule of thumb, if your company has big bucks to spend, choose a major agency. They have the most services to offer. If the budget is small, choose a smaller agency. The few dollars you do have to spend will get more respect there.

3. Make a list of the *advertising services* your company requires. Only interview agencies that offer those services.

4. Examine the agency's work for other clients. Does their *past performance* suggest they could turn out good stuff for your company? Don't be shy about requesting and calling the agency's clients for references.

5. It isn't absolutely necessary to use an agency that is *familiar with the company's industry*, but it often helps. The education process and the time required to get a campaign up and running is shorter. At the same time, make sure the agency is not working for your company's direct competitors or has no other commitments that could represent a conflict of interest.

6. A major advertising campaign often results in a kind of honeymoon between client and ad agency. Honeymoons, however, rarely last forever. Before running off to Niagara Falls, make sure that the two of *you are compatible*. Do you like the people you'll be working with at the agency? Do they like you, or are those smiles insincere?

MEDIA SELECTIONS AND WHY THEY ARE MADE

Media are the vehicles through which advertising is placed. Newspapers are a medium; so is radio. In fact, media are broken down into two broad categories:

- *Print media*, represented by magazines, newspapers, and other purveyors of the printed word.
- *Broadcast media*, represented primarily by radio and television.

Which one is most effective? There is no single best answer. Advertisers select certain media depending upon the kind of audiences they wish to reach. Someone advertising townhomes for sale in a retirement community would certainly not choose to deliver the company's message via a classic rock radio station. Someone advertising a Grateful Dead commemorative compact disk, however, might think that particular station represented an excellent choice.

Five questions to ask before making a media selection

When selecting media the advertiser must begin by asking certain questions. These questions are:

1. What audience do I want to reach?
2. What message (or sales pitch) do I want to deliver to this audience?
3. What response do I want to elicit?
4. How much money am I prepared to spend?
5. Where is the competition spending its advertising dollars, and are their ads effective?*

HOW TO USE NEWSPAPERS AND MAGAZINES

Except maybe for smoke signals, town criers and word-of-mouth, newspapers were here first. They are the old reliables. Included in this category are daily newspapers, Sunday papers, weeklies, giveaways, national dailies such as the *Wall Street Journal*, and special-interest papers. Some are prestigious publications which help shape our society and others are sleazy rags. They all derive their revenues through the advertising they run.

Do people actually read newspaper ads? According to McGraw-Hill, only 16 percent of newspaper readers ever read a *full-page ad*. Smaller ads attract even smaller audiences. As television takes a greater hold on all of us, there are fewer newspaper readers every day. So why should you consider advertising in a newspaper?

---

*Don't always assume that the competitor's ads are effective. If they appear to be reaching the target audience by using a certain medium, however, perhaps the company should be active in that arena too.

Advantages of newspaper advertising

Advertisers, such as retailers, choose newspapers because that's where some shoppers look when they're in the market to buy something. For example, many grocery shoppers are conditioned to look in certain days' issues of newspapers for supermarket ads offering weekly food sales. Shoppers in the market for homes will look in the Sunday real estate section. That makes the newspaper a valuable shopping guide. Advertisers can take advantage of newspaper readers' shopping habits to position their ads in sections where they are most likely to be read.

Newspapers offer territory flexibility. Advertisers can choose a newspaper whose circulation closely matches their marketing area. They're delivering their message to an audience within their marketing range, and that's the advertising power they're paying for. Newspapers also have the power of immediacy. They are journals of today and now.

If the company is a retailer or a service company, or if the company's product is one that is carried by retailers and shopped for by end-users, then newspapers are a good media choice.

Disadvantages of newspaper advertising

Newspapers have a short lifespan. Technically, the daily paper is current for 24 hours. Actually, most papers receive 20 to 30 minutes of attention, and that's not even close attention. Material is often scanned rather than read. Ads compete for attention not only with other ads, but with the substantive material a newspaper publishes. Whole sections are often passed over without ever being opened.

The cost of newspaper advertising

Newspaper advertising is usually sold by the column inch. Newspaper "space" salespeople offer contracts based on the volume of ads to be run. The more ads, the lower the cost per column inch. Newspapers may also charge different rates for different types of advertisers. For example, retail stores may pay a different rate than cigarette companies. Every advertiser within a category pays the same rate.

The expenses related to designing the ad, that is the charges for graphic arts work, copywriting, layout, and other production costs, must be added to actual space costs to determine the true costs of advertising. In some instances there are rebates from corporate advertising and "co-op" advertising that lower out-of-pocket advertising expense.

Ad frequency, size, and position

What determines whether an ad will be read? The big advertising agencies will claim that depends on how creative the ad is. (In other words, employ their services.) Certainly creativity is an important factor in grabbing a newspaper reader's attention, but other primary factors include where on the page the ad is positioned, the size of the ad, and how often it is run. The top of the page and the outer edge of the page are considered the best positions for an ad—the eye is naturally drawn to these areas. Bigger ads capture more attention than smaller ones. The more times an ad is run, the greater the probability that the information contained in that ad will be retained by the reader.

Designing a newspaper ad

An amateurish ad is just money down the drain. Those who have no experience designing ads should leave the job to professionals. For best results, use an ad agency or the resources of the newspaper itself. For those who want to do the job themselves anyway, most professionals suggest the following:

1. The content of the ad is all important. Make a dynamite offer. There's nothing more effective in marketing than providing the customer with genuine value.

2. Catch the reader's eye. Set the headline in big, bold print. This headline should include a statement that entices the reader.

3. Use plenty of white space around the printing. Don't make plowing through the ad a chore for the reader.

4. Keep sentences and paragraphs short. Follow Mies van der Rohe's dictum, *Less is more.* (Have you noticed that less isn't as much as it used to be?)

5. Emphasize key words and phrases through capitalizing them, using bold type, underlining, reverse printing, and so forth. Also use check marks, asterisks, and other symbols to draw attention to key statements.

How to use television

Advantages of television advertising

Television's primary advantage is that it delivers a large audience. Even local television programs in major markets can reach hundreds of thousands of people. The average household now watches more than seven hours of TV every day. That makes television the medium of first choice to advertise consumer type products that are used by large segments of the population. This is the medium for national-brand toothpaste, mouthwash, and nationally distributed cookies.

Another of television's advantages is that it gives the seller an opportunity to actually show and demonstrate the product. Drama can be used in developing the scripts. People can be shown using the product and loving every minute of the experience.

Being on the tube also gives a product a kind of legitimacy. Some people feel that if a product has been shown on TV it must be good. Remember what we said earlier about advertising giving a product credibility? No medium lends more credibility to a product than television.

Disadvantages of television advertising

Advertising on television is so costly that the product must have broad appeal to make the expense worthwhile. Only companies with large advertising budgets need apply here. Even the spot ad run on the 2:00 A.M. horror movie show may cost more than the company can afford if the spot is to be played often enough to be effective.

Television is a broad-brush medium. Although many TV shows are aimed at specific audiences, the ability to target particular market segments is not as precise as with some other media. Cable television is beginning to change that.

The ads on television come not as in single spies, but as battalions. This continual assault has hardened some viewers against all ads. They use the time when commercials are aired to channel surf, to raid the refrigerator, to finally talk to the kid about the failing report card, and so forth. The rise of the remote control has changed all the rules about grabbing the viewer's attention.

Ad production costs are incredibly expensive. The slick commercials shown on national television today cost as much as some B movies did a few years ago.

The ads, once aired, disappear into the ozone. That makes it difficult to get an immediate viewer response. Phone numbers, addresses, and other information about placing orders disappear too.

The cost of television advertising

TV ad costs are based on amount of time the commercial will be run, the size of the audience that the program delivers, the identity of that audience, and the popularity of the particular program. For example, the most expensive time slot of all is advertising during a Super Bowl. This is because the program is delivering a very large audience, the audience can be identified as mainly active males, and there's a prestige for the product that comes with being associated with this major sports event.*

Companies who wish to run many ads on TV may purchase a specific number of spots at a discount depending upon the quantity purchased. The lower the rate, the less control the company has over when these ads may be run. Those advertisers who bought time cheap shouldn't be surprised if the ad is run at 3:00 A.M. during a break from a rerun of a black-and-white Perry Mason episode.

Designing a TV ad

The length of the average TV spot is 30 seconds. That puts a constraint on the message to be delivered and provides a creative challenge to ad production companies. The ad must be simple, containing one or two ideas at most. It must grab viewers' attention before they run off to grab a sandwich and beer. Drama is used extensively. Those 30-second spots often tell a story. "Experts," that is actors who appear to be doctors and other professionals, are used to sell products. Testimonials by prominent personalities are offered to give products more credibility. Some strong personalities, however, can draw attention away from the product onto themselves. This is known as the "vampire" effect, and ad creators must watch out for it.

---

*TV stations attempt to extend those high advertising dollars with "before-and-after" programming meant to attract the audience earlier and keep it from straying later. Panels of pundits come on to make pre-game predictions and stay to make after-game analyses. Advertisers don't pay quite the same rate for these shows because there is an audience falloff, but the rates are still much higher than normal charges.

Production values are very important to TV ads, and they are becoming more expensive to create every year. In some instances, big-name film directors and actors are used to work on an ad. This raises the ante for all advertisers because ads compete for the viewers' attention.

Time costs are so expensive that many advertisers design a "long" ad of 30 to 60 seconds, run it until an audience is familiar with it, then run a shortened version of 15 seconds. Only the key ingredients remain in this shortened version. The idea is to use repetition to imprint the message in the viewer's mind.

Television advertising alternatives

Local cable channels offer lower time costs. These channels deliver viewers in specific geographic areas or appeal to specific audience segments. This gives marketers more demographic control over their advertising programs. Some cable channels provide national coverage. The television "shopping clubs" have proven successful in making fortunes for their promoters and providing a viable marketing tool for many different vendors. In recent years, however, their popularity has waned. Turn on a shopping network today and the products being offered seem to consist entirely of costume jewelry and collectibles. This is no accident. The viewer has difficulty comparison shopping these kind of products, which suggests they are high-profit.

The infomercial, a half-hour or longer program dedicated to selling a product, has become a very popular TV marketing method. This kind of "show" uses every minute of time to extol the virtues of a product and to motivate people to buy it right now. Cosmetics, exercise equipment, cooking utensils, consultation with psychics, and just plain gimmicks are marketed in this manner. Fading personalities give testimonials. (Like Branson, Missouri, infomercials are havens for fading stars.) Some of these personalities claim they have even personally developed the product.

HOW TO USE RADIO ADVERTISING

Those who, a few years ago, predicted the death of radio were dead wrong. Radio is powerful and it is growing. It has become what is called a "portable" medium. People carry radios everywhere. They listen to radios at work and during recreation. Just about every worker driving to and from the job listens to the car radio on both journeys. Radio is so pervasive it reaches almost 95 percent of the adult population every day.

Advantages of radio

The strength of radio lies in its ability to deliver a message over and over at a relatively inexpensive cost. That makes it popular with advertisers who believe that repetition is the key to a successful ad campaign. Radio is also effective at reaching specific groups, as long as the categories are broad. For example, young people and working stiffs are two groups proven to be frequent radio listeners. Because radios are portable, it can reach listeners everywhere. It also reaches audiences that other media miss.

The radio station has become an integral part of the local community. Stations feature local news, rhapsodize about the local sports teams, employ local personalities, and participate in local events. Using radio can help advertisers become part of the local community.

Production costs associated with delivering the advertising message are also much lower than with television. That means there is more flexibility in experimentation, changing scripts, the time the message is delivered, and fine-tuning offers until a formula that works is discovered.

Disadvantages of radio

Radio's major disadvantage is that, like television, once the message is delivered, it's lost in the ozone. A reader can go back to take a second look at a newspaper ad. That television commercial at least offers a visual image that helps the viewer retain the message. Not so with radio. The message disintegrates. Another problem with radio is that FCC regulations limit stations to 50,000 watts of sending power. Signals can't get over that faraway hill and that limits audience size.

Tips on how to use radio

Radio isn't the best choice if the message is complicated. Keep the company's story simple. Emphasize one idea at a time. Use repetition. Develop a simple theme and repeat it again and again.

Buying radio time

Radio advertising costs—all advertising costs really—are based on the audience the program delivers and the amount of advertising purchased. More spots will cost the advertiser more dollars, but at a lower cost per minute. Targeting to reach specific audience segments at specific times will also up the ante.

When buying radio time the important thing to understand is that the rates are negotiable. The radio time salesperson will have a rate card to flash at the advertiser, but these rates are not chiseled in granite. Deals can be made. Take the approach that the rate card is absolutely the most the company is to pay and a point from which to negotiate. During prime listening hours, there may not be enough leverage to negotiate special pricing. During less attractive times, anything goes. The bigger the financial commitment the company is prepared to make, the more leverage possible when negotiating. Shop for the best deal and let the time salespeople know that the rates are being shopped.

Five decisions to make when buying radio time

The radio time buyer has a wide variety of choices. Some of these choices are:

1. Which station will be used? This will depend on the kind of audience the company wishes to reach. The format of the station will shape the audience.

2. What times of day or night will the ad be on the air? More radios are turned on between the early morning hours of 6:00 A.M. to 10:00 A.M. and during the late afternoon between 4:00 P.M. and 7:00 P.M. The audience is large during these time periods because that's when people are driving to and from work.

3. Will the ads be run on an AM or FM station? Again, the decision depends on the desired audience. FM may be the best buy if the product is geared toward a young audience.

4. What days of the week will the ad be run? The day as well as the time and the station programming all shape the audience.

5. How much is the company prepared to pay? Budgets will determine the length of the message and how often it can be delivered.

Eleven tips for writing and delivering radio scripts

Radio commercials normally run 30 or 60 seconds, though there are some 10-second and 15-second spots. Here are some tips for script writers:

1. The key to a successful ad is product and company identification. Repeat the product name, the price, the phone number, and the company name many times during the ad. Some experts believe the product name should be mentioned every ten seconds.

2. Use a hook that captures the listener's attention in the first few seconds.

3. Don't confuse the audience with too much information. Don't talk about a whole host of products in one commercial. If the price is mentioned, keep it to a single price.

4. Avoid trite superlatives such as "wonderful," "beat," "quality," "great," and so forth.

5. Avoid words that sound like other words. Remember, the message disappears into the ozone. Don't leave the audience wondering what was said.

6. Be sincere. Nothing sells better than good value, honestly presented.

7. Don't use comparisons with competitors. Why give them free air time?

8. Don't try to cram too much information into a single commercial. Everyone has heard one of those commercials in which the announcer makes a rapid-fire, breathless delivery. Okay, he's virtuoso of the vocal chords. But how much information was retained by listeners?

9. Don't use the company's money to underwrite your debut as a performer. Keep the immediate family out of it too—even if your daughter is a cutie-pie. The purpose of the advertising is to sell a product, not build egos. Use professional announcers to read the commercial. Try to get one with a distinctive voice. Local personalities are good choices because they have already developed credibility with their audiences. That credibility rubs off on the products they advertise.

10. Music works. Jingles are popular because they help listeners retain the ad's message.

11. Repeat the commercial many times. If there's not enough money for many ads, then maybe radio is the wrong vehicle.

How to use Yellow Pages advertising

The Yellow Pages are phone directories listing of local businesses. They are organized according to the products and services these businesses offer. Some companies put their entire advertising budgets into Yellow Pages directories. This strategy makes sense in specific industries. In consumer service industries, such as roofers, pest control, plumbers, and so forth, Yellow Pages ads are the primary method through which customers are attracted. Even some intangibles, such as automobile insurance, are sold through this medium.

Advantages of Yellow Pages advertising

The Yellow Pages directories are semi-permanent in that they remain in a household for a full year. An ad placed at the beginning of the year may get results in August. Yellow Pages readers are always shoppers. They have already decided they want to buy something when they open the directory. This makes them highly qualified prospects. The Yellow Pages also serves local communities. Advertisers who wish to limit the geographic area they cover do well with this medium.

Disadvantages of Yellow Pages advertising

The Yellow Pages lists ads by business categories. Every dry cleaner ad is displayed next to another dry cleaner ad. That means readers see all the competitive ads every time they open the book to find any company. Many advertisers using other media, such as radio, will encourage prospects to look up the company phone number and address in the "white pages" so they won't be distracted by these competitive ads.

The past few years have seen an explosion of Yellow Pages directories. Some are effective in distributing their books to the buying public and others are not. An expensive ad in a poorly distributed directory is wasted money.

The purpose of Yellow Pages advertising

The purpose of the Yellow Pages ad is to entice the shopper to call your company instead of your competitor. Remember, when people open up a directory they are prepared to buy something.

Designing the Yellow Pages ad

Experienced marketers don't use subtlety when designing a Yellow Pages ad. They pull out their automatic pistols and empty the full clip. Yellow Pages ads require boldness. Users are looking for something. Good ads make that something easy to find.

Experienced advertisers use ads that refine the proposition to a few words. The company's phone number is prominently listed and highlighted. Borders, clever graphics, and other eyecatchers are often used to make the ad stand out. The company's address is listed so customers can visit or mail in orders. Service businesses should list the geographic areas they cover. If companies make in-house calls, they should try to appear "local." Shoppers suspect that they'll be charged for travel time. List the company's credentials, i.e., how long in business, if bonded, kind of licensing, and if approved by groups such as AAA.

What to do when the Yellow Pages shopper calls

Smart marketers recognize that the job is only half done when the prospect calls the Yellow Pages advertiser. What happens when the phone is answered determines whether the company gets the business or the prospect lets those fingers continue walking. These marketers train their telephone people to be prepared for those calls. They are ready, they are informed, they are courteous, they ask for the business.

TELEMARKETING

Everyone who, when just about ready to sit down to dinner, has received a call from a telemarketer selling long-distance telephone service or soliciting for a credit card company probably has a negative reaction to the process. Boiler room sharpies hawking swampland, aluminum siding, and penny stocks have contributed to telemarketing's poor reputation. It is, however, an economical, efficient way to reach many prospects quickly.

The sales message is delivered directly to the prospect and it allows the prospect to ask questions in return. Objections can be answered and information exchanged. That makes telemarketing an interactive medium. These are reasons why it has become a thirteen-billion-dollar-a-year industry.

Some companies rely entirely on telemarketing to put their products before the buying public. It's a middle marketing course, cheaper than a face-to-face sales call and more expensive than direct mail.

Other companies use telemarketing in conjunction with other forms of advertising and marketing programs to make all programs more effective. For example, the telemarketer may call the prospect a few days after a direct mail piece has been delivered: "What other information can I give you about our proposition?" The conversation could lead to:

- An order.
- An appointment for a personal call.
- A turn-down.
- Information about the ad campaign that will be useful in making it more effective, or in making a decision to deep-six it.
- A combination of some of the above.

Telemarketing scripts

The first step in a telemarketing campaign is the preparation of the script that will be used by the telemarketers. (That caller asking for a donation to the Widows and Orphans Fund is not just "winging it.") This script should be pliable enough to allow for a variety of responses by the prospect. Some scripts have "branches," with the telemarketer following one branch with a positive response to a question and another branch with a negative response. Each branch diverges and perhaps leads to still other branches. But all branches, we hope, arrive at the destination: an order or a commitment of some kind by the prospect.

Good telemarketing scripts start with an opening hook or a question. These hooks give the listener a good reason to stay on the line. They often flatter the listener by asking for an opinion—that's why the "survey" approach is so popular. The product or service and the benefits offered are presented early in the conversation. Some telemarketers tinker with scripts until they find the benefits of the offer that are the best motivators in buying decisions. The offer and terms are stated clearly. A reason is given why a decision on the offer is needed immediately.

Often, several products or services may be included in one phone call. The telemarketer has a primary objective and a fall-back option of a lower-cost deal if the prospect is reluctant.

When the scripts are well written, the entire presentation is simple. Short words, sentences, and familiar phrases are used. The telemarketer periodically solicits responses from the prospect to make sure the presentation is being followed. Questions are answered with questions: "You can't afford to re-roof now? We have any easy payment program that spreads the cost over seven years. It's just a few bucks a month." The prospect's responses are fed back to him or her to show they have been heard and understood.

Finally, the telemarketer closes or asks for the order. An "order" isn't always a commitment to buy something. The telemarketer may be trying to set up visits for an in-home sales counselor. If agreement is made for an appointment, that telemarketer has made the "sale." Closing may be done in a variety of ways depending on how the conversation has progressed. Good scripts will have identified the best close for the situation.

Choosing the prospects

The best way to increase the effectiveness of a telemarketing campaign is select prospects from a list of people who may have some interest in your product or service. The Mercedes dealer soliciting prospects to come in to the show room to see a new $75,000 model should not telemarket to those living on minimum incomes. How does the Mercedes dealer find out who to call? *Demographics!* Lists of high-income people, including those who have purchased luxury cars in the past, are available from database companies.

Hiring telemarketers

The next step in the process is to hire good telemarketers. They aren't easy to find. People with clear voices, pleasant dispositions, and determination are needed. Telemarketers perform hard, stressful jobs and are faced with countless rejections. People can only take so much of it each day. Many companies use telemarketers on daily shifts of four to six hours because they become "burned out" by the number of calls they're required to make.

Some companies use professional telemarketing agencies rather than an in-house staff. The advantage to using an agency is that they are experienced, they already have staff, which means they can get up and running faster, and they know what works and what doesn't. The disadvantage is that some control of the process is lost.

Agencies are often the best choice for a temporary campaign or blitz effort. Those companies and marketers who plan to rely on continual heavy use of telemarketing should consider in-house staffs.

How to use direct mail

Every day our mailboxes are filled with envelopes hinting at promise. Inside these envelopes are "incredible offers" that demand our immediate action. We glance at these solicitations for a few seconds, find them resistible, then toss them in the garbage. One out of a hundred attracts our interest. We call that company to place an order or ask for more information.

I've just described the direct-mail industry. Marketers send out mail in huge quantities in the hope of attracting one or two buyers out of every hundred pieces mailed. The low percentage of success is compensated for by the sheer volume of letters mailed.

Direct mail is one of the most effective ways to target a specific group of prospects. Database companies maintain enormous lists of individuals, companies, and organizations separated into various categories. These lists are sold to advertisers who wish to send out solicitations. Lists can be purchased for doctors, lawyers, or Indian chiefs. It's possible to pick the kind of industries that are prospects for the company's products and even to identify the names of individuals or job titles within those companies. Mail can be directed to different parts of the country, to specific zip codes, different ethnic groups, various political persuasions, and so forth.

Direct mail is a personal form of advertising because the message can be slanted to the type of individual receiving the mailing. It fits very well into a localized advertising program or a national campaign, and it works well in conjunction with other marketing programs.

Disadvantages of direct-mail advertising

A great many pieces must be mailed to get one "hit," and postage isn't getting any cheaper. The sheer volume of mail being sent every day works against the effectiveness of an individual piece. Much direct mail gets relegated to the "circular file" without ever being opened. Advertisers must resort to clever tactics to entice recipients to read the material. For example, some advertisers send direct-mail pieces that appear to be checks.

Five situations in which direct mail can be effective

How can a marketer know when direct mail is appropriate? The following are five situations in which direct mail has proven effective:

1. When the company wants to deliver a message to a specific marketing area or class of prospect. Direct mail can pinpoint better than any other medium.

2. When the company wants to sell something directly to end users without third-party involvement.

3. When the company wants to create a friendly environment for a salesperson's follow-up call.

4. When the company wants to restrict an offer to a localized area.

5. When the message to be delivered is complex or requires detail. Lengthy explanations are possible in direct-mail campaigns.

How to conduct a direct-mail campaign: Obtaining the mailing list

The most important ingredient in a direct-mail campaign is a current mailing list that correctly identifies the target market. These lists may be accumulated from company compilations of prospects, customers, and suspects. Lists may also be purchased from mailing-list brokers, magazines, newspapers, and specialized database companies.

The Yellow Pages of phone directories contain the names of database companies that offer mailing lists for sale. Most of these companies acquire their lists by purchasing them from other sources. For example, a mailing-list broker may purchase the list of everyone who has bought a hunting license from a state. They would then resell this list to advertisers targeting hunters.

Lists are supplied on printout sheets, on adhesive labels, and on floppy disks. They are usually inexpensive, but are often restricted to one-time use. How will the company that sold the list know if it used a second time? The lists are "salted" with the names of bogus companies. A few copies of every mailing goes directly to the database company. The company that tries an unauthorized mailing gets a bill for that second use.

Many list brokers provide a complete mailing service for their customers: writing copy, printing, stuffing envelopes, stamping, sorting, and delivering mail to the post office. Often their charges are less expensive and faster than doing the work in-house.

The three parts of a direct-mail campaign

A direct-mail package will consists of three parts. These parts are:

1. The offer letter.
2. The description or picture of the product being offered.
3. The return piece or action the company wants the mail recipient to take.

Each part of the package is important, but the offer letter is paramount.

Seven tips on writing a direct-mail piece

The direct-mail marketer has only a few seconds to grab the reader's attention when the mailing piece is opened. Here's how to make every offer letter an attention getter:

1. The offer is everything. Make it irresistible. Get the deal out in the open in the very first paragraph. Excite the prospect!

2. Keep the paragraphs short. The direct-mail piece should never be confused with a Russian novel.

3. Keep the text chummy and personal. An overly formal letter may turn off the reader.

4. Don't worry about going on for pages if that's the length needed to tell the company's story.

5. Add a postscript with a strong close. Even people who don't read the letter will scan the postscript.

6. Personalize the letter. Address it to a specific individual in the home or company who is being targeted. (The direct-mail piece that is almost a waste of money is the one addressed to "resident.")

7. Prove any claims with testimonials, third-party studies, independent reports, survey results, and so forth.

The value of the product brochure

The product brochure in the direct-mail package is a representation of the company and what it has to offer. Don't skimp when putting one together. Use the best material to create the most attractive presentation possible. The brochures, however, should not be composed of many pages. A heavy brochure will add to mailing cost, which is the biggest expense in a direct-mail campaign.

The direct-mail response form

The offer letter and the product rendering are designed to motivate the recipient to take some action. Make it something easy for that recipient to do. That's where the third part of the direct-mail package, the response form, becomes important. If the purpose of the mailing is to entice the recipient to buy something, include an order blank that's simple to fill out. Have you ever noticed those solicitations for credit cards and magazine subscriptions? All the recipient need do to order is to check off a box and put the form in a self-addressed envelope.

Two ways to increase direct-mail response

In many cases a "good" response to a mailing is a one- or two-percent return. That means ninety-eight to ninety-nine percent of the letters will be thrown away. Rejected! There are two ways to improve this percentage:

1. Conduct test mailings before embarking on a big mailing program. Experiment with different lists, different offer letters, and different brochures until a formula that works is found. Then, and only then, do the mass mailing.

2. Follow up on the direct-mail piece with phone calls. Make the same appeal in the phone call that was made in the mailing. Follow-up phone calls can double and even triple the response to a direct-mail piece.

Cutting direct-mail costs

Direct mail is expensive, primarily because of the cost to send the offering, and postage isn't getting any cheaper. Cut costs by using third-class mail. Mail costs can also be trimmed by sorting the mail before it is delivered to the post office. Contact the local postmaster for their requirements and cost-saving tips.

ADVERTISING BUDGETS

An advertising budget is the amount of money that is allocated to marketing communications for a specific period, usually a year. This budget is just part of the expense for a complete marketing program that normally includes things like trade shows, point-of-purchase displays, buyer incentives, and commissions.

In large companies, advertising managers fight for their share of the total marketing budget with other departmental managers. These managers with other responsibilities naturally think that a better bang for the buck can be achieved by throwing dollars their way. So there is the eternal internal squabble over which programs are the most effective.

Good advertising managers avoid this inter-mural competition. They recognize that marketing programs work best when they work in conjunction with one another. *Good* managers seek the exact amount needed to do the job. *Good* managers do not try to hog money from other departments nor do they pad the budget on the assumption that whatever number they project will be cut.

How much, exactly, should be allocated to an advertising budget? There is no exact figure and no magic formula. There are several accepted methods for calculating budgets. These methods are:

Six ways to develop an advertising budget

1. *Percentage-of-sales budget.* This is the most common way to develop an advertising budget, probably because it so easy to calculate. Just take the total sales for the company, plug in a percentage for advertising, and the budgeting task is completed. For example, $5 million in annual sales with 2 percent allocated to advertising would result in a $100,000 budget.

Will it be in line with what others are spending? Industry trade associations, trade magazines, and consultants usually track what other companies in that line spend on advertising so individual companies can get information on industry averages. Industry averages are helpful in developing marketing strategies. (Spend more on advertising to attract more potential customers. Spend less on advertising to reduce costs and make the product more price competitive.)

The one vital decision the ad manager must make when developing a percentage-of-sales budget is whether to use past sales, what the company did last year, or projected sales, what the company expects to do next year. The projected sales approach is a necessity when launching new products because there is no sales history on which to base a number.

2. *Historical budget.* This budgeting method is also easy. Just review what was spent on advertising last year, add a certain percentage for anticipated improvement or inflation, and the budget job is done. The nice thing about this kind of budget is that it usually wins quick approval from senior management. They're operating in familiar territory. Look out, however, for criticism from the people upstairs when last year's budget didn't get the job done.

3. *Let's-copy-what-the-other-guy-does budget.* This all-to-common reactive marketing technique is based on too much concern over what the competition is doing. ("Those SOB's are spending tons of money so we're going to outspend them!") The problem with this approach is that it is based on emotion rather than an organized marketing plan. At least the other guy has some plan attached to his program.

4. *Catch-as-catch-can budgeting.* The system is total disorganization; there is no annual budget *per se.* Advertising is decided by whim or when there are a few extra bucks in the company till. Some who use this method justify it on the basis of seeking "targets of opportunity," but they really mean they're too lazy, or too inept, to develop a real program.

5. *Unit-of-sales budget.* This budgeting method determines a specific amount needed to sell a single unit of the product. For example, if the company sells computers it might allocate one dollar in advertising for each computer sold. When targets are set, say to sell five million units, the ad budget automatically becomes five million dollars. This method is similar to the percentage-of-sales budgets. It has the added advantage to multiproduct companies of more precisely allocating cost of advertising to each product in the company's line.

6. *Build-up budget.* This budgeting method builds up steam depending upon the success of the advertising program. It's a "let's-ride-a-winning-horse" budget. Advertising budgets are set, and the results of advertising campaigns closely monitored. When programs that are successful, that is when they result in more product sales than anticipated, more money is allocated and the advertising is expanded. If more sales result, the budget is raised again and advertising is expanded still further. The program is continued just as long as sales continue to escalate. The program also works in reverse. When sales are disappointing, the advertising budget is curtailed.

TEN TIPS FOR WRITING DYNAMITE COPY

The basic consideration that guides copywriting is the intent of the advertising. What is the hoped-for result? Media considerations also determine copy. Material in a classified ad to be run in a daily newspaper probably wouldn't be effective for an ad to be run on television. The target audience is an equally important consideration. So before sitting down to the word processor, the copywriter must ask, "Where will this ad appear, who am I trying to reach with it, and what do I hope to accomplish?"

There are, however, certain criteria that are useful when preparing copy for any purpose in any medium and in communicating with any audience.

1. Appeal to the reader's emotion. When selling products directly, promise benefits.

2. Communicate eagerness and enthusiasm.

3. List features, especially when the company offers more features than the competition. Also emphasize how the reader's life will be made better with the purchase of your product.

4. If the price is to be included, save it for the end of the ad. The price can be a turn-off if it appears before the copy explains the product's benefits.

5. Mention a pending event that makes the reader take action immediately: "Sale ends Saturday."

6. Explain the product's superiority over the competition, but don't give the competition too much attention. Remember, your company is paying for the ad.

7. Include a toll-free number in the ad so people can call in orders.

8. Make sure the ad's production values are first rate.

9. Don't copy the competition's style. The audience may become confused.

10. Be entertaining. You're competing with countless other ads.

The most important tip of all for new marketers is to employ a copywriting professional who has experience with the specific medium in which the ad will be run. Demand samples of past work. Don't necessarily believe the jack-of-all-trades who claims that "copy is copy."

THE DIFFERENCE BETWEEN CONSUMER ADVERTISING AND BUSINESS-TO-BUSINESS ADVERTISING

Advertising aimed at consumers is different than advertising aimed at businesses. That's because consumers buy to please themselves. They don't need to justify their purchasing decisions, except perhaps to their spouses. Advertising to consumers, therefore, works best when it includes a strong emotional appeal. ("This after-shave will make you more attractive to women.")

Buying decisions made by a company manager, however, are *supposed* to be based on the organization's need. Some experts believe that *all* decisions are based on emotion. Logical reasons to support those decisions are plugged in after the fact.

Advertisers must be aware of the corporate mentality. Managers in corporations have two primary objectives:

- They want to take credit for things that go right.
- They want to avoid blame for things that go wrong.

These twin objectives should be in the marketing manager's mind when designing an ad campaign aimed at business.

Three basic ingredients of a business-to-business ad

1. The ad should enthusiastically *list the multiple benefits* that will come to the company that buys the advertised product. The biggest problem business advertisers face is corporate inertia. Corporate managers use the philosophy of "if it ain't broke, don't fix it" as an excuse to avoid doing anything, including making improvements that could benefit the organization. That's why the business-oriented ad must be powerful, even overwhelming in listing the advantages the product or service offers.

2. To allay the prospect's fear about making a mistake, *include testimonials* from current satisfied customers. ("XYZ company saved 30 percent on their warehousing expenses.")

3. *Address major needs and offer major solutions.* Corporate managers see no point in changing vendors and risking their own reputations to save pennies. This is why approaching a major corporation with the sales pitch— "We can save you a few bucks if you switch from your current vendor"— almost never works. These managers need more dramatic reasons. Don't promise minor miracles.

Some advertisers play the ambition card by suggesting that the decision maker who buys the product is destined for personal success.

CO-OP ADVERTISING

Cooperative advertising is a marketing program in which manufacturers pay part of a reseller's advertising costs. The amounts allowed are usually related to the dollar value of the products the reseller purchased. For example, if the manufacturer offers a 3-percent advertising allowance and the reseller purchases $100,000 worth of merchandise, that reseller is entitled to $3,000 in co-op ad money.

The money usually comes with strings attached. For example, the reseller is often required to put up matching funds and there are restrictions on where, when, and how the advertising can be used. If the reseller makes an inappropriate media choice or didn't approve the ad copy, the manufacturer can reject the allowance.

Advantages of co-op advertising

1. Co-op advertising helps with product sell-through and that ensures the reseller will be placing more orders next month. Nothing is more important than sell-through. That big order the reseller placed means nothing if the product doesn't move off the reseller's shelves.

2. Co-op advertising makes sure the product gets advertising exposure in local publications, on radio stations, and on cable television. Often, the reseller knows which local media choices are the most effective.

3. The program helps build reseller loyalty. The reseller knows that the product supplier will help his organization move product.

4. Because the reseller must usually match funds on a dollar-for-dollar basis, the marketing manager's advertising budget goes further.

Disadvantages of co-op advertising

1. Co-op ads are often not carefully controlled and the quality of the ads can deteriorate. The company image on product ads may not be displayed as desired.

2. The reseller decides on the media to be used and what goes in the ad.

3. Occasionally, the reseller has an agenda other than selling the company's product.

4. Co-op dollars are sometimes completely wasted on foolish programs that contribute nothing to the sale of the company's product.

Seven ways to make co-op advertising more effective

The thing that makes advertising managers nervous about co-op advertising is that they lose control. The following are six ways to work with resellers to help them make the ads more effective:

1. Provide the reseller with finished copy ads including layout, copywriting, camera-ready art, and even suggested price points.

2. Require prior approval on all ads before release of co-op funds. That way the advertising manager will know what goes into the ad.

3. Help the reseller select appropriate media. Take suggestions, but check them out for yourself.

4. Have the account salespeople check with resellers to make sure their co-op funds are being used. Wasted co-op money is an indication that the reseller is not promoting the company's products.

5. Track the results of co-op reseller ads for their effectiveness. Don't be afraid to borrow successful ideas from one reseller and pass them along to another.

6. Coordinate co-op reseller ads with specific buying seasons and holidays.

7. Suggest specific promotions at specific price points. Make sure the profits in these promotions make sense to the reseller.

ADVERTISING TO ATTRACT CUSTOMERS VERSUS ADVERTISING TO RETAIN CUSTOMERS

Advertising to attract new customers and advertising to retain existing customers isn't necessarily the same. It's wonderful when one program can accomplish both objectives, but this result can't always be expected. That's because the goals, although similar, are not identical. The new customer must be persuaded to change what is being done now. The existing customer must be persuaded to keep from changing.

The job of persuading prospects to become customers is infinitely harder. People only change when they are given a powerful reason for doing so.

Advertising to potential customers should emphasize the product's benefits and how "safe" it is to do business with the company. The ads should recite the company's track record. Success stories should be offered. The twin messages are that it's safe to come over here, and you'll enjoy substantial benefits if you do.

Existing customers know about the product and how the company performs. They're more concerned about a confirmation of their judgment and what the future holds. Old customers need to be reassured that the company is still a presence in the industry. To retain customers, run "institutional" type ads in prestigious industry magazines. These ads should focus more on image and future than on current product.

Some cross-pollination inevitably occurs when running both types of ads. The institutional-type ad aimed at current customers makes the prospect feel that the company is still a reliable supplier. The product-type ad aimed at prospects may acquaint an existing customer with additional applications.

CATALOGS

The typical catalog includes illustrations of products, descriptive copy, prices, and order forms. They are used to sell every kind of merchandise from shoe laces to tractors.

Sears Roebuck, and a few other companies, made the merchandise catalog as common in every American home as the family Bible. These catalog merchandisers provided a valuable service to their customers, particularly in rural areas where there were few retail stores. They offered quality merchandise of every type at competitive prices. Sears became the most powerful retailer in the world on the strength of its catalog.

That time in the sun is long past. Malls moved into the suburbs and, even in rural areas, goods became available from a variety of sources. The sheer number of pages and variety of merchandise offered made the general-purpose catalog expensive to produce and distribute. Major catalog houses were limited to two issues a year, which locked in product prices for six months. That's not responsive in today's fast-paced, competitive economy. Eventually, general merchandise catalogs declined as a marketing tool.

This marketing method, however, is alive and well through the emergence and success of special interest catalogs. Companies, such as Lands' End and The Sharper Image, have thrived by targeting specific market segments. Their catalogs don't try to target everyone. The merchandise in them appeals to upwardly mobile customers with large discretionary incomes. The catalogs themselves are perhaps one-tenth the size of a Sears Catalog, but they contain high-quality graphics and almost poetic copy. Four-color photos and high-quality glossy paper are used. Browsing through one is entertainment.

The success of any catalog depends upon the issuer's customer list. It must conform to the niche the marketer has selected. Lands' End must seek out the upscale casual clothes buyer. The Sharper Image must find the gadget lover.

Not all catalogs are distributed via the mail. Stores, such as Sears and J.C. Penney, have catalogs available at their retail outlets. Customers can pick them up as they shop. Catalogs have become so expensive to create that both Sears and Penney charge new customers a fee for them. The money is applied to the customer's first order.

Many customers use catalog or arm-chair shopping as a convenience. They're saved the bother of visiting a mall or traveling downtown. The holiday season is a particularly busy period for catalog distribution. The issuers want to get the catalogs before their customers so they can order presents in time for Christmas or other festive occasions.

Almost any company can use catalogs as a marketing tool. For example, a one- to four-page catalog slipped in the shipping container when a product is sold informs the customer about the company's other products. This simple marketing advertising strategy is particularly effective when the sold product uses consumable supplies. A supply catalog and an order form sent along with the product will increase supply volume.

Four major advantages of catalog advertising

1. Unlike many other media choices, catalogs are often retained by shoppers for long periods. They work for the marketer month after month after month.

2. The catalog issuer can reduce expenses by eliminating retail outlets. Mail-order operations don't require substantial investments in real estate.

3. Catalogs are an effective method for increasing add-on sales.

4. Through carefully assembled customer lists, catalogs can target specific market segments. Products that appeal to these markets can be selected.

Six disadvantages of catalogs

1. Even small catalogs are expensive to produce and distribute.

2. Many people who receive catalogs never order from them, although the catalog issuers prune their mailing lists periodically.

3. It's difficult and expensive to develop an effective mailing list.

4. Returns from catalog sales are higher than in retail outlets. Sometimes that poetic copy is *too* effective.

5. Trials and tests to find winning formulas are also expensive.

6. Prices offered in the catalog are locked in for the duration.

Ten tips for making catalog marketing more effective

1. Specialize in a specific market segment. Sears, Penney, and Montgomery Ward are still circulating their general merchandise catalogs, but the fact that they now charge for them should tell the marketer something. Special-interest catalogs are where the action is.

2. Accumulate a customer list that is interested in the products or services the company offers. Or, tailor the products offered to the customer list you all ready possess.

3. Hire the best copywriters and graphic artists your company can afford.

4. Make it easy to order and then make it even easier. The order form should be easy to fill out. Get a toll-free number so customers can phone in their orders. Experiment with the Internet and World Wide Web as ordering vehicles.

5. Have a liberal return policy. Customers don't get to see the merchandise until it arrives on their doorstep. They need to be confident the stuff can be returned.

6. Make sure the products offered for sale are readily available. Customers abhor back orders.

7. Invest in a good order fulfillment system. The only thing worse than putting an item on back order is sending out the wrong merchandise.

8. Describe the product fully. Let customers know what they're going to get, including how much it weighs and how tall it is. A complete description will cut down on returns.

9. Specialize in items that aren't readily available through normal retail sources. Why should customers order a product from a mail-order company if they can buy it at local mall and have it the same day?

10. Offer genuine value. Give customers their money's worth.

CARD DECKS

The use of "card decks" as a marketing tool has become explosive. Card decks are groups of post cards with advertising messages on the back and the advertiser's business address on the front. The decks are sent to prospects in "bundles" of up to seventy cards. The cards usually offer the prospect information about a product or service, a sale price on an item, a free sample, and so forth. The prospect shuffles through the cards and hopefully responds to a few.

Advantages of card decks

1. Card decks are an extremely low-cost advertising medium. They frequently pull in between a 1-percent to 2-percent response, which is comparable with other direct-mail media that cost a good deal more.

2. The decks are interactive in that they require the prospect to fill out a name and phone number and perhaps even answer a question or two. This makes respondents highly qualified prospects.

3. Results are easy to measure. It's also easy and costs little to test various offers, copy, and even markets.

Advertisers trying to sell their products through card deck advertising find the decks work best with items that sell for less than $100. They are also effective for:

- Generating sales leads.
- Introducing new products.
- Distributing literature and catalogs.
- Making other advertising programs more effective.

Disadvantages of card decks

1. Many recipients of card decks simply throw the entire deck away without ever glancing at the material.

2. Many card-deck offers draw far less than 1-percent response.

3. Card-deck promoters often include advertising from direct competitors in the same deck.

4. They are not effective at selling high-priced items, perhaps because there is a cut-rate aura about the process.

5. When products are ordered through card-deck advertising, the rate of return may be as high as 50 percent.

Four ways to make card-deck advertising more effective

1. When considering card-deck advertising, investigate the markets the deck will reach. Check out the promoters' mailing list, the other advertisers in the deck, and the print quality.

2. Test various decks for the ones that produce the best results.

3. Test various offers, headlines, and price points. With card decks, this testing is inexpensive.

4. Remember that the reader is doing a fast shuffle through a large group of cards. The reader's eyes may rest on any single card for less than a second. Use big headlines and bold offers that cry out for the reader's attention.

BILLBOARDS

Billboards bring advertising to the great outdoors. They are constructed primarily along highways and city streets where they are seen by car drivers, passengers, and pedestrians. What marketers like about billboards is that they are an intrusive medium that cannot be ignored, up there broadcasting the advertiser's message twenty-four hours a day (if they are lighted).

Billboards are priced according to monthly exposures, that is the number of people who can be expected to see that billboard over a 30-day period. The more traffic passing a particular point, the more a billboard located there will cost the advertiser.

The most important consideration in billboard advertising is the location of the billboard. The question of whether the billboard will be downtown or on the Interstate or elsewhere depends on the product offered and the purpose of the ad. A billboard advertising a motel will certainly do better on the highway close to the exit where the motel is located. A billboard advertising appliances might do best in the city, preferably close to the appliance store.

Advantages of billboard advertising

1. Billboards are a low-cost medium when considering the number of people they reach.

2. They are good choices for both local and national advertising programs.

3. They are an extremely visual medium and their size helps establish the advertiser's reputation as a substantial company. That makes billboards a good choice for the image-building type of ads.

4. In the case of motels, restaurants, tourist shops, campgrounds, and other local businesses that depend on highway traffic, there is no better advertising choice.

5. The size of a billboard means the advertiser's message can be bold.

6. The medium allows the advertiser to use many creative techniques to draw attention to the sign.

Disadvantages of billboard advertising

1. It is often difficult to measure the impact of billboard advertising, particularly with image-building ads.

2. The exposure to a billboard ad is often from a fast-moving vehicle. The ad is behind the reader in the twinkling of an eye, and that eye should always be on the road.

3. The proliferation of billboards lessens the impact of any one sign.

4. Billboards have high production costs.

5. Good locations must be locked in with long-term contracts. If the company's advertising program changes, the marketing manager is still stuck with the billboards.

Six ways to make billboards more effective

1. Consult with traffic experts to pick out the most desirable locations.

2. Make the message bold and dramatic, short on copy and high on graphics.

3. Increase readership by placing the billboard close to a traffic stop, toll booth, or other location where traffic is forced to slow down.

4. Use bright colors.

5. Hire a professional to design the billboard.

6. Take advantage of technology to be creative.

SIGNS

One of the first things most business owners do when starting an enterprise is to erect a sign. "Putting up a shingle" is a potent symbol that the company is open and ready for business. The sign ties a company to a location and gives potential customers information about the type of business in that location.

Some businesses, small retailers in particular, depend almost entirely on their signs to bring them customers. The sign is street advertising that brings these retailers foot traffic. Large organizations use signs to establish image. The local offices of major companies will use the same sign nationwide to help establish a distinct corporate identity. One of the oldest advertising cliches is that the sign is a "silent salesman."

Advantages of signs

1. Signs are inexpensive, simple to use, and always on the job.

2. They are effective in alerting customers about the type of business in the location.

3. They help attract impulse buyers who may not have considered a purchase until the sign was spotted.

Disadvantages of signs

There are no disadvantages to signs, unless you're the CIA.

Six ways to make signs more effective

1. Erect the sign where it will be seen by the most people.

2. Bigger is better with signs. Get the largest sign you can afford.

3. Refine the message to a few words. This is not the medium for *War and Peace*.

4. Periodically change some element or information in the sign to maintain interest. Eventually, a permanent sign that never changes becomes an ignored part of the background.

5. Use strategically located multiple signs to direct traffic to the business location.

6. Keep the sign in good repair. Nothing telegraphs a failing business like a broken sign.

Media costs versus productivity

Media costs are usually calculated on the price paid to reach one thousand people. For example, if a newspaper has a circulation of 500,000 readers and the cost for an ad is $500, the cost per thousand readers is $1.00. (That's a pretty good deal—grab it!)

Cost per thousand, however, is only part of the story. The daily newspaper in a major metropolitan city may have a circulation of a million or more. Their ad rates may be high, but the cost per thousand readers is relatively low because of this circulation. It's an efficient medium for products and services that appeal to a broad segment of the population.

This same newspaper may not be so efficient for products that appeal to those with special interests. A magazine aimed at duck hunters may have a circulation of less than 50,000. Their ad costs to reach one thousand of their readers will be much higher, but *all their readers are duck hunters*. If the company is in the business of manufacturing duck decoys, which publication do you think would give the marketer more bang for the advertising buck?

When making media selections marketing managers must measure not only the cost for reaching an audience, but the kind of audience they're reaching. Measure the productivity of the medium, not just the raw numbers.

Institutional advertising

Institutional or corporate ads focus on the company's image. They are not intended to sell product directly, but rather to promote a warm, fuzzy, positive feeling about the organization. Some typical institutional-type messages include:

- We're a great company and we're doing wonderful things.
- We're a credit to the community.
- We're bigger than you thought we were.
- We're on the cutting edge of the future.

- Boy, can you trust us.
- Investing in our company is a great idea.

Many good institutional ads use a slogan. This slogan is repeated over and over, in some instances until it becomes part of the popular culture ("Things go better with Coke"). The slogan should be used on all forms of the company advertising and in all promotions.

All the experts agree that an institutional ad must be run frequently to be effective. Remember, the purpose of the campaign is not to get a customer to rush out and buy a product, but rather to implant a favorable image of the company in the customer's mind that will last forever.

HOW MUCH ADVERTISING IS ENOUGH?

American companies spend about 150 billion dollars a year on advertising, but industry experts are insatiable. They believe that no amount of advertising is ever enough. These people are paid a percentage of the advertising placed, so their argument is based on self-interest. There is no question that more advertising produces better results than less advertising. There are those unpleasant constraints, however, called *budgets* that require every marketing manager to work within limitations. Simply throwing money at problems is never a satisfactory solution.

We believe enough advertising is the amount needed to reach the company's goals. So how much advertising is that? To phrase the question in a way more pleasing to bean counters, What is the least amount that can be spent on advertising and still have it be effective?

Dr. Jeffrey Lint, a marketing consultant, believes that advertising must reach a prospect a minimum of seven times within a year and a half to be effective. That is the amount of repetition needed for a message to sink in.

One of the reasons this repetition is necessary is that, like all creatures, humans react to their environment. The volume of advertising in all media has caused us to develop a protective shield that "tunes out" what we don't choose to see or hear. We're like those sea anemones that fold up at the slightest touch, only we do it when we hear an advertising message.

Those seven contacts are merely a guideline. The contacts needn't be the identical ad, but each ad should convey a similar message. Varying the ads but delivering the same message is a creative challenge for the marketing manager.

Chapter Three

PROMOTION AND PUBLIC RELATIONS

PUBLIC RELATIONS

Public relations is often considered a synonym for lies and deception. This is a false impression. Actually, the good PR firm relies on openness and candor to help their clients in the following areas:

- To stand apart from the competition.
- To build confidence in their client companies.
- To develop a positive image (build a solid reputation) of their client companies and their product lines.
- In a few instances, the role of public relations is to limit the impact of negative developments. This effort is frequently called "damage control."

Professional publicists, such as Stephen Berg, define public relations as "positioning through journalism." It is a more subtle persuasion than advertising because PR firms do not pay for space or time in a communication medium. Their job is to convince an editor, reporter, or commentator to refer to the company, or its products, in a positive light.

The advantage of a product or company mentioned as part of a news story, as opposed to advertising in that same medium, is credibility. We have grown cynical of advertising claims. The news story is far more likely to be read or listened to. What's even more important, information in a news context is far more likely to be believed.

Some companies, with the connivance of the media, try to disguise their advertising as hard news. Skeptical? Just open the Sunday real estate section of any major metropolitan newspaper and read the planted stories about various new home developments. The word "advertisement" will appear in small print just under the headline.

THE PRESS RELEASE

The basic weapon in the arsenal of the public relations manager is the press release. This is an information package about a company, or its products, presented so that the material appears to be news. The press release is prepared by a publicist and most often mass-mailed "for immediate release" to the media. The hope is that at least part of the information in the release will be used by some editors.

Why do publications and other communication media accept these obvious attempts by PR firms to promote a product or company? Thrift. Many publications, who often don't have large budgets, depend on press releases for some portion of their editorial content. Press releases are a good source of information on what's new and what's interesting. There would be a lot of blank space and dead air without them.

Many editors are lazy and copy the material in a press release word for word. That means the company's story is told just the way the publicist wants it told. The bigger problem is getting the story into print at all.

Nine topics that will help get a press release into print or on the air

Thousands, make that tens of thousands, of press releases hit editors' desks every year. What factors decide which releases get attention? Business editors are like any other journalists in that they want to report on the new, the innovative, and the interesting. Their job is to entertain and inform their readers. That's why trade journals will almost always use a press release sent by a major industry player. What the 800-pound gorilla does is always news.

Smaller companies don't have the same advantage. They must craft their press releases more carefully. Some things that make a press release publishable include:

1. A new product announcement.
2. A major personnel change. (Hiring a new janitor doesn't qualify.)
3. A major policy change that affects the way the company does business.
4. A new company venture.
5. A new system.
6. A success story.
7. The purchase of another company.
8. The sale of a division.
9. The company's community involvement.

Of course there are other "newsworthy" events. Getting into print or mentioned on the air depends upon the publicist's imagination.

How to create a press release

The easiest way to create a press release is also the most obvious: Hire an experienced PR firm and let them handle the chore. A good firm not only knows how to write copy and how to put a press release together, they also know where to send it. Their media contacts are invaluable, particularly for companies just starting out. The chances of getting the company's story into print or on the air are much improved when using professionals.

A do-it-yourself press release

For those who feel they have the gift for writing persuasive prose, here's a primer on press release format:

1. Start off with a blank sheet of paper. (Stuck already? The blank piece of paper is God's way of telling the copywriter just how hard it is to be God.)

2. At the top of the paper, type the words, "PRESS RELEASE." Make sure this is centered and capitalized. Your document now begins to assume an air of importance.

3. Next, type the word "FROM" followed by the name and address of your company.

4. At the right hand corner of the page, type the name and phone number of a contact at your company. This information gives editors someone to call in case they have a question about the release.

5. If it's okay for the editor to publish the information right away, space down two spaces and type in "For immediate release." If the release is related to a future event, say the Fourth of July, indicate the date it can be run.

6. The headline, all caps and no more than two lines, comes next. Craft headlines carefully. They should be a short synopsis of the material in the story. Their job is to capture the attention of the editor. A clever headline that the editor can use verbatim has a better chance of being published.

7. Space down a few more lines and begin typing the story. Write it in short paragraphs which the editor can select for use as space allows. Keep sentences and paragraphs short. Avoid hyperbole. Double space so the editor can pencil in any changes.

8. Type in "END" when you are finished so the editor knows there's no more to come.

9. Send the press release to every respectable publication that might possibly use it.

New product announcements

One of the easiest press releases to get into print or on the air is a new product announcement. If the product has just been introduced to the market, reporting on it is considered genuine news by editors, particularly to the trade journals who report on that industry. Some publications will run new product announcements at no charge and track the leads that result from the story. Their space people will then try to sell advertising based on the results.

The new product announcement should include the following:

1. Information about the new product.
2. What the new product does and the benefits it provides.
3. A fact or specification sheet on the product.
3. What product the new product replaces, if pertinent.
4. A picture or drawing of the product.
5. A positive quote about the product, even if that quote is from someone in the company. (" 'The Aviary Flush will change bird cage cleaning forever,' said company president, Ken Canary.")
6. Information about the company.

Seven hints on how to get a press release into print

Considering the blizzard of press releases they receive every day, how do editors decide which ones deserve publication and which ones get relegated to the circular file? The first, most important criterion is that the information appears newsworthy. If the release contains material editors think their readers will find worthwhile, in it goes. Here are some additional criteria:

1. Write copy that follows the style of the publication. The less editing the material requires, the better chance it has of being published.

2. Take your best shot early. Put the nitty-gritty, eye-catching information into the first sentence.

3. Be neat. Double-space the typed copy. Make it easy for editors to read.

4. Forget hyperbole. Editors won't give free space to what they consider to be out-and-out advertising copy.

5. Be brief. If the editors want a feature article on the subject, they will assign it—and pay for it!

6. Include photographs and other displays. With the success of *USA Today*, every publication is trying to be more "visual."

7. Send the material to the right department editor. If you don't know who that is, do a little digging. Putting the material in the right hands is more than half the battle.

PRESS KITS

Press kits are what the name implies: packets of information given to reporters in the hope that some of it will get published. Kits are used extensively at industry conventions and new product launches. The press kit is usually packaged in a 9-by-12-inch folder, which means it can contain more pages and be more detailed than a press release.

The traditional kit contains information about the product, perhaps even data on the entire product line, material about the company, product brochures and catalogs, glossy photos of the products, maybe even a handsome picture of company headquarters or the CEO looking bottom-line serious in his Armani suit. They are meant to offer reporters a more complete picture of the organization or the product that is about to be launched. Often, press kits are used as handouts after a briefing by a company representative, saving the poor reporter the burden of taking notes.

THE PLANTED ARTICLE

Public relations at its best is the use of the planted magazine article to provide a positive image of the organization and its management. The article appears to be normal reporting, written by someone on the publication's staff, or by a freelance reporter. The tone is positive, but the article does not appear to be slanted. Typical topics include highlighting a manufacturing process, describing a business turnaround, providing information on a new product or system, or profiling a company's senior-level executive. Some CEOs are so anxious to be "profiled" in this manner that they pay public relations firms who can manage it big fees.

Many of these planted articles are actually written by public relations firms who then try to place them with various trade publications. It's a trade-off that benefits all parties. The trade publication gets a polished article on a subject of interest to the readers. The company gets some positive publicity. The PR firm gets paid for its efforts.

WHAT TO CONSIDER BEFORE HIRING A PR FIRM

Firms that go outside their own organizations for public relations expertise must first decide what they want the PR firm to accomplish and what degree of cooperation they're prepared to offer to reach these goals. (First rule of PR: don't stonewall your own PR firm.) If the goal is to polish the CEO's image, and that one is fairly common, then the CEO has to make herself available to:

- Members of the PR firm.
- To the press.
- To security analysts.
- To watch-dog groups.
- To government regulators.
- To others as the PR firm suggests.

CEOs should realize in advance that all of this accessibility will be time consuming and they must make the appropriate commitments. Secrecy is the enemy of positive PR. CEOs must learn how to appear before the media and others, and how to *appear* to be candid. A good PR firm can help senior managers learn this facility.

Eight hints when hiring a PR firm

Here are additional points to remember when hiring any PR firm.

1. PR firms only give advice. They don't, and they shouldn't, run your company. If, however, the advice of the PR firm isn't trusted, get another.

2. Get a member of the PR firm involved on the new product planning team. PR people may not know how the whiz-bang works, but they may provide valuable advice on how to sell it.

3. Good PR firms take advantage of publicity opportunities. That means they must have access to senior-level decision makers who can authorize courses of action without relying on committees who require days of deliberations.

4. Get references. Check the PR firm's current list of clients. Are these clients happy with the firm's work? Check former clients too. Why did they leave?

5. Meet the movers and shakers at the agency. Do you like and understand one another? If there's no rapport, you haven't found the right agency.

6. Discuss the company's game plan and let the PR firm explain how they see their role in making it happen.

7. Learn how the agency bills their clients. Do they charge by the hour? On a monthly retainer? What will you be getting for your money? (The fees are likely going to be higher than you thought they were going to be.)

8. Make sure that key agency people are available when you need them. If they're always spending time with "more important" clients, get an agency where your firm is a more important client.

Marketing promotions

Promotion is a marriage of convenience between advertising and public relations. Like all advertising, promotion is designed to move product, but the public relations part in the equation sets up other goals. These goals could include:

- Increasing product or brand recognition.
- Shoring up the company image.
- Strengthening the company's relationship with resellers.
- Developing a database.
- Any combination of the above.

Many promotions require the customer to take some action. This action could be to:

- Clip a coupon and take it to the store for a discount on the product.
- Enter a name and address in a contest.
- Buy one—get one free.
- Send in a form and receive a factory rebate.
- Mail in for something free, such as book of recipes.
- Come to a location to see a personality perform.
- Phone a toll-free number for information.
- Access an Internet website for details.

The common denominator in all of the above is that the customer becomes involved.

Most promotions offer the customer something extra but are valid only for a short time. The promotions urge customers to take advantage of this additional value while they can.

How cosmetic companies promote their products

Cosmetic companies' marketing tactics are an example of how companies can promote products without resorting to price cuts. Any woman can tell you that the premier cosmetics companies never, ever discount their prices. For a cosmetics company, a $10 mascara is $10 for 365 days a year—unless the price goes up. The strategy behind this one-price marketing policy is that the companies don't want women to hold off buying these "necessities" in the hope that a sale is on the horizon.

When the cosmetics companies seek to hype sales, they do so by offering various promotions. One of the most popular is a "gift with purchase." Buy a lipstick or eyeliner (at a certain minimum price) and the cosmetics company throws in a free gift. This gift often includes kits, bags, or packages filled with more cosmetics, including samples of new products. The promotion not only results in additional sales, but helps the company introduce new products to loyal customers.

Another type of promotion popular with cosmetics companies is a "purchase with purchase." In this type of promotion the customer must buy a product at the regular price to get the opportunity to buy another special product at a price that appears to be less than its value. Like most promotions, the purchase-with-purchase offer is available for a short time.

Gift-with-purchase and purchase-with-purchase deals are frequently run during holiday seasons. The customer purchases a bottle of cologne for Auntie Sue as a Christmas gift and receives a free clutch purse for herself.

COUPONS

Every Sunday newspaper carries pages and pages of cents-off coupons, mostly for supermarket items. Thrifty customers clip these coupons to take with them when they shop. Store chains process the coupons, receiving their value back, plus a processing fee, from the manufacturer. Occasionally the manufacturers will grumble and threaten to discontinue their coupons, but faced with competitors who won't do likewise, they never follow through.

Marketers use coupons to encourage shoppers to try or keep using their products. They are effective in promoting the sale of brand-new products and hyping the sale of familiar ones.

Americans like the coupons. Some shoppers keep them neatly organized into product categories. They won't buy a product that doesn't offer some sort of discount. Other shoppers use coupons to lower the cost of an item that they might not otherwise purchase. For these reasons, coupons will remain a popular promotion method.

TIE-INS

Tie-ins are sales promotions that are wedded to another event. For example, whenever a new Disney movie debuts, a fast-food chain, such as Burger King, may offer free dolls in the likeness of characters featured in that movie. To qualify, customers must purchase a "kid's meal."

Both organizations profit. The fast-food chain gets additional traffic in its restaurants and the movie studio receives free publicity related to its new release. Most tie-in promotions are related to some phase of the entertainment industry. These include those promotions related to major sporting events, live performances by music personalities, and so forth. Retailers, for example, will often offer free or cut-rate tickets to sporting events and live concerts as a way of encouraging customers to patronize their shops.

Tie-ins are also used for promotional packaging. For example, when *The Lost World,* a movie about dinosaurs, was released, all manner of familiar products, such as bags of potato chips, appeared decorated with pictures of *Lost World* dinosaurs. Some packaging was even in the shape of dinosaurs.

Marketers must move quickly on tie-in promotions. A current event tie-in promotion will produce a surge of interest, but this interest is usually short-lived. When the movie, or other event, has faded, the promotion is dead.

CONTESTS AND SWEEPSTAKES

Contests and sweepstakes offer customers the opportunity to win a prize. This prize can be cash, a vacation trip, a sports car, a shopping spree, or whatever. Usually, the only thing customers must do to enter the contest is submit their names and addresses. (This has the added benefit of providing the company running the contest with a customer database.) No purchase is necessary; laws forbid this requirement. The odds of winning are infinitesimal, but millions of people enter contests in the hope of getting something for nothing.

Marketers use contests to introduce a new product or to stimulate sales of an existing product. They are effective for this purpose. Even with the no-purchase-required stipulation, many customers buy the product because they feel that using the "official entry form" enhances their chances of winning. Some companies get around the no-purchase-required rule by placing contest entry forms inside their product. The entry form could be part of the box, inside the box, or underneath the lid. The companies stay legal by offering to mail a free entry form to anyone who writes to request one.

Considering the interest they generate, sweepstakes contests are relatively inexpensive to run. Some companies, particularly a few selling magazine subscriptions, market exclusively through sweepstakes. They must be on to something, because their prizes get larger every year.

The problem with contests is that there are very few winners in proportion to the number of entries. Many people simply ignore contests for this reason. There are also a number of contest mavens who spent much of their spare time entering every contest offered a myriad of times. Their sheer volume of entries means they win a disproportionate share of the prizes. This kind of "professional" contestant has no real interest in the product. They seldom become good customers.

FREE ADVICE

One of the oldest business clichés is that, "free advice is worth what you pay for it." Contrary to this conventional wisdom, many marketers find that free advice pays very well. The difference is that they are dispensing free advice, not paying for it.

Free advice as a marketing tactic is popular with the cosmetics companies that were profiled earlier. Customers are encouraged to come in for advice on skin care or to receive a free make-over by a "beauty consultant." Theoretically the customer is under no obligation by accepting this offer, but most women who accept the free offer leave the store laden with a bag of cosmetics they have purchased.

The insurance agent who offers to come to a prospect's home for a "free evaluation" of the prospect's insurance needs is also using the free advice technique. The agent inevitably concludes that the prospect is under-insured.

Seminars

A variation, and a good one, of the free advice giveaway is the free seminar. Equipment manufacturers and resellers invite prospects to "free" sessions during which products are demonstrated. The features and benefits of these products or services are explained and various concerns are answered. Often, refreshments are served. There may even be a shill or two in the audience throwing up lollipop questions or offering testimonials.

The incentive for those who attend is that they will receive valuable information. Some information is offered to keep the attendees in their seats. The real goal for the seminar giver, however, is to convert these information seekers into customers.

Free seminars are used to attract customers for many types of services such as writing "living wills," for offering investment opportunities, for enrolling senior citizens in health-care plans, and for selling time-shares in vacation properties.

The seminars work because they get a great many prospects together at one time. The prospects are made to feel important, but they are a captive audience. The company's best salespeople and senior executives can be in attendance to participate, to answer questions, to make suggestions, and to try to close deals. The presentations, including the questions-and-answers session, can be rehearsed until they are letter perfect.

The disadvantage of seminars is that they have often been used in an unethical manner to separate senior citizens, and others, from their money. In the pursuit of a buck, high-pressure tactics are sometimes used and unsubstantiated claims are made.

FREE SAMPLES

"Free" is the most exciting word in the English language. Just mention it and watch people scramble to take advantage of whatever it is that is being offered. Many marketers use this excitement to acquaint customers with new products by offering free, introductory samples. These samples usually come in special, smaller packages that are designed to give the customer a "taste" of the product and, it is hoped, a hankering for more.

Free samples are also used to encourage impulse purchases. The supermarket dispensing morsels of Cheddar cheese or smoked sausage is hoping their customers will add these items to tonight's menu.

Offering free samples not only introduces a product to consumers, but often gives marketers an idea of the public's reaction to it. A questionnaire may be included with the sample.

Distribution of free samples is often handled in one of the following ways:

1. *Clip-out coupons in newspapers and magazines.* Customers bring the coupon into the store and are not charged for the item when they check out. The advantage of this method is that only people who are interested in the product bother to take advantage of the offer.

2. *Actual product sample delivered with the daily paper.* The advantage of this method is that the entire circulation of the newspaper receives a sample.

3. *In-store personnel who pass out the samples to shoppers.* The advantage of this method is that customers receive the free sample at the point of purchase.

4. *Rebate coupon that the shopper mails in with proof-of-purchase for a refund.* The problem with this method is that the customer has postage expense and often must wait for six to eight weeks for the refund. The marketer knows that not every rebate coupon will be redeemed, thus lowering promotional costs.

Free sample promotions work best when the samples are distributed in tandem with money-off coupons. The customer gets the first taste free and a discount on the first product purchased. The marketing strategy behind this approach is to establish customer buying habits.

"Free" as a motivator

"Free" certainly causes people to take notice. Use free samples to encourage customers to try a new product, to enlarge a customer base, to draw a crowd to a grand opening, or to create excitement: "The first fifty people in the store will receive a free digital watch."

A caution about "free"

Aside from the promotional cost, the danger of using free samples, even trial sizes, to enlarge the market for a current product is that distributing the samples sometimes temporarily drives down sales. Customers who normally buy the product will instead stockpile the freebies. They're out of the market until the freebies are depleted. Offering free samples repeatedly devalues the product. Why purchase something when it may be available later for no cost?

REBATES

Manufacturer rebates are still another popular promotion method. They are used with such diverse consumer products as wine, office machines, and computer software. Amounts of the rebate vary from one dollar to several hundred dollars.

In this type of promotion the customer who buys an item is given a mail-in form to be sent to the manufacturer along with the proof-of-purchase. (Rebates under one dollar don't work because the customer must spend 32 cents in postage to mail in the forms). When this mail-in form is received by the manufacturer, a check for the amount promised is sent to the end-user/customer. In effect, the customer has purchased the product at a discount.

Rebates are popular with resellers because they help move product, but it is the manufacturer who is responsible for paying for the discount. The reseller can maintain any profit margin it wishes. In the case of automobiles, the cost of the rebate is shared by the manufacturer and the dealer. That makes the rebate seem larger than it actually is because the dealer has less room to discount.

Manufacturers offer rebates because they are used as an incentive to encourage resellers to stock up on the product. ("You better take a gross. We're announcing a $50 rebate next week.") They are often used by the manufacturer to promote the sale of slow-moving products. Resellers may even strongly request that the manufacturers take this step when they have a problem with too much inventory.

Marketers know that a certain percentage of the rebate forms will never be completed and mailed by the customer, which means their promotional costs are reduced.

EIGHT RULES FOR EFFECTIVE PROMOTIONS

Types of promotion possibilities are only limited by the marketing manager's imagination. There are, however, rules that apply to any kind of promotion. Rules for making a promotion effective include:

1. *Keep the promotion simple.* Don't make it complicated for the customer to understand or to participate.

2. *Set specific goals.* What do you want the promotion to accomplish?

3. *One goal at a time please.* Setting multiple goals will only confuse the customers—and make the results harder to measure.

4. *Make sure that everybody's operating on the same wavelength.* Will the sales department have the brochures in time for the product launch? Are the point-of-purchase displays in place? Does telemarketing know about the special pricing? Are the resellers on board? (How many times have you walked into a department store to take advantage of a sale only to find that not one clerk in the place knows anything about it?)

5. *Know the target audience.* What will best appeal to the customers you're trying to reach? Are they looking for cents-off coupons? A chance to win a Hawaii vacation? Structure the promotion accordingly.

6. *Make the value real.* There are too many promotions offering phony discounts, bogus contests, and phantom giveaways. People see through these deceptive deals. When planning a promotion, don't bankrupt the company, but do offer something special.

7. *Select the media depending on the type of promotion.* Some promotions are best advertised in newspapers. Others are best suited to radio or television, or run at the point of purchase.

8. *Keep the offer related to the product that is being promoted.* Victoria's Secret wouldn't offer a free football to customers who purchase a silk negligee.

Chapter Four

PRODUCT DEVELOPMENT

Products are combustible. They provide the heat that energizes the company, but, after a time, the fire inevitably wanes into embers unless more fuel is added. That fuel is new products. Every company, regardless of its size, must have some sort of plan in place to develop and introduce new products. The process must be continuous, as normal and fundamental a part of business as making sales, taking inventory, and meeting payroll. Consider it corporate furnace stoking, a necessary chore to keep out the chill.

EIGHT THINGS NEW PRODUCTS DO FOR A COMPANY

1. New products are necessary for any commercial organization's continuity. The products of today won't be good enough to serve the markets of tomorrow.

2. New products allow the company to maintain and increase sales and profits.

3. New products are a morale booster. Developing and marketing new products are more interesting and exciting than working on the same old stuff.

4. New products allow the company to keep pace with its client industries and to maintain an industry image as an innovator.

5. New products allow the company to expand and to enter new markets.

6. New products expand the company's scope and help increase the sales and profits of the existing product line.

7. New products create renewed interest in the company. Customers and prospects are more willing to talk to company representatives.

8. New products occasionally change the focus of the company and take it in a new direction.

WHAT IS A NEW PRODUCT ANYWAY?

Not every new product need be revolutionary or a breakthrough. It isn't necessary to have Edison, Steinmetz, or Tesla working in the R & D lab, although that lineup wouldn't hurt any program. Often, a new product for a company is something as simple as slightly modifying an existing model by increasing its operating speed, shrinking its size, or adding a feature.

This category of new products that builds on past experience are called "evolutionary" because they are natural improvements. These improvements could be the result of customer requests, an advance in technology, or knowledge gained through the manufacturing process. For example, through experience, product manufacture can often be simplified, requiring fewer parts, less expensive materials, and shorter assembly time. These simplified versions cost less to make and can be offered to the marketplace at lower costs.

New products also don't necessarily involve hard goods. For a service-oriented organization, a new product might be a service not previously offered or another feature added to an existing service. An inventory management company might add cash management or payroll services for their clients. A dry cleaner might offer clothing alterations, minor repairs, or tuxedo rental. For a farmer's produce combine selling lettuce, a "new" product might be washed salad packaged with dressing.

SIX COMMON NEW PRODUCT CATEGORIES

Most marketers divide new products into six general categories. These categories are:

1. *Revolutionary products that bring about fundamental changes in the way things are done.** These kinds of products shake up an industry—maybe even an entire culture. The Model T Ford is a good example. There were automobiles before the Model T, but Henry Ford's vision of a motor car affordable to the masses transformed our society. Many new industries were born as a result of this revolution and many others perished.

2. *Breakthrough products that have a dramatic impact on the company's status.* The breakthrough product performs a function infinitely better than any product previously available. The breakthrough product operates at twice the speed, uses one-tenth the energy, or cuts the price to the end user by more than half.

The breakthrough product is wildly successful because it is a dramatic improvement and the marketplace instantly recognizes the value it offers. Sales skyrocket, profits soar, and the company that introduced it is changed forever. Every marketer dreams of managing at least one breakthrough product during his or her career.

3. *Evolutionary products that are natural developments or extensions of the current product line.* More horsepower is added to the motor, the capacity of the input or output mechanism is increased, memory is added, and so forth.

Market conditions often dictate these advancements. For example, the 100-watt light bulb has been around for decades. The 100-watt light bulb that uses vastly less energy is a fairly recent development of the need to conserve power.

4. *Modified products that improve their company's competitive position.* This category is what "new and improved" is all about. It often involves product changes dictated by the marketing department.

---

*Marketers should not expect immediate acceptance of revolutionary products. They often fail because the marketplace isn't ready for them.

Additions are made to make the products sexier or to give the marketer a different platform. For example, raisins or sugar coating are added to corn flakes. Perfume is added to cleaning soap. Rice is parboiled to make it "instant."

5. *Products that are new to the company, but not new to the marketplace.* Not everyone can be first out of the box with a new product. Often, the biggest improvements in a product come not from the company that introduced it, but from an outfit that came late to the dance and had to create something better to compete.*

Instead of blazing the trail, Big Blue graciously permits other companies to conduct very expensive market research for them. The process saves many missteps. When they observe that a product has a good future, IBM relies on their reputation and marketing muscle to help them catch up quickly. This tactic ensures that any new product they introduce offers a substantial market opportunity.

6. *Products that are repackaged old-hat products masquerading as new.* Some marketers will try to revive a slumping or mature product by repackaging it and trying to sell it into a different marketplace. For example, a national baker might take a popular cookie and package it in a "snack size" container that is convenient to toss into children's school lunchboxes.

The safety razor is another good example of successful repackaging. The male market for the safety razor has long been saturated. This market can only expand to the extent that the population expands. In fact, it is subject to contraction as electric razors capture a market share. Along came the marketers with a simple idea. They packaged the safety razor in a box printed with flowers and other soft designs. They curved the handle and colored it in pastel shades. They ran ads showing women with bare, attractive legs using the product. Suddenly that familiar, rugged, face-scraping utensil became an aid to feminine beauty, a dainty "lady's razor." Hallelujah! The potential market had just doubled.

---

*Some companies avoid being first in favor of being best. For example, IBM is seldom found occupying the cutting edge when it comes to new products. Its corporate philosophy seems to reflect that cautious wisdom: "The pioneers are the guys with the arrows in their backs."

SEVEN THINGS EVERY COMPANY MUST DO TO BRING NEW PRODUCTS TO MARKET

Like all things that grow, new products thrive best in friendly environments. The following is the corporate mind-set that nurtures new product development.

1. The company must be in constant contact with its customers and the industries it serves. If the company's focus is on solving customer problems, it will create products that offer value.

2. The company must believe in assuming reasonable risk. Those employees who try and succeed are rewarded. Those who try and fail are not punished. (There is a saying at General Electric that no one is qualified to be president of the company unless he or she is responsible for at least one million-dollar mistake.)

3. The company must have people in the organization who are specifically dedicated to bringing new products to market. These people could be product managers, planners, members of a new products team, and the engineers and scientists over at the skunk works. In a one-person outfit, product planning must be the responsibility of the lone star who runs the show.

4. The company must be willing to spend money on new product development. How much money? Sony, for example, employs more than nine thousand scientists and engineers. This company spends about 5.7 percent of its total revenue, which equates to $1.5 billion a year, to support R & D. The investment results in four new products introduced by Sony *every business day*.

New product budgets must be maintained even when profits are down. This is the last place to cut back because new products are needed to bring the company back up.

5. The company must be willing to conduct market research to determine if planned new products are, indeed, what customers actually want. Products created in a corporate vacuum suffocate for lack of air.

6. Companies must take steps to remove new product development from the corporate political arena. Any backstabbing or glory grabs should be strongly discouraged.

7. Companies must make new products, which may currently exist only on a drawing board, part of future forecasts for sales and profits. Putting them in the future forecast ensures their current development.

THREE THINGS THAT WORK AGAINST NEW PRODUCT DEVELOPMENT

Ever notice that some companies continually lag behind their peers in the introduction of new products? There are many reasons why some companies are always behind the curve. Here are three of the most common:

1. Fear of failure, or a corporate culture in which failure is punished. Why stick your neck out when it's likely to be lopped off? Past mistakes tend to make planners more cautious. Sure, the mistakes should be analyzed and lessons learned, but they are no reason to stop trying.

2. Bean counters in charge who want only to maximize profits today. If the company's P & L statement is being polished up for Wall Street, or to make it an attractive takeover candidate, new product development often suffers.

3. There is nobody in charge who is able and willing to pull the trigger on new product commitments. Some companies give committees the responsibility for new product development. That's okay just as long as someone who can make decisions is in charge of the committee.

PRODUCT DEVELOPMENT AND RETURN ON INVESTMENT (ROI)

One of the ways the Japanese drive competitors to their knees is through the relentless introduction of new products and models. While many American companies try to squeeze a certain lifespan out of a product to pay for its development costs and provide a proper return on investment, the Japanese amortize development costs over much shorter periods. The result is that they spit out new products at a dizzying pace, each new model a bit sexier than its predecessor. The competitor who sets her sights on a particular Japanese product is likely aiming at the wrong target.

The fact is that new product development requires a continual dialogue (or battle) between marketing and finance about realistic product lifespans and the return on investment. One way to win the dialogue is get a senior person from finance on the new product development team.*

PRODUCT DEVELOPMENT AND DUCK HUNTING

Product development teams aiming at the competition have the same problem that a hunter has when trying to knock a duck out of the sky. If the hunter aims directly at the duck, he'll miss badly because the duck will have flown past that point by the time the shot arrives. The hunter must lead the duck, that is *anticipate* its arrival at a different point in the sky and aim accordingly.

Like the duck hunter, development teams can't aim their big guns at products currently on the market, unless they can produce them cheaper. They must anticipate what is likely to be available from the competition when the company's product will be ready to be launched and surpass that competitive entry. This concept is called "leapfrogging." In some industries, two or more competitors are engaged in continual leapfrogging, springing to new positions off one another's backs.

THE IMPORTANCE OF TIMING WHEN BRINGING NEW PRODUCTS TO MARKET

Got a revolutionary idea for a product that will shake up the industry? Don't crank up the production line just yet. No matter how good that product is, it could be quite a while before the marketplace accepts it. Here's one example:

If there is any one product responsible for waylaying the "paperless office" so widely predicted by industry experts twenty years ago, it is the fax machine. Every office and many homes have a fax. The technology is ancient. The idea behind facsimile transmission has been around for more than 150 years. The first photograph was delivered via fax more than 85 years ago. Wire photos, sent by a kind of fax transmission, have been used

---

*Marketers who wish to amortize development costs over shorter lifespans must be prepared to set higher prices for their products. This is the trade-off that financing will demand.

by newspapers and police departments for more than fifty years. Yet facsimile machines didn't become an integral part of most offices until just a few years ago. Anyone manufacturing fax machines before that time had a tough sell into a limited market.

There are reasons why it took the market such a long time to accept fax systems. In those early years there were no standards for fax machines. Every fax machine manufacturer used a different signal for sending and receiving. To communicate with one another, two machines had to be made by the same manufacturer. That constraint severely limited the machine's usefulness. A few companies used them to communicate between the home office and branches. Fax machines were also expensive to buy and operate. They were competing with the U.S. Post Office when the message wasn't urgent and with Western Union when it was.

It was only when international standards were adopted that allowed all fax machines to "talk" to one another, regardless of their manufacture, that the industry exploded. When every machine used the same sending and receiving codes, a machine made by Panasonic could send a fax to a machine made by Hewlett Packard. That meant any two companies with fax machines made by different companies could send paper messages to one another.

When office machine manufacturers saw the market opportunity in compatible fax transmission, more companies entered the arena to produce product. The additional competition made the machines less expensive. More features were added making the machines even simpler to use. Compared to fax, Western Union was inconvenient. The Post Office became less desirable. In a few years every business *had* to have a fax.

The point is that timing is an important ingredient when bringing a revolutionary new product to market. Conditions must be right if the marketplace is to accept the product. In the case of fax machines, the critical timing factor was when communications standards were set.

A CAVEAT ON REVOLUTIONARY PRODUCTS

Have you invented something that's going to replace the automobile? Don't count on immediate market acceptance even if your product produces dramatic results. Your product is revolutionary, and revolutions upset the existing order. They don't necessarily succeed.

In some instances, a revolutionary product changes the destiny of the company. Xerox is an example. The Xerox plain-paper copier turned a 13-

million-dollar a year "nice little" company into a business giant with annual sales far in excess of ten billion dollars.*

Revolutionary products, however, can also unravel the structure and profitability of an organization. That's because it's difficult to predict market acceptance of a totally new concept, and it's hard to anticipate the impact of true innovation on the current product line.

Questions to ask about revolutionary products

The questions that marketers must ask about revolutionary products before bringing them to market are:

1. Is the market ready for it?
2. Will the market pay for it?
3. Does it offer a real advantage to the customer over what is available now?
4. Are we satisfied that it really works?
5. Can we make and sell it in profitable quantities?
6. Is it priced so customers perceive it as a value? If not, is there another way, such as leasing, to solve the pricing problem?
7. How will it impact the current product line?
8. Will educating and training our customers and prospects about this innovation take up all our time and attention? (Research this one carefully; innovative products consume time.)
9. Will it mark our company as a pioneer and help distinguish us from the competition?
10. Will it be an easy product for our competitors to copy?
11. Is the competition already working on something similar? (That, by itself, doesn't necessarily mean your company must follow suit. As Napolean said, "Never interrupt the enemy when he is making mistakes.")
12. Can the product be suppressed for a time while older, more profitable products are maintained? (If the innovation offers true benefits not now available, the answer to the suppression question is almost always no. Sorry, you conspiracy buffs, but there is no really cheap alternative to gasoline that is being suppressed by the oil companies.)
13. What effect is the innovation likely to have on the company's bottom line, both near term and long range?

---

*It's important to distinguish between product improvement and genuine revolutionary innovation. Product improvement is almost always a good thing for the company.

WHAT EVERY MARKETER SHOULD KNOW ABOUT RESEARCH AND DEVELOPMENT

The research and development team are those scientists and engineers who occupy the laboratory they won't let ordinary folks near. They're the ivory-tower team working on the secret stuff that will knock the socks off the competition. They are tinkering with the motors of the vehicles that will transport the company to tomorrow.

Actually, the name of the department is misleading. Most company R & D operations are strictly devoted to developing new products. They should properly be called product development laboratories. Only a few, such as Lucent Technologies (formerly Bell Labs), engage in basic research.

The average percentage spent on R & D for large companies is 3.9 percent of sales. Small companies, with under $100 million in sales, invest an average of 8.7 percent. In high-technology industries, the average spent is much larger. How much is your company spending?

Ten pearls of wisdom regarding research and development

A research and development department can be any size from Sony's nine thousand scientists and engineers to a single would-be entrepreneur who tinkers in the garage on weekends. (If any reader thinks less of the latter, consider the two Steves, Messrs. Wozniak and Jobs who developed the Apple computer in a garage.)

A good R & D department will result in a steady flow of new products. A poor one will represent a direct cash drain, badly conceived products and marketing dollars spent traveling down blind alleys. For those responsible for establishing or running an R & D operation, here are thoughts on making it more effective.

1. When hiring for the R & D team, stay away from too many specialists. Often, a specialist's scope is too narrow to be truly innovative.

2. Base product development on the perceived need for something. Products in search of a market are tough to sell.

3. Put the money into development rather than surroundings. The R & D center doesn't have to be a palace. Too many companies build Taj Mahals badly disguised as laboratories.

4. Be reconciled to the fact that only one out of every twenty to twenty-five ideas will ever result in a product coming to market.

5. Be further reconciled to the fact that fourteen out of every fifteen products will fail.

6. If the company can afford to employ several teams working independently on the same project, do it. Competition works in R & D too!

7. Get senior management involved. At most U.S. companies, senior management gives the majority of their time and attention to current products. Japanese managers know better. They devote the majority of time to new products.

8. Engage in market research, but keep intelligence gathering to reasonable time limits. Waiting until everything is known is waiting too long because *all* the facts are never in. Extreme caution could cost the company a jump on the market. Go with hunches. Treasure inspiration.

9. Wait until the last minute before freezing specifications on a new product. Once the specifications are set in concrete, so are the minds working on the project. Keeping the architecture open keeps the creative juices flowing.

10. Stamp out the N.I.H. (not invented here) factor. Good ideas can come from any source. A great many ideas will come from customers, from company employees, and others who are not "designated inventors."

SIX QUESTIONS TO ASK BEFORE SPENDING A DIME ON DEVELOPMENT

The company has a promising idea for a new product. What comes next? The traditional answer is "market research." There are, however, logical questions that should be asked even before investing in market research. These questions are:

1. Who will buy this product? (This one is a variation of that basic marketing query "Where will the customers come from?")

2. Can we make this product or provide this service in a cost-effective manner? The ability of managers to realistically assess their organization's capabilities is vital when contemplating new products. Stretches are okay. Wild leaps into the unknown usually result in a crash to the canyon floor.

3. What impact would this product have on our current product line? Would the company be killing the golden goose to lay a rotten egg?

4. What sales channels would be used to move this product? New channels which the company hasn't used before may not be as easy to penetrate as you imagined. In the words of Little Richard, "The other guy's grass may look greener, but it's just as tough to cut."

5. When this product is ready for the market, will the market be ready for the product? Think about the duck hunting analogy.

6. Will this product give us a competitive edge? If the answer to this one is negative, why go any further?

FIVE SIGNS THAT INDICATE WHEN PRODUCTS ARE REACHING THE END OF THE LINE

How long will the current product line still be competitive? The answer is important because the marketer needs to know when, exactly, to introduce new products into the market.

Even when sales are satisfactory, there are signs that point to a product's inevitable decline. These signs are:

1. There are many competitive products coming on the market that are as good as, or even better than, those the company offers. This one obviously means trouble. Get over to the R & D laboratory fast to see what they have cooking that will help you counter. Don't count on the company's superior relationship with customers to help you carry the day. If the competition offers a better value in the form of superior features or lower pricing, the marketplace will react to it.

2. Sales volumes are still good, but profit margins are diminishing. The customers are demanding bigger discounts to order the same quantities.

3. Reseller inventories are becoming bloated. If sell-through isn't happening, orders will stop soon. (Advance orders are already declining.) Demands for returns and credits will start shortly thereafter.

4. The sales staff's complaints are rising. They want more bells and whistles on the product, or a giveaway price. Don't assume that everyone on the staff is making excuses. They may be reflecting the views of the marketplace.

5. It's hard to schedule appointments with prospects and customers to talk about the product. They're interested in other things.

PLANNED OBSOLESCENCE AS A MARKETING STRATEGY

Some companies schedule obsolescence just as rigidly as the factory workday is scheduled. These companies introduce new models at a relentless pace that crowd the old models off the shelves and out of the marketplace. Computer firms are a good example of this marketing strategy. Any PC that is more than two years old is an antique. They're not wanted by users who demand state-of-the-art hardware.

One of the things planned obsolescence accomplishes is to cause current customers to discard equipment that still has a useful life. It also reduces the number of industry players. Those companies that are not well funded just can't compete with the industry demand to remain "state-of-the-art."

SQUEEZING MAXIMUM MILEAGE OUT OF A PRODUCT

Other companies try to get maximum return from the investment in their existing products. They keep a product in the line just as long as sales volumes for the product are adequate. Tooling and development costs have been recovered and more profit comes to the bottom line. These products are considered "cash cows." The profits from them are often used to fund future developments.

Companies also use these products to attract price-conscious customers and to place additional pressure on the competition. An example of this strategy is how the Ford Motor Company positioned the Thunderbird. From 1987 to 1997, only cosmetic changes were made in each Thunderbird model year. When all tooling costs were amortized, Ford used the automobile as their low-price sporty-car leader. A "loaded" model was priced at less than full-size cars from other manufacturers. The design eventually got stale.

Fewer models were sold each year until Ford retired the Thunderbird at the end of 1997. It will come back in a few years with a complete makeover.

Bringing a new product to market

More than 80 percent of all planned products never make it to market. That's not necessarily a bad number. Aborting a poorly planned project is preferable to launching it and watching it die. There is less corporate pain and certainly less cost. The only thing that suffers when a project is aborted is corporate ego, and ego alone is no reason to waste millions.

Getting a new product to market necessarily involves many different departments or responsibilities. In a manufactured product the involved departments might include:

- Research & Development
- Marketing
- Finance
- Manufacturing
- Administration

Each department has a different focus, so who should determine if a potential product deserves to see the light of day? Many companies use committees or teams with representatives from each "discipline" to make this determination. The bigger the organization, the more likely the team approach will be used. Other companies will give the responsibility to a single person. This second approach will get new products into the marketplace faster. It doesn't necessarily guarantee that more new products will be successful. That depends on the ability of the project leader.

How to reduce the time it takes to get new products to market

"History exacts a penalty on those who are late," exhorted M. Gorbachev (who was late in recognizing that the Soviet Union was crumbling).

There is often a "window of opportunity" for new products. By that we mean that if the product is introduced within a certain time period it will succeed. If the product is late in arriving, other technologies and developments will surpass it. That means it's important to keep product development time to a minimum. The following are some time-saving hints:

1. No matter the size of the organization, have a specific path of approval for new products—and make the path short. Don't require sign-offs by everyone in the company from the janitor on up.

2. Set timetables, make them optimistic, and work like heck to meet them.

3. Develop a sense of urgency and convey it to everyone in the organization.

4. Take calculated risks. It's impossible to nail down everything.

5. Avoid the committee approach unless the committee has a strong leader with the authority to override objections.

ELEVEN PLACES WHERE NEW PRODUCT IDEAS COME FROM

Somewhere, in some mind, a light bulb is illuminated. Eureka! The idea for a new product is born. Here's where new ideas typically come from:

1. *R & D.* The boys and girls in the lab are always cooking up something.

2. *Market research.* Investigating what the marketplace wants and needs is one of the most common sources for new product ideas.

3. *Sales department.* The people on the front lines have a good feel for new products that will make their sales jobs easier.

4. *Product managers.* Anyone responsible for the care and feeding of a product line usually has a plan for that line's progression.

5. *Customers.* Those who are using a product often have the best ideas on how it can be improved.

6. *Prospects who didn't buy.* Listen to the objections when prospects tell salespeople why they turned down the product. These refusals may contain ideas for product improvement.

7. *Competition*. Many companies get ideas for new products from their competitors. (Never be too proud to steal a new idea, unless, of course, it is patented or copyrighted.)

8. *Company administrative employees*. Never ignore the person in the stockroom, the complaint clerk, or the guy on the shipping dock when one of these people makes a suggestion. Different job responsibilities give these employees perspectives that those in sales and marketing may lack.

9. *Publications*. Articles in industry magazines and newsletters may provide the source for a new product idea.

10. *Installation or service people*. Individuals responsible for the installation, repair, and maintenance of a product will often have insights on how it can be made better.

11. *Industry experts*. Some "gurus" offer legitimate vision as to where the industry is headed.

WHY NEW PRODUCTS FAIL

What makes one product introduction a hit while another is a miss? The answer to that can be illustrated by an old anecdote about a company that came out with a new dog food. The company hired the best veterinary nutritionists to develop a quality product. They used top artists to design the can labels. They recruited the best sales team money could buy to move the product. They spent millions on advertising. They priced the dog food at 20 percent under the competition.

The product still failed miserably. At a meeting to discuss the horrible results, the director of marketing asked if anyone on the sales team could explain the failure. One veteran salesman shouted out, "The dogs don't like it."

This ancient story explains everything: New products fail because they don't address the needs of the marketplace. The dogs must like it. How can the marketer determine the dogs' taste in advance? Market testing. Check out the dogs' reaction to the product at a dog pound. A kennel. The dog show. Give samples to vets.

WHERE DO BAD IDEAS COME FROM?

"Nothing is as powerful as a bad idea whose time has come."
Victor Hugo, paraphrased by the author

We have all heard about major marketing blunders such as the Edsel and New Coke. These ideas must have, at one time, seemed brilliant to the companies and marketing teams that conceived them. The best minds in these organizations thought these products were unconditional winners. Marketing research agreed. Millions of dollars, make that tens of millions, were spent in promoting the products to an unappreciative public. The products bombed. How could the best and brightest marketing managers and all the market research be so wrong? Here's how:

1. *Hubris*. The Greeks believed this fancy name for arrogance was a fatal flaw. Some organizations believe that if they like a new product idea, the public will necessarily love it. This malady is found most often in organizations with large market share.

2. *Compromise*. Finance has one idea. Manufacturing has another. Marketing wants something in between. The result is a product that no one, especially the buying public, wants. This malady is found most often in organizations that relegate new product decisions to committees.

3. *Elmer's Glue technology*. Some organizations will simply paste on a new feature, or new skin, to a mature product and hope the marketplace doesn't recognize that it's an old shoe in a new box. This malady is most prevalent in organizations that are trying to cut down on their engineering and R & D expenses.

4. *Assumptions, assumptions, assumptions*. Some organizations don't do any market research at all. They just assume that if their management likes the product, the marketplace will necessarily love it. This fanciful attitude is seen most often in some small companies that don't believe in, or don't understand, market research.

5. *The 800-pound gorilla loves it*. There are powerful people in some organizations who can ram a new product through the pipeline because of their forceful personalities. Just because some guy can shout everyone down, doesn't mean he can't have a bad idea. This malady is found in every size and type of organization. If the product fails, the 800-pound gorilla wanders off to another part of the jungle for a time.

6. *Impatience.* Some products take time to develop. The fact that the product isn't an instant winner doesn't automatically make it a loser. This malady is most often found in organizations where the people in finance rule the roost: "You aren't meeting your projections on this product. Let's pull the plug."

7. *Let's make it because we can make it.* These are products in search of an application. Some companies actually bring products to the market and hope that their customers find a use for them. This malady is most commonly found in companies in which engineering is top dog.

8. *Sloppy research.* Want to live on false hope? Send your sales team out with a prototype product and tell them to ask their customers and prospects whether they would buy this product if it were available at such-and-such a price. The sales team usually comes back with healthy projections. These projections may not be realized when the product is brought to market. Customer surveys, by themselves, are not enough. They rarely produce accurate results. What customers say they will buy and what they will actually buy are two different things.

9. *The emperor has no clothes.* Sometimes a new product just isn't any good, but no one in the organization will willingly acknowledge that fact. There is too much time and money (and careers) invested in the product to simply admit failure and move on to something else.

10. *Poor marketing.* Good products don't sell themselves, particularly when the marketplace isn't acquainted with them. If the marketing manager has chosen the wrong sales channels, or created an ineffective advertising campaign, or selected the wrong price points, or not reached prospects and customers with the company's story, the product will fail.

TEST MARKETING

Test marketing means bringing out a product in limited supply or limiting the introduction of a product to a specific geographic area. It allows the marketer to determine customer acceptance of the product. Test markets also allow the marketer to experiment with various price points (the marketer wants to know which price produces maximum sales volume and maximum profit), with packaging options, with the sales channels that will move the most product, with the optimum sizes that will produce the most profit, and so forth. Test marketing then is a vehicle that allows marketers to hedge their bets.

Test marketing is used most frequently in consumer products, such as breakfast cereals, though it is becoming more common in industrial products. Companies, such as McDonalds, will test customer acceptance of various new food items in a few cities before placing these items on their national menus. They'll also test various pricing combinations (milk shake, quarter-pounder, and small fries for $2.99) for customer acceptance.

Five reasons why test marketing increases the chance of success

Companies don't engage in test marketing merely because their marketers are cowards who are afraid of failure. There are genuine benefits. These are:

1. Testing limits the company's financial exposure in introducing a new product. Information is gathered on just how well the market will accept this product.

2. Test markets reveal if modifications in the product, the pricing, or the packaging are needed before a national rollout.

3. If the company is a start-up operation, test marketing may be the only way to prove to potential investors that the product is a winner.

4. Test marketing can test other aspects of the marketing campaign, including the advertising.

5. Test marketing allows the marketer to make more accurate sales projections when the national rollout is conducted. The warehouse won't be stacked with unsold product, nor will the file cabinets overflow with backorders.

Five reasons why test marketing is a mistake

Test marketing is no panacea; it also has a downside. There are good reasons why some companies bypass the test marketing step and take their products directly to the national arena. These reasons are:

1. Test marketing gives the competition advance information on the company's new product. They have time to react. There could be a competitive product on the market before your company has instituted a national rollout.

2. Test marketing is expensive. Some tests cost into seven figures. Why not use that money on a national rollout?

3. The tests aren't pure anymore. Modern communications have eliminated the pristine, isolated market.

4. The competition may attempt to skew the results. The information from the test may be poisoned.

5. Caution is costly. Test markets delay a product introduction by six to twelve months. In today's fast-paced business world, the product may be obsolete by the time it is given the green light.

Alternatives to test marketing

When test marketing runs into seven figures, gives the competition advance warning, and delays a product's entry into the market, you can bet that smart marketers will try to develop alternatives. These alternatives include:

1. *Consumer panels*. This method involves sitting a group of consumers around a table, feeding them coffee, and asking them a series of questions about a proposed new product:

- What would a fair price for that product be?
- Would they buy it?
- How would they use it?
- Did they prefer one package design over another?

Often, when this questioning is going on, the marketers are behind one-way mirrors watching the reactions.

2. *Consumer test stores*. Remember when you played "store" as a child? This is a similar game designed for grown-ups. A play store is set up, consumers are given "money" to use at that store, and then they are turned loose to see what they buy. Is this situation artificial? Of course it is. The results, however, do give marketing managers some insight as to what attracts consumers to a product.

3. *Customer site tests.* This method is often used with industrial products. Cooperative customers are given new product models and asked to use them in their operations. The customer will then record what was liked and disliked about the product.

4. *Reseller test marketing.* When products are sold to end-users through resellers, consultations with the buyers of these groups almost constitute a market study. Savvy buyers know what kind of products they can resell and at what price points.

5. *Company wise-man market testing.* Some marketers bring in top salespeople and regional managers for a discussion of a new product. These are the people in tune with the marketplace. They often have insights as to what will sell and what will fail.

THE PRODUCT LAUNCH LAUNDRY LIST

If marketing is both an art and a science, the "artsy" part involves launching a new product. In a way, introducing a new product is like bringing a baby into the world. Yesterday, the infant didn't exist. Today, it's alive and kicking, an entity, a part of the world. Like the infant, new products require intensive care and feeding to survive. Here are the things that need to be done:

1. The company's advertising agency should be involved throughout the planning process. If the project is confidential, limit the information to senior-level agency staff members.

2. The product must be set to go. This seems an obvious requirement, but some companies introduce new products while the lab is still tinkering with various versions.

3. If the company plans to test market, these tests must be completed before the national rollout. The results should be in and conclusions drawn from these results.

4. Manufacturing must be prepared to make the product. This means all suppliers must be in place and production capacity allocated. It also means that marketing must make accurate sales projections so manufacturing knows how many items to crank out each month.

5. The pricing and packaging must be finalized. Perhaps any test marketing revealed the best price points and most effective packaging choices.

6. The sales channels must be selected. For most companies, the channels used for the current product line will be the natural choices for new entries. When the products are truly different from previous offerings, new channels may be better suited.

7. The sales force must be educated and trained in the product. Other company personnel who normally are in contact with customers and prospects should also be trained. Nothing suggests a disorganized operation more than uninformed personnel.

8. The advertising campaign must be in place, including media selections, literature, promotions, and introductory offers.

9. Inventory must be available to satisfy the demand. Remember, backorders discourage customers.

TIMING NEW PRODUCT INTRODUCTIONS

The marketer must give careful consideration to timing when introducing new products. Those artificial Christmas trees won't do well if released to the market in July no matter how "life-like" they look. Specific timing factors should include:

1. *Seasonal considerations.* New products should arrive on the shelves or at resellers just before the beginning of a selling season.

2. *Promotional tie-ins.* Can the product introduction be tied to another event to give it more exposure?

3. *National conventions and trade shows.* Many companies introduce new products at trade shows and conventions because they can be seen by a large number of potential buyers in a short period of time.

4. *Media schedules.* Advertising campaigns must be planned months in advance. If specific issues of various publications are desired, the advance requirement may be even longer.

MARKETING PROBLEMS WITH NEW PRODUCTS IN NEW COMPANIES

Often, the reason a new company is formed is because the founder has an idea for a new product. If the founder has years of experience in the industry, this idea may be based on perceived need. In this kind of start-up the product may be developed very quickly (large corporations take note) because new product development is the organization's entire focus. There is also natural anxiety in any new company about bringing the product to market and generating revenue. This often leads to:

1. The hasty release of the product before it has been fully tested. If the product is deficient in any way, it acquires a poor reputation. Some products never recover from this bad beginning.

2. Inadequate market research as to where the customers are and what would induce them to buy.

3. Incorrect pricing that doesn't allow sufficient profit margins, or too-high prices that turn off potential buyers.

4. Wrong media choices in advertising. Deciding where to advertise new products isn't as simple as it appears.

5. Insufficient marketing budgets.

6. No fall-back marketing plan in the event the product isn't an immediate success.

7. Panic at the first sign of trouble.

All of these scenarios are why there is such a high failure rate in new products. The fault lies not only with the product itself, but also with the attempts to market it.

MARKETING PROBLEMS WITH NEW PRODUCTS IN LARGE COMPANIES

Big companies take longer to bring new products to market. In some instances they take so long, the marketplace has passed them by. Often, the delay is a function of their size, though recently the team concept has provided some large companies with a dash of entrepreneurial spirit. The specific problems big companies have in marketing new products include:

1. Committees are used to determine which new products should be developed, and these committees take forever to make decisions. Every department is represented, but there's really no one in charge.

2. The corporate culture is such that the smart political play is to avoid making mistakes.

3. Marketers demand too much research before making a decision.

4. Senior management demands guarantees.

PRICING CRITERIA FOR NEW PRODUCTS

The first pricing criterion is to price a new product so that it produces a profit at the projected sales volume. If the product can't make money for the company, why make it? Beyond that obvious requirement, there are many marketing considerations when developing new product pricing.

1. What kind of product is it? Marketers can charge (and get) higher prices at higher margins for innovative products that offer substantially more benefits than existing products. "Me-too" entries that merely mirror other products currently available must be priced more aggressively. Commodity products must be priced according to the competitive situation and available supplies.

2. The price for the product must be considered a value to potential buyers.

3. The price should recover the company's investment in the desired time period, based on projected sales.

4. The price should maintain desired profit margins. If the product is sold through reseller channels, the price must also allow the resellers to maintain their desired profit margins.

5. The price should discourage the competition from entering the marketplace. When introducing a revolutionary product that will set the industry on its ear, it's tempting to skim extra profits by pricing it at higher than normal margins. High profits, however, are like tossing chum and blood in the ocean. The sharks (the competition) will come circling, anxious to take a bite out of the market. A more thoughtful, long-term policy is to price revolutionary products low enough to discourage competitors from trying to copy it. Lowering the price automatically raises the ante for other companies!

Reasons to set high prices for new products

Here's why some marketers like to start out with high prices when introducing a new product.

1. The marketplace will accept the high prices. Completely new products are novelties that command a premium. Why not take advantage of the demand? Charge as much as the market will bear.

2. There's not enough product to go around anyway. It takes time to ramp up production.

3. High prices give a product prestige.

4. Resellers will mark it up anyway. Why should they get the extra profit?

5. Costs are recovered faster.

6. The product may only have a short lifespan. Maximum profits must be made while the product is still "hot."

7. There's room to cut the price later if the marketplace resists.

8. High prices allow additional funds for advertising, promotion, and distribution.

9. Senior management loves high margins. Marketers and product managers who can deliver them are looked on with fondness and favor.

10. High prices make the sales force justify its existence. They have to go out and explain why the product offers genuine value.

Five reasons why marketers recommend low pricing

1. Low pricing keeps the pikers out of the game. The competition will hesitate to make an investment in a "me-too'" entry if they can't see good profit margins.

2. If the company is introducing a "me-too" product, it must deliver it at a still lower price to gain market share.

3. A low price attracts more customers. They perceive that the product offers a better value.

4. Low pricing enforces corporate discipline and efficiency. That spirit of economy spills over to other operations.

5. Low pricing increases sales volume. More customers are attracted because they perceive that the product offers value.

PRODUCT-LINE PRICING AND NEW PRODUCTS

Pricing issues are addressed more fully in the following chapter, but we touch on it here as pricing strategy relates to new products.

Most new products take their place in an existing product lineup. There may be other products in the line with fewer or more features, but with similar characteristics. The products are priced from basic to deluxe models according to the features and benefits they offer.

The goal of the marketer is to sell projected quantities of the entire product line while maintaining desired overall profit margins. This goal gets tricky because the margins for various models may differ. The advanced, or deluxe, model may carry a higher margin with the higher price rationalized to the consumer on the basis of the additional features offered. The trimmed-down, economy version may be priced at lower margins, which often produces higher unit sales. In these instances, the prices charged may not be directly related to the cost of manufacturing each model. Strategy, rather than cost, dictates the price.

It's up to the marketer to accurately forecast unit sales for each model so that desired profit margins are achieved. When the sales for one product does not meet projected volumes, the price is often tweaked until the volumes are in balance and overall margins are achieved.

The introduction of a new model often forces the marketer to recalculate pricing for the entire line. New models may impact the sales volumes of older models whose prices may need to be adjusted. A new product, improperly priced, can upset the existing balance. Some models may no longer be viable. It is best for the marketer to work out any price adjustments in advance, before the new model is introduced. Price changes that are reactive to situations are often too late to stem the tide.

NEW MODELS AND CLOSEOUTS

Shortly before a new model or product is to be introduced many marketers offer closeout pricing on existing models which will be less attractive once the new units become available. Reducing the price early is better than being stuck with obsolete inventory gathering dust in the warehouse.

Chapter Five

PRICE AND PROFIT

HOW PRICES ARE SET

In a market-based economy, price is everything. Price determines which products get made and in what quantities. Price even determines how products will be made. For example, any company selling disposable razors must make the razor's body out of molded plastic. Manufacturing the product out of a higher-cost material, or in a different way, would make it noncompetitive. Price even determines who the customers will be. The price for a Rolls Royce limits potential buyers to those at the upper end of the income ladder.

As anyone who has shopped in a supermarket knows, price is never a constant. Weekly specials announce price changes. Vegetables and fruits are less expensive in summertime. Suppliers seek to reduce excess inventories and cut prices. The cost of cattle feed rises and hamburger becomes dear. The variables are endless.

What are the factors that determine the current price? The traditional wisdom holds that price is dictated by supply and demand. The greater the supply, the lower the price. The greater the demand, the higher the price. Supply-side economists believe these two factors work against one another to produce a natural equilibrium. When prices for a product are high, more companies rush into the market thus increasing the supply and lowering the price. When prices (and profits) are low, companies abandon the market thereby lowering the supply and raising the price. This is a simplistic explanation for how prices are established, valid perhaps for a less complicated age.

Today, the old law of supply and demand hasn't quite been repealed, but some marketers feel it should be under judicial review. New products are introduced at a dizzying pace. Demand often isn't a natural phenomenon, but rather is created by clever marketers through advertising, through promotions, and through aggressive sales tactics.

Even in commodity-type products, where supply and demand supposedly operate in a pure form, marketers upset the natural balance. Supplies are sometimes artificially limited to create temporary shortages. Indeed, an entire industry, such as manufacturing and selling collectibles, is based on the "limited edition" concept.

Petroleum and coffee, along with other products, have been deliberately withheld from the market to increase demand. The federal government buys commodities, such as wheat, cheese, and butter, and stores the surplus in warehouses to keep the prices artificially high. Subsidies are provided to keep farmers from growing too much of certain crops.

When supply and demand are manipulated, the old equations don't work. The point is that price isn't something that just happens over which the marketer has no control. Price must be as carefully planned and controlled as advertising, promotion, and selecting distribution channels.

SETTING PRICES

Setting prices for products is probably the marketer's most important, difficult, and vexing job. The "right" price for a product accomplishes the following objectives:

1. It is low enough so customers perceive that the related product or service offers real value. In other words, the price must be low enough to stimulate demand.

2. It discourages the competition from entering or staying in the market. Keep in mind that high profits attract imitators who are anxious to get in on a good thing.

3. It discourages customers from seeking alternatives to the entire product category. When the price for a ball game ticket rises too high, people will go to the movies instead. When the price for a movie ticket goes out of sight, people will stay home and watch television.

4. It produces maximum profit for the company.

5. It sustains production and helps the company achieve its desired sales volumes.

These five objectives are a tall order, so let's see how they can be accomplished.

COST-BASED PRICING

When establishing pricing, many marketers work backwards from the above list of objectives, beginning with formulas that will bring the company maximum profit. The first thing that must be known in establishing profit margins is the cost of the product. For a manufacturer, that cost is how much money it takes to make the product. For a wholesaler, or retailer, product cost is the price of purchase. For a service provider, that cost is labor costs plus administrative expenses.

Even this number is a variable because the cost for making the product could be affected by the volume produced or purchased. Make or buy a large quantity and the cost per unit diminishes. Make or buy only a few and the cost per unit rises. So the marketer needs still more information before establishing cost-based price. He or she must know how much the unit will cost at various volume levels. Fortunately, this information is relatively easy to obtain from manufacturing or purchasing. Here's the kind of data they'll provide to the marketer:

$$10,000 \text{ units} = X \text{ cost per unit}$$
$$5,000 \text{ units} = X+ \text{ cost per unit}$$
$$1,000 \text{ units} = X++ \text{ cost per unit}$$

With this data in hand, the marketer must make the first hard decision. He or she must now project the number of units that will be sold. The raw cost for product is plugged in at that number.

Next, marketing expenses must be added. Here are the questions the marketer must answer:

- How much money will be allocated to advertise the product?
- How many dollars for promotions?
- How much for distribution?
- What about other marketing expenses, such as literature?

All of these expenses must be prorated over the total number of units that are projected to be sold. It seems simple, but here the marketer working on the problem encounters another of those vexing variables. The more money spent on advertising and promoting the product, the more units that are likely to be sold. The greater the quantity of units sold, the lower the prorated promotional costs per unit. There's a point of diminishing returns, of course, and many marketers try to allocate advertising and promotional dollars right up to this point. The hard part is knowing exactly where this point is located.

Most marketers develop cost models based on varying volume scenarios:

	5,000 pcs	10,000 pcs	20,000 pcs
Manufacturing cost:	_____	_____	_____
Marketing cost:	_____	_____	_____
Burden:	_____	_____	_____
Total cost:	_____	_____	_____

The marketer cannot ignore *burden* when setting prices. This is the cost for running an operation, including charges for office or plant space, electricity, and administrative services. These fixed costs are usually prorated over the number of units projected to be sold.

When all product costs have been calculated, there is still one important number to plug in. Senior management thinks it's the most important number of all: profit margin. How much money would the company realistically like to make on this product? That figure, added to the others, is the price the company would like to charge for the product. Cost-based pricing then is a combination of:

- Raw manufacturing or acquisition costs.
- Burden.
- Advertising and promotional costs.
- Distribution costs.
- Profit margins.

OUTSIDE FACTORS THAT AFFECT PRICING DECISIONS

In the best of all possible worlds, companies would price every product in the line at full profit margins, sell all they can make, and declare big dividends every year. There are several rude realities that prevent this delicious world from being realized. These realities are:

1. *Competition.* Competitive factors play a large role in pricing decisions. There is no point in the company pricing itself out of the market. If the price for the company's product is not in line with competitive pricing, customers will vote for the other guy with their pocketbooks and purchase orders.

2. *Perceived value.* Customers must perceive the value of the product as being greater than the purchase price, or they won't part with their money to buy it. Often, perceived value has little to do with the marketer's cost for providing the product. Systems-related products, for example, may save customers millions of dollars, but, often, they cost the supplying vendors relatively little. The vendors are charging for their knowledge. Management consulting is another "product" that falls into this same category.

3. *Alternatives.* There's always a third or even a fourth way to do things. When prices get too high for an entire product category, people will seek out these alternatives. During the last gasoline crisis, when prices skyrocketed and supplies were scarce, some people opted to walk or to use bicycles.

The competition, perceived value, and alternatives keep companies from charging whatever they wish for products. Why don't grocers charge a million dollars for a banana? Because no one, not even wealthy gorillas, would buy it.

PROFIT MARGINS AND ENTERING MARKETS

Many marketers develop cost-based pricing, plug in necessary profit margins, than compare the resulting figure with the existing prices for comparative competitive products. This kind of exercise is a peek at the realities of life. It often precedes a decision on whether to enter a new market or offer a new product. The company may see what the competition has available and decide that the proposed new product can't be sold at the margins it requires. The project is abandoned before any real harm is done. That's one reason why companies who control market share tend to keep their prices low. They want to discourage competitive entries.

Why costs sometime decline and why it matters to marketing

Experience making and marketing a product often translates to lower production and marketing costs down the line. If other factors, such as material costs, are constant, these reductions are even predictable. Marketers can assume that the cost of making the product six months from now won't be as much as the cost of making it today. Some marketers use this "experience curve" to plan lower pricing for a product after it has been on the market for some time. The lower pricing also leads to higher volumes, which, in turn, reduces production costs still further. These planned reductions help the company maintain and even increase market share.

The impact of eliminating products on profit margins

Many marketers try to maintain similar margin levels for every product in the line. When some products can't be sold at the desirable profit margins, they believe these products should be eliminated. The problem is that many costs for marketing a product line are shared by every product in the line. Eliminating a few poorly performing products puts a greater cost burden on every other product. Thus, eliminating one product often *reduces* margins for every other product, creating exactly the opposite result the marketer wanted. Many products also build traffic for other, higher-margin products in the line.

Eliminating low-margin products also often creates "gaps" in the line. Prospects perceive the lineup as incomplete and may not consider the company as a supplier when doing "one-stop shopping." In this way, eliminating a product or products solely for margin reasons may result in lessening demand for the entire product line.

"BLACK COCAINE" PRODUCTS

An office machine manufacturer I once represented offered a line of toner cartridges used in laser printers and fax machines. This supply item is a commodity which is offered by a great many vendors. Everybody sells them and everybody uses them. The cartridges had no positive impact on the rest of the company's product line. Nobody bought an office machine from the company because we supplied toner. It was merely an item that added sales volume. In addition to original equipment manufacturers, there were a fair number of small, garage-type operations refilling and selling used cartridges.

Price and availability were the primary considerations when customers made toner cartridge purchasing decisions. For my company, sales volumes were high, but profit margins were infinitesimal because there were so many other vendors in the game.

We in field management at the company called the product "black cocaine." We were all hooked on the sales volume it provided. Toner sales became a way to save quota in a tough month.

That volume came at a cost. Very little profit trickled down to the bottom line because prices had to be so low. Selling toner took time and attention away from the company's more profitable products. It also took administrative effort and warehouse space, and it absorbed our customers' credit limits. The situation became so serious that management first reduced sales commissions, then stopped giving quota credit toward toner sales.

Eventually, the company discontinued the product. Sales volume suffered for a time, but the remaining volume became more profitable. We were forced to concentrate on the things the company did best.

Many companies have at least one "black cocaine" item in their lineup. These items contribute sales volume, but very little profit. They don't add anything to the product lineup and they may even give the company a reputation it doesn't want. These products should be eliminated because they deflect from the company's purpose. Sales volumes may be temporarily affected, but the company is not in business to make sales; it is in business to turn a profit.

PRICE AND THE PERCEPTION OF VALUE

Do you want a reputation for quality? Price the product sky high. Lacking any other information, consumers assume that high price is synonymous with high quality and high quality is considered synonymous with better value. Many companies use marketing strategies that take advantage of this consumer perception. The elegant shop with swank appointments in the best part of town uses outrageous prices as part of its aura of exclusivity, style, and quality. If it offered lower prices, customers who seek out this sort of atmosphere would be disappointed and shop elsewhere.

Marketers also use this perception to reposition products. A soup manufacturer may repackage a canned soup in a fancy glass jar that reveals the ingredients, add a homespun label that says "All Natural" or "Mother's Kitchen," place the product in the grocer's gourmet foods section, and triple the price. Same soup, but now it has panache.

PRICE COMPARISONS

Consumers don't live in vacuums. They are continually bombarded with prices everywhere they turn. This exposure gives them a perception, or reference point, of what familiar products should cost. When they're exposed to a new product, they automatically compare the offering price to other prices for the same category of product. For example, if most national brands of catsup are selling for $1.49 for a 16-ounce bottle, consumers will use this price as a reference point to determine if a weekly sale or new offering represents a better value. A $4.00 bottle of catsup will seem expensive, whereas one selling for $1.00 will appear to be a bargain.

That doesn't mean a new supplier cannot charge more than $1.49 a bottle. High prices don't always equate to market rejection. An attractive package, an exotic blend of spices, or a clever advertising campaign ("America's Olympic swim team trains hard by practicing every day in a pool of our thick, rich catsup. During competition, swimming in water becomes child's play.") might allow the marketer to double, or even triple, the price and still attract customers. The higher price would lead some consumers to assume that the product offered better quality.

Consumers also perceive low and high pricing limits for products. Marketing catsup at ten cents a bottle won't work because consumers would assume it was a poor-quality product, perhaps mostly colored water. Marketing it at $10.00 a bottle won't work either, because consumers would consider purchasing catsup at that price a wasteful extravagance.

Some consumers will always buy the lowest price products in that product category. Consumers who buy quality, however, are still interested in bargains. The Armani suit, marked down from $2,000 to $1,200 will attract buyers.

Marketers can get premium prices for products which have sustained the perception of quality over long periods. Some Japanese products, such as automobiles, have acquired a reputation for quality and often are priced higher than comparable American models.

Marketers work for years to achieve a high-quality reputation. Maintaining high prices is part of the strategy. That means resisting the impulse to lower pricing when sales are slow. Sales events must be programmed, preferably at the same time every year, so customers are assured that quality hasn't diminished.

THE PROBLEMS WITH LOW INTRODUCTORY PRICING

There's an old marketing adage, "It is easier to trade down than it is to trade up." That simply means it's easier to get buyers to accept lower prices than it is to get them to swallow higher ones. Seem obvious? Nevertheless, many marketers bring a new product to market with "special, low introductory prices." The idea is that customers will be tempted to try the product because it is a bargain.

Unfortunately, this strategy often doesn't work. Many studies show that initial low pricing, which is later raised after the introduction, often produces poorer long-term sales volume. Buyers become accustomed to the discount and consider the normal pricing an increase. If the price is going to be higher over the life of the product, introduce consumers to this price immediately. Offer coupons, contests, promotional tie-ins, and other inducements to encourage consumers to try a product.

PRICING NEW PRODUCTS

Pricing new products when similar products are currently on the market is simpler than pricing products for which there is no frame of reference. A new catsup manufacturer knows the prices competitors charge for their products. The marketing decisions necessary were based on how the marketer wishes to position the product vis-a-vis the competition. The marketer must decide which factors he wants to compete on:

- Price
- Quality
- Exotic taste
- Unusual packaging
- Big advertising budget

In each instance the marketer knows the competition and has a marketing strategy. Prices can be set accordingly.

When introducing a product for which there is no current direct competition, the pricing decisions become more difficult. The market is unknown, the demand has yet to be created, and customers may find applications for the product that the company had not considered.

Despite all the unknowns, what the marketer must first do to develop new product pricing is to estimate the demand. This may be the age of scientific advancement, but estimating the demand for an innovative product is still largely a matter of intuition and past experience. The marketer's confidence in his or her ability to create demand may play a large role in the price figure selected.

Estimating demand is only the first step in the process. A systematic approach to innovative product pricing is as follows:

1. Estimate demand.*
2. Select target markets.
3. Select distribution channels.
4. Determine an overall pricing policy. High prices to maximize profits over a short period, low prices to maximize sales volume and discourage competition, or something in between.
5. Estimate probable life expectancy of the product and costs over that period.
6. Estimate competitive entry points.
7. Select a specific price.
8. Schedule price adjustments as the product matures.

SKIMMING PROFITS FOR FAD-RELATED PRODUCTS

Innovative products can often command a premium price simply because they are new. There is a segment of the population that always wants to be first to own something. Marketers can take advantage of this desire to make excellent margins for short periods.

---

*Use market research to get information on possible demand for a completely new product. This research could include focus groups, test marketing, and surveys. Will the information be accurate? Well, these methods beat looking at sheep entrails.

The first ballpoint pens were introduced shortly after World War II. The technology was new to the public. The first pens were a leaky mess, but they were priced at up to fifty dollars each because they promised "a lifetime supply of ink." Many were sold, even at these premium prices. The price came down rapidly, and today's ballpoint stick pen selling for eighty-nine cents is a vastly superior product than its ink-dripping ancestor.

The window of opportunity for skimming, however, doesn't last long. Products don't have the sparkle of novelty for long. The more stylish or fad-related the product is, the shorter its lifespan. Marketers should recognize this phenomenon and program price reductions as interest in the product wanes. Here's a sample pricing schedule for a fad-related product:

1. *Skimming.* Set initial high prices, make high margins. When it works, life is sweet.

2. *Offer substantial price reductions at the first sign that sales volume has peaked.* Margins are still good during this period.

3. *Close-out pricing as sales decline.* Margins are now mediocre, but the primary objective is to get rid of remaining inventory. On fad products, don't wait too long to pull the trigger on this last reduction.

Penetration pricing

A penetration pricing policy sets the product entry prices low, at acceptable but not spectacular margins. This pricing strategy is often used in one or more of the following circumstances:

1. The company expects the product to have a long lifespan.
2. The company anticipates costs savings may occur as experience is gained manufacturing the product.
3. Low prices may increase sales volumes by accelerating customer demand for the product.
4. The competition has a comparable product currently in the market and low pricing is needed to gain market share.

5. The competition may announce a comparable product soon and low pricing may discourage this entry.
6. The company doesn't have a reputation in this product category. A low price is needed to gain attention.
7. The marketplace simply won't accept a higher price.

BREAK-EVEN POINTS

There are many costs associated with introducing a new product. What is the best strategy for recovering these development costs? The boys upstairs wearing the green eyeshades want all costs recovered as quickly as possible. If it were up to them, they'd pile every penny onto the first unit sold: "That first unit is $1,270,493.42, but you can have the second one for $5.95."

In most instances, however, sanity and the marketing manager's outraged screams prevail and development costs are prorated over the number of units sold. If product development costs are one million dollars and the company expects to sell one million units, development costs would add one dollar to every unit.

Unfortunately, most equations are not as simple as this example. Projecting a larger quantity would lower the prorated costs. Here's how the math works on a development cost of one million dollars:

1,000,000 units = $1.00 per unit
2,000,000 units = $0.50 per unit
4,000,000 units = $0.25 per unit

Projecting a larger number of units would lower the offering price thus making the product more attractive to buyers, which, in turn, would help the marketer sell more units. The point is that any change in the price will change the break-even point.

It's tempting for marketers to project large sales volumes for new products so that prices can be kept competitive—the triumph of optimism over reality. The problem with this temptation is that senior management expects marketers to make all their projections come true. Those marketers who are wrong with one projection find it difficult to get management's acceptance on future high projections.

PRICE POINTS

Most products have price thresholds, that is, points at which the majority of customers will resist any further increases by reducing purchases and, conversely, breakthrough prices at which customers will perceive the product offering an extraordinary value.

These price points are most critical with nonessential goods. Customers may complain, but they will pay the going price for bread and milk. If the price of cocoa rises too high, however, many consumers will simply stop buying it.

Smart marketers are aware of these thresholds and develop their pricing strategies accordingly. When current prices for a product are at or near what marketers consider a critical price point, most will do everything possible, including eating a bit of margin, to avoid any further increases.

Marketers will also encourage the development of products to be sold at certain price points. They will often manipulate features, alter designs, or use different manufacturing techniques and less expensive materials to meet their price goals.

When laser printers were first developed, they sold for several thousand dollars. Marketers knew the commercial market would triple if products were available for under one thousand dollars, a price that would make the product attractive to small and home offices. When that goal was achieved, the next threshold was a $500 laser printer. That price made the product attractive to computer hobbyists. Now, there are $299 laser printers on the market. At this price point, however, laser printers compete with a different technology: inkjet printers.

FIVE PRICING OPTIONS WHEN COSTS CHANGE

When the manufacturer's costs rise for a product and that product is at or near a price resistance point, marketers have several options. They can:

1. *Raise the price accordingly and lower volume projections.* At the same time, marketers will be praying that competitors will raise their prices.

2. *Eat the cost increase and lower profit margins.* When cost increases appear temporary, many marketers will choose this option to maintain price uniformity. This option may be downright necessary when a fierce competitor simply won't raise prices. Marketers who use it regularly, however, should keep their résumés polished.

3. *Maintain the price, but change the product to lower the cost.* This option, which is really a disguised price increase, explains why there are "pound" cans of coffee with only ten or eleven ounces of product in them.

4. *Change the terms of sale to lower marketing ancillary costs.* "Cash only. No credit cards accepted."

5. *Raise the price, but change the product to give it the appearance of improved quality.* An example might be a richer-looking package, or an improved skin design.

FOUR WAYS TO INTRODUCE HIGHER PRICES

When price increases are absolutely, positively necessary, there are several ways they can be introduced to make them more palatable to customers. These ways are:

1. Make an announcement alerting all customers that a price increase is about to take place and explaining the reasons why one is necessary. This method works best with commercial accounts. It gives customers an opportunity to stock up at current pricing. There is less resistance because, "hey, we warned you this was coming."

2. Make an immediate price increase announcement followed by a "sale" that brings the product temporarily back to the old price. This tactic is frequently used with consumer products to acquaint customers with the new, higher pricing.

3. Announce an immediate price increase in conjunction with some kind of promotion, such as cents-off coupons, that brings the pricing down to old levels. This tactic also acquaints customers with new pricing.

4. Add something to the product that makes it "new and improved." Redesign the package to make the product appear "richer" and therefore worth more money.

CHANNEL PRICING

Let's begin with a definition: A sales channel is a distribution network through which goods and services are moved. If a computer manufacturer offers its products to end-user customers through direct-mail catalogs, that is the channel of distribution it has chosen.

Many manufacturers sell their products through several different channels. Office equipment manufacturers, for example, may sell their products through wholesalers, mass merchants, traditional retailers, and office equipment dealers. Each of these entities may perform different marketing services for the manufacturer:

- The wholesaler might warehouse equipment, ship in low quantities, and supply credit to small dealers which the manufacturer could not economically handle.
- The office equipment dealer might supply installation and maintenance to end-user customers.
- The retail store might have a liberal return policy that encourages customers to make buying decisions.
- The mass merchant may advertise extensively.

What the marketer must recognize is that, because they don't operate in the same manner, different channels require different profit margins. The price that manufacturers charge these channels must vary accordingly. For example:

- True wholesalers can operate with 12- to 15-percent margins because they merely warehouse and ship.
- A retail department store situated in a high-rent mall requires profit margins of more than 40 percent.
- Dealers who install and service equipment need high margins to pay for the personal time and attention they give to customers.
- Mass merchants need margins somewhere in between.

How can the manufacturer satisfy the margin requirements of each of these channels and still price products so no federal laws are broken? One popular way is by making minor cosmetic changes in a product, that is adding or deleting a feature, and dedicating that model to only one channel. It has the appearance of being exclusive, but it rolls off the same assembly line as models dedicated to other channels.

Channel price points

Manufacturers and wholesalers cannot legally dictate the retail prices merchants charge for their products. Still, they recognize that unless the merchants make their required margins on a product, they won't continue to carry it. What marketers can do is to develop products with pricing that meets the following objectives:

1. The price to the merchant meets the supplier's profit margin objectives.
2. The price charged by the supplier allows the merchant to offer a price to the end-user that meets the merchant's profit objectives.
3. The retail price is attractive enough so the end-user considers the product a good value.
4. The price to the end-user keeps the product moving through the distribution channel. (If this doesn't happen, all the rest is meaningless.)

These four objectives explain why many products are developed with specific price points in mind.

FUNCTIONAL DISCOUNTS

All discounts are price reductions. The price charged by the manufacturer for product to various channels should reflect the service the channel offers that helps the manufacturer move product. For example, a manufacturer might offer a dealer an allowance for installing equipment at an end-user location or for training end-user personnel in the operation of the equipment. Allowances for these kinds of services are called *functional discounts*. They are becoming less common because the lines between wholesaler, retailer, and mass merchant are becoming blurred.

QUANTITY DISCOUNTS

The most popular type of discount offered by suppliers is the quantity discount. These are the easiest discounts for the marketer to calculate, the easiest for customers to understand, and easiest for the company to administer. Quantity discounts also have a positive impact on sales volume. Customers will often structure their purchases to take advantage of a specific discount schedule. Here's what a quantity discount schedule looks like:

1–11 units: $20.00 ea.

12–99 units: $17.00 ea.

99+ units: $15.00 ea.

Some marketers schedule price break quantities just over their customers' normal level of needs. The customer who needs ten units is tempted to purchase a dozen because buying the extra two units means all twelve receive a 15-percent discount.

Suppliers cannot discriminate by offering a quantity discount to one customer and refusing that same discount to others. If a discount price schedule is available to one customer, it must be available to all.

Marketers who wish to reward particular large-volume customers may, however, establish a quantity discount schedule that is only significant to a select few customers because they are the only ones with the financial resources or marketing muscle to buy in such large amounts.

Blanket order discounts

Some sellers will allow quantity discounts on blanket orders. Under this arrangement, the customer contracts to purchase a specified quantity of product over an agreed-upon period of time. This arrangement benefits both parties in that it guarantees quantity pricing for the customer while locking in that customer for the seller. Problems can occur, however, when the customer does not take the agreed-upon quantity. The sales contract should address this possibility with possible penalties (such as back billing) spelled out.

Quantity discounts and profit margins

Quantity discounts have an impact on profit margins. Marketers must be careful not to make their high quantity discount schedules too attractive. Too many customers will ignore the lower quantity levels and order at the best prices. This will lower the company's profit margins. A well-thought-out discount schedule makes it practical for customers to buy at any quantity price level, including a single unit. At any price break, the product must still be considered a value by the customer.

To get an ideal order mix, the marketer must review customers' past buying habits, forecast probable orders at each quantity break, and work out prices that will bring desired margins based on that forecast. Keep in mind that high-volume orders require less handling and lower administrative costs than small orders, which help make the lower margin on these orders more acceptable.

Quantity discounts and competition among resellers

When Wal-Mart waltzes into a small town, the independent merchants disappear. They can't compete because Wal-Mart buys products in such large quantities; Wal-Mart always qualifies for their suppliers' best discount schedules. (In many instances, the best discount schedules offered by vendors aren't good enough for Wal-Mart purchasing agents. They insist that their suppliers sharpen their pencils and offer even greater discounts. In return, they usually deliver terrific sales volume.)

The small reseller often can't buy the product from the supplier at the price Wal-Mart, and other mass merchants in its league, are charging their end-user customers. That's because of the great disparity between the quantity-one price offered to small dealers and the large-volume discount offered to the mass merchants.

Marketers who wish to keep many channels of distribution open, and the small merchant afloat, can't permit the "super store" to eat up the small fry. Automobile manufacturers recognize this danger and price their products to dealers so that the smallest can compete with the largest. This still permits their dealers to cut prices by selling at lower margins or by taking advantage of operating efficiency. They can't, however, cut prices so dramatically that the little guy is forced to close shop.

Those marketers who are lured by the big volumes delivered by some mass merchants and who give them extraordinary price breaks are putting all their eggs in one basket. The problem is that it's a low-margin basket. Perhaps, however, this battle has already been lost. Small, independent operators are going the way of the dodo. Good-bye, "Mom and Pop."

TERM DISCOUNTS

Discounts for cash with order or for rapid payment, say within ten days, are popular both with customers, who pay less for the product, and with the company's financial people, who like to get money for merchandise as soon as possible.

These discounts are usually contained in the price quotation to the customer (2 percent ten days, net thirty). This advice tells the customer that a 2-percent discount may be taken if payment is made in ten days and that the seller expects full payment within thirty days.

Paying shipping charges (FOB destination) is another popular discount method that reduces the price of the product to the customer. Marketers sometimes use this carrot to encourage higher volume purchases: "FOB destination on orders of 100 pieces or more."*

PROMOTIONAL DISCOUNTS OR ALLOWANCES

Many marketers will allow retailers a discount for their promotional efforts to move the product. These discounts further reduce the price of the product to the buyer. The most common method for handling these discounts is through co-op advertising funds. For information on how co-op advertising works, refer to Chapter Two.

STOCK ADJUSTMENTS AND "SELL-THROUGH"

It's up to the marketer not merely to set up distribution channels, but to make sure that products are flowing through these channels into the hands of end-users. This is called the "sell-through factor." Much of a marketer's time and effort are spent in constructing advertising, promotional, and other marketing programs to make sure that sell-through occurs. If the products won't move off the resellers' shelves, they won't buy more. It's as simple as that.

What do you do when the product isn't moving through the distribution channel? Resellers don't like products sitting in inventory gathering dust. When that happens they're likely to ask the marketer to do one of two things:

1. Take the product back and issue a credit.
2. Adjust the reseller's price of the product down so it can be offered to end-users for less money.

In many companies, the trucks run in only one direction. That is, the suppliers are not willing to accept return merchandise which they would then have to restock, and resell to somebody else. Often, they will offer the

---

*The more distance between supplier and market, the more difficult it is to make the sale. Paying the buyer's shipping costs alleviates this problem.

reseller a rebate on merchandise already purchased, but in turn will ask the reseller to advertise the product for sale at a price that will move it out quickly, but not so low that it will destroy the market. These stock adjustments can be expensive for the product supplier, but they're often a better solution than alienating an important customer.

When manufacturers refuse to accept the return of slow-moving merchandise, some mass merchants often threaten to advertise this merchandise for such a low price that it ruins the market for everyone. This is blatant extortion because every other reseller with this product currently in inventory now loses money. Those resellers become reluctant to buy from the manufacturer ever again.

A marketing truth: *If resellers don't find the relationship profitable, they will cease doing business with a supplier.*

Mix-and-match discounts

Some marketers will allow their customers to pick and choose among various models in the product line and offer a discount based upon the total quantity purchased. This makes qualifying for discounts much simpler and establishes the company as an outfit that is easy to work with.

"Baker's dozen" discounts

One popular discount that lowers the cost of product to the reseller is the "baker's dozen" promotion. In this promotion the reseller buys twelve units and receives the thirteenth at no charge. Both marketers and resellers like this discount because it is so easy to understand and to execute. Senior management is not nearly so fond of it because the extra unit at no charge represents a sizable discount that impacts profit margins.

Four ways to discount
to meet competitive pressure

What do you do when the competition comes out with a new model that runs at twice the speed and sells for half the price? We hope your company is working on a product that will meet this competitive challenge, but what is the best answer for selling an existing product that is no longer price competitive? If the marketplace no longer considers the product a value vis-à-vis the competition, it won't sell. There are several short-term solutions to this problem:

1. Immediately lower the price of the product to resellers and suggest that they pass along this reduction in terms of lower costs to end-users. When discounting slow-moving products, remember an old marketing maxim: The first discount is the cheapest. That means make the initial discount deep enough so it moves out all the existing inventory.

2. "Bundle" the product with what had been optional equipment or peripherals and thus make the base price more difficult for prospects to discern.

3. Offer liberal financial terms, such as little or no interest for six months or a year, to tempt buyers. If the product isn't selling, better that it sits in another outfit's warehouse rather than yours.

4. Offer services, which had been extra, such as installation, and longer warranty periods at no charge or at a reduced rate. This is a discount in that it costs the company money, but it maintains the price integrity of the product.

Every one of the above solutions is a discount, but only the first appears to be so.

PRICING MATURE PRODUCTS

As products become long in the tooth, that is, when the market is near saturation or alternative products are beginning to eat into market share, it's time to consider a new pricing strategy. Raising the price usually doesn't make any sense, unless costs have risen significantly and there's no other choice. A price increase will only lower demand. A price reduction, however, may improve sales volume or squeeze a few more years of sales productivity out of Old Faithful. This sustained volume will come, unfortunately, at the expense of profit margin.

Many marketers try to maximize profit contribution toward the end of a product's life cycle by "cheapening" it. That is, they drive down cost of manufacture by using less expensive materials, reducing manufacturing time and inspections, changing the packaging, lowering marketing costs associated with the product, and generally cutting corners. The problem with this approach is that a cheapened product can have a negative impact on the company's reputation as a supplier of quality products. The extra margin obtained may be very costly in the long run.

PRICING AND PRODUCTION

Price is always related to circumstance. The internal circumstances of the company are factors that should be considered when pricing products. The following are three situations that could affect the marketer's pricing decisions:

1. When the company's production line is operating two shifts, the plant is working weekends, and the company is still falling behind meeting demand, it's not the right time to consider price reductions. In fact, it may be wise to consider raising prices—perhaps the product offers too much of a value at the existing price. A slightly reduced volume at higher margins may be more profitable, and certainly less hectic, for the company. It also might be prudent to consider subcontracting some of the work to other firms. If quality can be maintained, this option could greatly improve margins over short periods. One caveat: The marketer must be careful that a new competitor isn't being created by turning over business to the subcontractor.

2. When the plant is operating at or near capacity, but on a single shift, now is the time to think about maximizing profits through manufacturing cost reductions, material and engineering changes, more efficient marketing methods, and so forth.

3. If the plant, however, is operating at less than 50 percent of capacity and the source of the next order is a complete mystery to the sales department, a price decrease may be what's needed to get things humming. Margins may decline, but there are certain fixed costs associated with operating a production facility. These costs must be covered by maintaining a minimum volume of business. If the only way to get that business is through lowering prices, the marketer must be prepared to bite that bullet. Prices cannot, of course, be lowered beyond the break-even point; but idle production time is just like excess inventory gathering dust on warehouse shelves. It's a serious problem that must be solved.

Price reductions on excess inventory

When the sales forecasts are dead wrong and merchandise begins to pile up in the warehouse, the marketer is faced with difficult choices. One option is to tough out the situation, maintain current pricing, and gradually reduce inventory over a period of time. This option works best with product lines that are fairly static with few changes from model year to model year. It is a disaster with technological products, such as personal computers, which advance dramatically every six months or so.

A second option is to lower prices, be reconciled to a reduced margin—or no margin at all—and clear out those mangy dogs ASAP. This option is almost mandatory with products in industries that change rapidly, or products that can be "dated." It is often a weak solution if sales are just going through the doldrums. Marketers who use it too often find themselves on the carpet making weak explanations to senior management.

Discounts on government bids

Most government agencies, at all levels, use competitive bidding to award contracts for goods and services. Many of these contracts represent very large sales volumes of seven, eight, and even nine figures. They are hotly contested by vendors.

The stories about ten-thousand-dollar toilet seats aside, government agencies expect lower prices than those offered to commercial accounts. The competitive (sealed) bid process ensures these low prices because contract awards are usually made to the lowest qualified bidder.

When bidding a government contract of any substantial size, marketers must use a sharp pencil because it's a certainty that the competition will hone their pencils to a fine point. Normal profit margins, except for defense contractors who enjoy a special relationship with the federal government, are not possible.

Many marketers who'd like a share of the volume business that the government marketplace represents try once or twice to enter this arena, then quickly retreat because they are not successful. They feel they've cut margins to the bone and some other bidder still walked away with the deal. How did these other suppliers bid prices that were so low?

The answer is simple: Some marketers use different costing methods when calculating the prices for important bid contracts. They take out many of the costs associated with doing business with commercial companies. For example, advertising and other marketing costs are sometimes eliminated because no advertising is needed for products delivered to the government. Inventory maintenance costs are also sometimes deducted. Sales commission is drastically reduced. Here's one way a bid price may be developed:

Government bid pricing sheet

Manufacturing cost for product   _____

   Plus total overhead and burden   _____

   Less advertising costs   _____

   Less marketing costs   _____

Bid cost for product   _____

% margin need to make job worthwhile   _____

Final bid price   _____

PRICING TO GAIN MARKET SHARE

Market share pricing is a long-term strategy designed to gain domination over a market. It is often gained at the expense of short-term margins and profits. The theory is that if the company is considered the prominent supplier of a product, and much of the competition is driven out of the market, long-term profits and high margins will naturally occur. This theory is valid. The company that owns the market calls the tune. It sets prices and decides when new models and products are introduced. It is proactive while all others in that market react to what the leader has done. Here's a fairly common strategy to gain market share:

1. Market share prices are set low initially to discourage others from entering the market.

2. New product models and innovations are introduced at a dizzying pace to increase the cost of entry for the competition.

3. The company establishes "user groups" who have a vested interest in maintaining the status quo.

4. The company allocates large sums to advertising to develop a reputation as the premier supplier.

5. When competitors do enter the market with products, the company leaks advance information of super models now on the drawing board or nearing production. (The cynical name for these products is "vaporware.")

6. The company controls the consumable supplies used by the product and obtains very high margins on these.

7. As market share soars, the company increases the profit margins on the product.

Market share pricing is best employed when the company has a technological edge others can't easily meet, or when it is the low-cost producer. Some companies who are now low-cost producers use it to gain entry into a market. They consider their low margins part of the cost of entry.

Ten terrible truths about pricing

The following are ten terrible truths, delivered in no particular order, associated with pricing. Most marketers, in their hearts, know these truths to be so, though some will quarrel with number ten.

1. Any successful product producing good profit margins will be imitated. The juicier the margins, the faster the imitators will come out of the woodwork.

2. Senior management expects marketers to deliver high sales volumes at high margins. If that's a surprise, get into another field of endeavor.

3. No matter how low the price is set, some competitor, somewhere, will sell the product for less.

4. The competition will find a way to *not* match that price increase your company is forced to make because of increased costs.

5. No matter how closely the secret is kept, the competition will, simultaneously, match any price reductions that your company offers.

6. Today, mass merchants and other big reseller distributors have the power over manufacturers. They, in effect, set the prices they will pay for products.

7. A sharp price drop isn't the only way to discount a slow-moving product.

8. Accurate forecasts before the fact are the key to avoiding drastic discounts later.

9. The company's administrative departments are always willing to allocate extra burden to products for internal services which marketers don't need.

10. Market share is a good thing to strive for, but it isn't an organized religion. (We couldn't find it mentioned anywhere in the Bible, Koran, Veda, or Talmud.)

Chapter Six

DIRECT MARKETING

WHAT DIRECT MARKETING IS

Direct marketing is the attempt to reach *individual* prospects to sell them products or services. It is the effort on the part of the seller to connect with the potential buyer. The pitchman on the street corner selling umbrellas on a rainy day is engaged in direct marketing. Here are some other examples:

1. The outside salesperson calling on a corporate account, or the door-to-door vacuum cleaner salesperson (are there any of these dinosaurs left?) are both engaged in the most fundamental form of direct marketing.

2. The bulk-rate letters delivered to hundreds of millions of mail boxes all over the country offering magazine subscriptions, time-share condos in Arizona, a free automobile transmission inspection, gorgeous aluminum siding that "never needs painting," and so forth are all examples of direct marketing.

3. The telemarketing phone calls, usually arriving just when you sit down to dinner, offering a no-fee credit card, a chance to win a Buick, or a year's membership in a gym are further examples of direct marketing.

4. The handbill passed out a street corner by a local merchant is one of the most basic forms of direct marketing.

What direct marketing is not

The magazine or newspaper advertisement is not direct marketing because it targets all readers of the publication rather than individuals.

Radio and television advertising is not direct marketing.

Any third-party situation in which the product supplier sells to a retailer or distributor who in turn sells to the end-user is not direct marketing. In other words, if something gets between seller and potential buyer, it isn't direct marketing.

The purposes of direct marketing

Marketers use direct marketing techniques to accomplish various objectives. These objectives include the following:

1. *Building market share.* Companies entering new markets with new products might focus on building sales volume rather than making profits in the near term. One way to accomplish this might be to flood potential customers with direct-mail letters describing the product and making attractive offers. These companies might even be prepared to lose money for a time while they are creating a customer base and product name recognition.

2. *Maximizing profit.* Companies with an established customer base and a mature product line might concentrate their direct marketing efforts on their existing customers, rather than trying to acquire new ones, in an attempt to "milk" as much profit as possible from the product line before it dies a natural death. These companies would not buy prospect mailing lists.

3. *Image building.* Companies often use direct marketing to build their image or establish a positive identity for a particular product.

Six popular direct-marketing methods

Direct marketing means telling the company's story about the product directly to a potential user. There are many methods for accomplishing this objective. Some of these methods, such as direct mail and telemarketing, were reviewed in our earlier chapter on advertising. In this chapter, the focus is on how these methods are related to bringing the company's message to the potential buyer.

The problem direct marketers face is how to reach zillions of potential users, separate them into likely and unlikely prospects, and reach the likely ones with a persuasive sales message.

The first constraint is that the message must be delivered at a reasonable cost. The following are the popular vehicles for accomplishing this objective:

1. *Direct mail.* Hundreds of millions of direct-mail pieces are sent out every year, but each piece is directed to an individual, a household, or a business. A direct-mail piece delivers a written and graphic message and a call to action of the part of the recipient.

2. *Telemarketing.* The phone call reaches into the home or the business and allows the seller to speak personally with the prospect. The message can be altered, depending upon the prospect's responses.

3. *The direct sales call.* Face-to-face selling is still the most popular method for persuading corporate decision makers to buy a product. It is the most personal selling method, the most effective—and the most expensive. For some product categories, the personal call cannot be replaced by other methods.

4. *Catalogs.* Catalog mailings are made to database lists of likely customers for the type of merchandise offered. The lists are continually pruned as those who order from the catalog receive new catalog issues, while those who do not buy anything are dropped from the lists.

5. *Handbills.* This inexpensive marketing "technique" is included because it is surprisingly effective, particularly useful for local merchants who are trying to reach potential customers within a small geographic area. For example, except for the kid on the corner (a marketing director in the making) dispensing handbills, passers-by might never realize that the corner butcher shop is offering special prices on spring lamb this week.

6. *Facsimile transmission.* This is a hybrid direct marketing technique, half telemarketing, half direct-mail letter. With the broadcasting feature now found on many fax machines, one message can be delivered to many different recipients. The messages can be programmed to be sent off hours when phone rates are low. Sending a sales message via fax to selected prospects has become so popular that many fax machines now include a "lock-out" feature that inhibits the reception of "junk fax."

WHAT MAKES DIRECT MARKETING EFFECTIVE

Direct marketing is popular with marketers not only because the sales message is delivered to the potential buyer, but also because that message can be controlled in the following ways:

- The content of the program can be controlled.
- The timing of the program can be changed as needed. Direct marketing is one of easiest and most effective methods for exploiting targets of opportunity.
- The cost of the program can be contained.
- The results of the program are predictable.

THE DIFFICULTY WITH DIRECT MARKETING

Direct marketing can be effective, but it is no panacea. No matter how many millions of direct-mail letters are sent, or how many phone call solicitations are made, all direct marketing is targeted toward individual prospects. The difficulty is in selecting those prospects who are most likely to buy the proposition. The targets may be selected in bulk, but the prospects must be sold one at a time. That constraint requires common-sense analysis of the prospect base and sometimes good old-fashioned intuition. For example, it doesn't take a marketing genius to conclude that customers who bought personal computers several years ago might be receptive to an attractive offer for a memory upgrade. Targeting owners of Jaguar Touring Cars for offers of sets of English leather luggage might not be so apparent a play, but it doesn't mean the right kind of deal wouldn't be successful.

MARKET TESTING

Market testing is a system for reducing failure rates. Results become predictable because of program testing. For example, direct-mail marketers rarely send out large volumes of direct-mail pieces without first conducting "sample" mailings. In these samples various offers are sent to small segments of the database (mailing list) to measure their effectiveness. Different wording is tried, the offer is changed, and experiments are made with the graphics (people want to see what they're buying). Small samples of these variations are sent to different market segments. What works is repeated in volume. What doesn't work is dropped.

Telemarketers sample by experimenting with the sales pitch, the responses to the prospect's responses, and the demographics of whom they call. Only when the tests indicate that a program will be successful, are large expenditures made.

THE RESPONSE RATE

The magic number, the one all direct marketers try to predict, is the response rate that any program will produce. The response rate is simply the percentage of prospects who will be turned into customers as a result of the program. ("If we send out a hundred thousand pieces, we should get back a thousand orders.") The goal isn't always to get an order. On a business-to-business direct-marketing program, a response might be an inquiry from the prospect.

The cost of the program is measured against the profit to be made by the predicted number of responses. If profit can be made, the program goes forward. If not, the program is junked, unless there are other objectives.

Statistically, the number of responses can be surprisingly low and the program will still be considered a success. For example, a response rate of 2 percent on a direct-mail offering is usually considered excellent. Any market test that revealed this response rate is probable would normally result in the program going forward.

BUSINESS-TO-BUSINESS DIRECT MARKETING

Business-to-business marketing simply means one company trying to sell its products or services directly to another. The most popular method for this kind of marketing is the direct sales call. In direct calling, a representative of the organization trying to sell the product will make a personal visit to an individual in an organization who may be a prospect for buying it. The sales pitch is made face-to-face.

Eight reasons why direct calling is effective in business-to-business marketing

Direct calling offers the highest level of control of any direct marketing method. Here's why:

1. The sales message can be shaped to fit individual prospects.

2. The message can be delivered to various individuals and management levels within the prospect's organization and the message can be repeated as often as possible to get an audience with the prospect.

3. The prospects' needs and priorities can be determined through questioning and dialogue.

4. Personal relationships can be established.

5. Any impediments to making the sale can be revealed, giving the seller the opportunity to try to remove these impediments.

6. Repeated calls can be made for product categories that have long selling cycles. The sale can be "inched" forward through these follow-up calls.

7. The representative can report back to management the customer's reaction to the company's sales message.

8. The representative is in a good position to assess the chances (i.e. make a forecast) of obtaining any business from the prospect.

The problem with business-to-business marketing via direct calling

Direct calling on accounts is an expensive marketing method. It costs hundreds of dollars to make a single direct call and costs continue to rise. There is much wheel spinning. In many instances, a direct call does not result in a contact with a decision-maker. There is a tendency to dodge the sales rep. Many of today's decision-makers hide behind their receptionists, secretaries, and phone mail. They are impossible to reach behind these high "barricades."

How to reduce direct-calling expenses

As the personal call becomes more expensive, and less productive, companies experiment with other marketing methods to reduce their costs:

1. Telemarketing is used to set appointments for field salespeople.

2. Third-party vendors are appointed to sell the product. (The product supplier has now given up direct-marketing responsibility to the third-party vendor.)

3. Suppliers use a combination of both direct sales forces and third-party vendors. The large-volume accounts are kept direct. Others, with limited potential, are turned over to the third-party vendors.

Ten business-to-business direct-marketing challenges

Business-to-business direct marketing offers different challenges than marketing to consumers. Some of these challenges include:

1. The business customer will demand a higher level of services from his suppliers. Hit-and-run doesn't work in this marketplace.

2. Most business organizations have set up strict rules that guide their purchasing decisions. There are procedures and protocols that must be followed. These procedures serve as barriers to closing a sale quickly.

3. Most business organizations place great importance on a supplier's reliability, reputation, industry experience, and product quality. These factors, and not low price alone, determine the product's value to the buying company.

4. Buying decisions take longer. Sales are seldom made in a single call.

5. It is more difficult to reach decision-makers. The direct-mail piece or the phone call directed to a home will usually reach the head of household. The decision-makers in business organizations are much more elusive. In many instances, the decision-maker is a committee.

6. The decision-makers in business organizations are often well informed about the product or service that is being offered. They are not swayed by emotional appeals and they want to do business with salespeople who are industry and/or product experts.

7. Avoidance of risk is often one of the biggest factors in a business organization's buying decision. This take-no-chances mentality gives a greater edge to established suppliers and proven products.

8. Business organizations have their own agendas and time schedules. Those who wish to become their suppliers must dance to their rhythms.

9. One slipup and you're gone. Mistakes and misinformation are not tolerated by business organizations. There are too many competitors waiting in the wings for a chance at the business.

10. Once a relationship is established, business organizations change suppliers reluctantly—unless mistakes are made. This gives their competent suppliers a better opportunity to obtain repeat business and makes it more difficult for newcomers to break in.

Marketers seeking to do business with the corporate world must recognize, and deal with, the above challenges.

Five steps toward developing business-to-business direct-marketing programs

1. The marketer's first job in dealing with these challenges is to shape the company's image as a valuable business partner. The image of the product as a valuable commodity must be shaped as well. Without the right company and product image, even persistent representatives won't get a hearing from desirable corporate prospects. Shaping the company's image as a valuable industry player won't hurt either.

2. Get the right attitude. The marketer must develop patience. This market won't produce quick results.

3. The marketer must prepare the sales staff with a complete program that answers business prospects' concerns. For example, when selling products to mass merchants for resale, the company must have a co-op advertising program for moving the product off the mass merchant's shelves, a quantity discount program, a store clerk sales training program, a warranty program, a return program, and so forth. There's no point in talking to a mass merchant about taking on the company's product line unless these programs are in place.

4. The marketer must convince top management that the business-to-business marketing program is a long-term investment, not just a toss of the dice to produce a quick profit. In other words, the marketer must also sell top management on the value of patience.

5. The marketer must make it easy for the prospect to buy: "You want it, you got it." Don't encumber business customers with your company's red tape.

BUSINESS-TO-BUSINESS TELEMARKETING

The cost of the direct sales call has risen so quickly that many companies are using alternative methods for contacting their corporate customers. One of the fastest growing methods is telemarketing. Once almost exclusively used to reach and sell to consumers, telemarketing to business entities is becoming very popular. It is much less expensive than a personal sales call and, with the right product or purpose, can be just as effective.

What works in business-to-business telemarketing

1. Telemarketing can be effective in selling supply and other types of repeat items to established customers and new prospects. It works best when the prospect is familiar with the product, knows how it is used, and has a need for it. Phone calls to check on inventory levels, to offer special pricing, or to warn about an impending event are usually not regarded as intrusive but rather as the supplier providing a valuable service to the end-user.

2. Telemarketing can be effective when used to set up appointments with corporate prospects for visits by a company field representative. This activity is called "birddogging." Birddogging permits more of the field person's time to be spent in front of prospects and customers. The prospect knows what to expect because the subject matter of the call has been defined.

3. Telemarketing works when the company name, the product offered, or both, are easily recognized by the person on the other end of the line.

4. Telemarketing works best when the call is directed toward a specific individual in the targeted organization. An exploratory call asking for "the director of human resources" is not as effective as an exploratory call asking for "Mary Smith, your director of human resources."

When business-to-business telemarketing doesn't work

There are circumstances when business-to-business telemarketing is a waste of time and money. These circumstances include the following:

1. Telemarketing isn't effective for selling concepts and intangibles. New ideas and systems can't be explained very well over the phone. They require face-to-face contact.

2. Telemarketing isn't effective for selling any product or service that can't be closed in a single call. The longer the selling the cycle, the less effective telemarketing is.

3. Telemarketing isn't effective when the business prospect on the other end of the line has never heard of the company the telemarketer represents or the brand product being pitched.

4. Business-to-business telemarketing isn't effective for selling big-ticket items. General Electric doesn't sell any ten-million-dollar gas turbine generators on the basis of a brilliantly worded direct-mail pitch. Rule of thumb: The more costly the product, the greater the need for face-to-face contact.

BUSINESS-TO-BUSINESS DIRECT MAIL

Direct mail to consumers and direct mail to industry are often used for different purposes. They both solicit a call to action on the part of the recipient, but the action requested is not the same.

The direct-mail package to a consumer often tries to solicit an order: "Here it is, buy it. You'll love it and if you don't, send it back at no obligation."

Direct mail to a business organization often tries to solicit an inquiry: "Call us for a free consultation on our revolutionary shelving system that will increase your company's usable warehouse space by twenty percent." The aim is to gain an appointment for a salesperson.

Because of the difference in desired end results, direct-mail packages to consumers will usually include an order form while the packages to businesses will include a reply card. Both may include a toll-free telephone number for those prospects willing to pick up the phone.

The message in the two packages will reflect these different goals. The consumer direct-mail letter will focus on the product and its features. The pitch may be based on emotion: "Be fashionable," or "be first," or "reduce the fear of," are typical emotional appeals. Most direct-mail pieces to consumers will end the solicitation with what the marketer hopes is an irresistible offer to buy right now: "The first fifty respondents will receive a genuine leather clutch purse as a bonus."

The direct-mail letter to business will also mention the product and its features, but it will emphasize the benefits these features bring to purchasers. The appeal will still be based on emotion, but that emotion will be better disguised: "When you do business with us, you're in safe hands." The names of other companies (success stories) who use and like the product may be highlighted. The price, so important in the direct-mail piece to consumers, will often not be included because price is not the business buyer's primary consideration. Besides, the delivered product may vary from customer to customer.

Ten secrets of an effective direct-mail piece

1. Write an attention-getting headline. Good headlines are short but dramatic. They promise a benefit, hint at a benefit, warn of a danger, ask a question, offer little-known wisdom, issue a command, or otherwise try to intrigue the recipient to read further.

2. Don't try to tell everything about the product in the headline; save some ammunition for the text.

3. Make the text relevant to the headline. Elaborate on the benefit to the recipient.

4. Describe the product or service. Don't be afraid to be eloquent. (In fact, never be afraid to be eloquent.)

5. Substantiate any claims made for the product or service. Quote studies, refer to happy users, offer testimonials, use comparison charts.

6. Include attractive graphics, photos, and illustrations. Show the product in its best light.

7. Sum up. Don't be afraid to repeat selling points that were made earlier.

8. Communicate a sense of urgency. Give the reader a strong reason to act immediately.

9. Add a kicker, one or more additional reasons why the reader should buy now.

10. Make it easy for the reader to order.

The strongest selling point of all

The single biggest factor in a direct-mail program is to provide satisfaction. Deliver the value promised in the direct-mail piece and not only will returns be dramatically reduced, but the customers will also be receptive to the next offer.

CATALOGS

The all-purpose catalog, such as the massive ones sent out by Sears and Wards, is near death, but special-interest catalogs have become one of the hottest vehicles for reaching special-interest customers. Got a list of duck hunters? Send them a spiffy four-color catalog illustrating hand-painted decoys, rain gear, Italian shotguns, lithographs of mallards in flight, waterproof boots, and so forth.

Computer catalog outfits, such as Gateway and Dell, are doing billions of dollars through merging catalog offerings with telemarketing sales.

Eight things that make a catalog operation successful

For those marketers contemplating a catalog operation, here's what makes one successful:

1. *The database.* The database. The database. The catalog must be mailed to the right list of potential customers. This database must be small and select so mailing costs don't eat up all profits. The marketer must know the interests (or desires) of the customer base better than they know them themselves.

2. *The right merchandise.* This merchandise must appeal to this database. It should not be readily available in department stores. It must be difficult for customers to make price comparisons.

3. *Good copywriting and brilliant illustrations.* The catalog itself must be a desirable possession, a possession that is kept as a reference until the next catalog is issued. Catalogs are keys to magic kingdoms. The customers must eagerly wait their arrival.

4. *The catalog house must respond quickly to orders.* Once the customer has made a buying decision, he or she wants the stuff right now!

5. *High-quality merchandise.* The products, once delivered to the customer, must not disappoint.

6. *A liberal return policy.* Catalog houses don't have the expense of retail locations, but they must take stuff back when the customer requests. The philosophy of the "trucks only run in one direction" won't make it in this industry.

7. *Merchandise with good profit margins.* Catalogs are not the vehicle for moving selling products at deep discounts. They can, however, be used for selling discontinued products or factory buy-outs that the merchant has picked up for distress prices.

8. *A good telemarketing crew.* Today, most of the orders are called in. Fast, courteous service from an informed staff is necessary to build a good catalog business.

HANDBILLS

Don't sneer at handbills. They are proof positive that any business, regardless of size, can engage in a direct marketing program. Standing on a busy street corner passing out handbills to whomever wanders by is an inexpensive, but surprisingly effective, direct-marketing technique. It works best for local retail merchants, but other types of businesses, such as auction houses, have had success with this kind of marketing. Here is why:

1. Handbill readership is high. Anyone who accepts one in the first place is likely to at least glance at the message it contains. Most handbills are passed out during early morning hours when people are going to work and in the early evening when they're coming home.

2. Retention is high. Those who are interested in what handbills offer often take them along for assurances that the merchant will honor the deal.

3. Handbills have an immediacy that attracts impulse buyers. ("This is the deal, it's for today only, and the store is only a few feet away.")

4. Changing the offer is inexpensive and can be done quickly. A different deal can be offered whenever the merchant chooses.

What makes a handbill successful

The key to making a handbill program successful is the deal that is being offered. A two-for-one pizza deal might attract workers coming home from a long day at the office and who may be too tired to cook.

HOW DIRECT MARKETING CAN BE USED FOR CAREER ENHANCEMENT

Direct marketing can be a fast track to a better career. As the personal sales call becomes ever more expensive, every company is seeking less costly methods for reaching and selling potential customers. Those who can successfully operate telemarketing, direct mail and other direct-marketing campaigns are increasingly in demand.

In any business, people are rewarded according to the contribution they make. One of the advantages of direct-marketing involvement is that contribution is easy to measure. The equation is simple: The company invests x amount of money in a direct-marketing program which returns x amount of sales and profit.

Direct marketers who can consistently develop and manage programs that finish on the plus side are very visible to top management. They are considered valuable employees who must be retained.

Of course, performance is important. Developing losing programs is likely to have a negative impact on a career. Limit the downside risk through extensive market testing.

Chapter Seven

MARKETING AND THE COMPETITION

HOW THE COMPETITION AFFECTS MARKETING PLANS

Why doesn't every company simply create a mediocre product, sell as many as its factories can knock out, price the product at 300-percent margins, and, each year, deliver the kind of profit that thrills and delights its stockholders? The answer to that naïve question is, of course, "market forces." This is nothing but a fancy term for competition, which is the yin and yang of commerce.

A reality of the business world is that there are many companies in the market making similar products. Visit a department store and look at the wide variety of available merchandise. Interested in a set of pots and pans? Your choices as a consumer are overwhelming. Do you prefer aluminum or thick-gauge steel? Do you want a modern nonstick surface or old-fashioned porcelain? Can you save a few bucks by buying an unfamiliar brand? How about a colorful enamel coating that coordinates with your kitchen's decorating scheme?

Each pot and pan manufacturer is competing with the others for the buyer's business. The mere fact of the competitors' presence is an incentive to provide better value and a constraint on prices. That means the competition must be carefully monitored at all times. That monitoring effort is called "competitive intelligence."

BIRDS OF A FEATHER: COMPETITIVE INTELLIGENCE AND MILITARY INTELLIGENCE

There are many acknowledged similarities between intelligence gathering in the marketplace and the same practice in the military. The first thing every general does when faced with a hostile force is to gather information. No effective leader would consider going into battle without knowing as much as possible about the other side. That same requirement holds true for marketing managers. You need information about the competition before you can set up and execute your own battle plan. What these companies are currently doing, what their strategic position is (their market share), and how they are likely to behave in the future affects every marketing manager's own planning.

We're certainly not suggesting that marketing managers must always react to what the competition does. It is far better that the other side reacts to your actions. Knee-jerk reactions, such as always matching the other side's pricing, and a steady stream of "me-too" products are poor substitutes for genuine strategic planning. Continually reacting to competitive action disrupts an organized program. Being aware of the competition, however, knowing their strengths and weaknesses, being able to predict their behavior, and so forth are all necessary to the marketing function.

COMPETITION IS NOT THE DEVIL INCARNATE: SEVEN GOOD THINGS COMPETITION BRINGS

Except in the minds and viscera of marketing managers, competition is a good thing. Competition is what makes capitalism work. It offers consumers a greater variety of choices, ensures that companies offer value, keeps a lid on runaway prices, and energizes the market with a constant flow of new products. Alas, competition gives marketing managers giant-sized headaches.

1. Competition is the reason why people such as marketing managers exist. Without competitors trying to waylay the company's customers, who needs a marketing manager?

2. Competition is the reason why many ill-conceived products never reach the market. What marketing manager worth his or her salt would authorize the development of a product, say a broom, that must be sold for fifteen dollars, knowing there was a ten-dollar competitive broom already available that offered superior features and swept up more dust?

3. Competition is the reason why products undergo constant improvement. The manufacturer that makes the ten-dollar broom will be constantly seeking ways to add features, improve performance, or reduce costs so the company's current market advantage can be maintained.

4. Competition fuels innovation. A competitor knowing that the broom-maker's advantage with manual models can never be overcome might decide to give up that battle and design an electric unit.

5. Competition improves service. Faced with a competitor or series of competitors offering similar products at similar pricing, one company might decide to focus on improved distribution, a toll-free information number, or a longer warranty as a way of distinguishing itself from the others.

6. Competition reduces inefficiency. The marketplace is merciless. The poorly run company, the badly designed or shoddy product, the ill-conceived marketing plan simply do not survive in a competitive marketplace.

7. Competition keeps a lid on prices. Bread and milk are absolute necessities of life so why isn't bread selling for five dollars a loaf and milk for eight dollars a quart? It is because the number of dairies and bakeries competing with one another simply won't permit this kind of price gouging.* Any increase in price by a single supplier will result in that supplier losing sales. Grocery store chains and other retailers continually monitor one another's prices to make sure they stay competitive. The bidders on large government contracts scribble numbers onto yellow pads when the bid results are read so they'll be more competitive next time.

---

*Price gouging and terrible service most typically occur where competition has been restricted or doesn't exist. Be a "captive customer" at a remote ski resort and you may pay twelve dollars for an underdone breakfast omelet because there is no other restaurant on that particular mountain top. During communism's heyday, the large state-run enterprises, which had no competitors, were notorious for their miserable service and their contempt for customers.

FOOTBALL VERSUS SOCCER:
ANALOGIES FOR TODAY'S COMPETITIVE ENVIRONMENT

One marketing man I know recently compared the competitive marketing strategy commonly used up to a few years ago to a football game. The offensive team huddled, a play was devised, the competition set up a defense to counter that play, the action took place, then both sides regrouped to assess the gain or loss. That was competitive strategy yesterday: a series of stops and starts with frequent time-outs for analysis and devising the next play.

Today, competitive marketing strategy is more like the game of soccer. The action in this sport is a continuous flow. A team is on offense one second, on defense the next. Decisions must be made on the run, while the ball is in play. Time-outs are yesterday's luxury. Instead of set plays, the players must make instant decisions based on constant change and an infinite number of variables.

WHERE HAVE ALL THE SANCTUARIES GONE?

One exception to the soccer–modern business analogy is that there are no sidelines away from the main action. If there is the tiniest bit of profit somewhere, someone, or some company, will be after it. For example, just a little more than a decade ago retail merchants in small towns could feel safe and secure and maybe even smug. Competition was limited because small town populations would support only so many pharmacies, so many food markets, shoe stores, clothing shops, hardware emporiums, and so forth. The established merchants in these small "sanctuaries" made comfortable livings. Their sales volumes were low, but margins were high. There was little reason to cut prices.

Along came Wal-Mart and a way of life changed by combining, in one location, most of the products and services previously offered by individual merchants. Wal-Mart's low prices, often less than a small merchant's wholesale cost, soon forced the individual merchants out of business. They had been blindsided by a marketing behemoth that arrived out of nowhere. Their comfort had only been false security.

The same fate has occurred to small retail merchants in big cities; their demise just hasn't been as well publicized. Mass merchants such as Office Depot and Office Max have meant the demise of independent office equipment and office supply dealers. The small hardware store has disappeared because of Builder's Square and Home Depot. The corner "eats" restaurant has given way to McDonalds and Burger King.

There's a lesson here for companies of all sizes, no matter how well they are positioned. Today's marketing managers must have their eyes peeled in every direction, including up and down. The next threat may come not from a known competitor, but from a completely unanticipated source.

TRACKING THE COMPETITION

Known competitors, of course, must always be carefully monitored. Keeping informed about competitive activity is part of the marketer's job. Here are the things the marketer must know about the competition:

Fifteen things every marketing manager needs to know about the competition

1. What success is the competition enjoying? Notice their failures too. It's a good way to avoid the other guys' mistakes.

2. What is their reputation in the industry? What do their customers like about them? Do they react quickly to problems? What are their soft spots?

3. What is their value added? The answer to this question is the key to why their products sell.

4. How do their products stack up against your company's lineup? How good is their product quality? Their service? Their follow-up? Their sales staff? Their management?

5. Who are their best customers? How loyal are these customers?

6. What market share do they own? Is this market share increasing? Decreasing? Staying about even?

7. How do they distribute their products? Are they selling direct or are they going through mass merchants? Where are their warehouses located? Do they use more than one sales channel?

8. What are their pricing policies? Are they aggressive? Do they normally match price cuts by their competitors? Do they tend to "eat" small cost increases or pass them along to their customers?

9. What kinds of promotions do they normally run? What times during the year do they run these promotions? Are their promotions successful? Do these promotions cut into your company's sales?

10. What are their typical product cycles? Do they normally introduce new products every two years? Every year? Every six months?

11. How much production capacity do they have? Where is their production located? Do they have production backlogs? Are they currently running double shifts, operating at 50 percent of capacity, or something in between?

12. How good is their R & D? Do they have a reputation for turning the industry on its ear every few years or so? Have they had any significant product failures?

13. Are they making a profit? If they are losing money, there's not much point in emulating what they're doing.

14. Do they deal in "vaporware"? In other words, do they spread rumors about new products to new customers long before these products are ready to be delivered.

15. What is their company size? Are they a big outfit or a small one? Are they a division of a larger corporate entity? The bigger the outfit, the more resources at their disposal, but their reaction time may be slower.

WHY COMPETITIVE INFORMATION IS NECESSARY

Marketing managers may complain that compiling the above information would leave little time for their other duties. Once a competitive information gathering system is set up, however, valuable data will come in from a variety of sources without too much additional effort on the part of the marketing manager.

Ten ways to gather competitive information

Competitive information gathering systems need not be complex and setting them up need not be difficult. There are a variety of sources from which good, solid material about the other side is available. In fact, the larger and more powerful the competitor, the more public information is available about it. Here are six typical sources:

1. *Annual reports.* If they're a public company, they must let their stockholders know how they are doing. Get a copy from your stockbroker, or read one at the public library. These published statements are a wealth of information. They report total sales, divisional sales, profits, problem areas, where offices and production facilities are located, and even what areas the company plans to emphasize the following year. You can always buy one share of their stock and attend the competition's annual meeting. As a stockholder, you're entitled to attend and you might even get a cup of coffee and a glazed doughnut.

Stockbrokers and investment firms also make independent reports and analyses of publicly traded companies. These reports can be more meaningful because they are written by unbiased observers.

2. *Sales literature.* Sales literature and specification sheets provide details on the competition's product features and benefits. Competitive sales literature should be required reading for every marketing manager. What claims does the competition make about its products? What does the sales literature tell you about the market the competition is after? If they're foolish enough to list prominent customers, these names can become your own hit list.

3. *Advertising.* The products the competition chooses to advertise, what features they brag about in the ads, the product applications they list, the media they select, and how much they advertise ("Hey, their ad budget must be triple the size of mine!") tell the marketer much about the other side's marketing strategy.

4. *Competitive products themselves.* When new competitive models are introduced, buy samples through legal sources and have the company laboratory analyze them. Run tests to check claims of speed, capacity, reliability, and so forth. Do the products live up to the claims made by advertising and product brochures? Take apart the products. Compare the construction and likely longevity to your company's own product lineup.

5. *Trade shows.* The competition's trade show booth will display their latest products, and perhaps even offer some pricing information. Stop by their booth during a slack period and see what's what.

But, don't play James Bond. When visiting a competitor at a trade show booth, always wear your name tag and reveal your company affiliation before asking any questions. Look at but don't touch their products. Avoid negative comments and product comparisons. Don't load up on their literature. Leave that task for a marketing support person. Also, when the competition gives you access to their trade booth, show them the same courtesy and give them access to yours.

6. *Friendly customers and dealers.* Count on it, your best customers, dealers, and distributors will be targeted for sales calls by the competition. Some of these customers, with whom you have personal relationships, may reveal the details of any offers and proposals.

7. *Trade publications.* Does your industry have a magazine or journal that reports on various happenings? These publications are good sources of information about the competition. If the competitor is prominent, information about it may be published in the national press, such as the *Wall Street Journal* or *Business Week*.

8. *Field sales force.* These are the men and women in the trenches, face to face with the enemy, and they are often the best source for what those wily coyotes have come up with this time. They know exactly why the prospect liked the other side's proposal better, when the competition introduces new models, the bells and whistles on those models, why they lost a deal because the competition cut prices to the bone, and much more valuable stuff. The field sales force can gather competitive literature, arrange to buy a competitor's product from a friendly dealer, learn first-hand about the competitor's dissatisfied customer, and so forth.

9. *Dissatisfied customers.* A disgruntled customer may give you a wealth of information about the competition's weak spots. Be careful about repeating what you've heard to others in the industry. When dissatisfied, former customers may tend to exaggerate their complaints.

10. *Industry insiders.* Salespeople for suppliers calling on both companies, friendly marketing managers working in the same industry with noncompeting products, contacts made at industry seminars, and a host of others may also provide valuable data about the competition.

What the marketing manager gains from competitive information

Those managers who have researched the competition are not likely to be blindsided. They'll not only know what the competition is doing currently, they'll also be able to construct a reasonable scenario about how the competition may react in any given situation. For example, the competitor whose plant is running at 40 percent of capacity, and with a past history of matching competitive price cuts dollar for dollar, is certainly likely to match any planned price cut on the part of the marketer. The competitor who traditionally revamps the product line every two years is probably ready to introduce new products soon if the current line is near the end of the two-year cycle.

THREE WAYS TO OBTAIN INFORMATION ABOUT COMPETITIVE PRICING STRATEGIES

Learning what the competition charges is always a good idea if for no other reason than to wave the information in front of your own top management with the complaint, "I told you those guys are undercutting us! If they can sell at these prices and make a profit, why can't we?" Quantity discount pricing is the most revealing because it indicates how low the other side is prepared to go.

Obtaining competitive pricing information is not difficult. Typical sources include:

1. *Published or advertised list prices.* Some companies advertise their prices in industry publications, or distribute their price sheets like confetti to one and all. Often, these price sheets won't show their very best schedules, but from a quantity-one price, it's not difficult to extrapolate large quantity discounts and even the other guy's profit margins.

2. *Government bids.* Do your competitors participate in bid requests from state, local, or federal government agencies? Then you have a wonderful source for obtaining inside pricing data. Bids to government entities are always public information. They usually are opened in a public session, read aloud, and then posted on a bulletin board. These bids, particularly if the quantity is large, will reveal your competition's best, low-down and dirty pricing.

3. *Competitive situations.* Competing for a lucrative account with an aggressive competitor? The prospect may not reveal exactly what the other guy is proposing—no, no, that would be unethical—but the prospect may drop tidbits of information, little manipulative hints here and there, to work one side against the other.

Two methods never to be used to acquire information about the competition

In the heat of battle, and under pressure to perform, some marketing managers may forget that certain practices are unethical and may be illegal. No matter the anxiety level, no matter how important it is for you to know, here are information sources to ignore:

1. *Don't buy secrets.* We assume you'd never consider buying the competition's price book, design plans, and so forth from one of the competitor's employees. Such action is both unethical and illegal. If offered such a deal, contact your company's legal department.

2. *Don't hire secrets!* There is another situation that sometimes tempts marketing managers because it isn't an outright exchange of cash for secrets. If a current or former employee for a competitor offers to provide you with the other side's price list, customer list, marketing plan, product design, or whatever in an exchange for a job, throw the bum out of your office. Not only is this unethical, but next week that bum will be taking secrets out of your shop.

In fact, never use unethical or illegal methods to gather information—or for that matter, in any other area of your conduct. Surely the company's product line is good enough, and you as marketing manager have a sufficient degree of competence to compete ethically.

How to know when the competition is likely to cut prices

The competition always seems to have a sixth sense about your company's pricing strategy. Any announcement of price reductions made by your company is matched by them within hours.

You can be just as prepared. Here are the circumstances in which the competition are likely to cut their prices.

Eleven tell-tale signs that indicate the competition is about to cut prices

1. If the competitor's resellers are overstocked with merchandise, or the competitor's own warehouses are stacked to ceiling with product, a price cut may be imminent. High inventories are a sign of slowing sales. What's the inventory situation in your own warehouse?

2. If the competitor's production facilities are operating at far below capacity, count on it: Their marketing manager is under pressure to bring in enough business to get the plant hopping. Low production means the other side may be calculating extra discounts this very minute.

3. If a traditionally slow buying season is approaching, the competition may be thinking about discounts to stimulate sales. This move may be anticipated by how the competition has handled slow seasons in the past.

4. If the competitor's product is a bit long in the tooth, that is, ripe for obsolescence, the competitor may cut prices to milk a bit more volume from the existing model before new models are announced.

5. If your company, or another operating in the same arena, introduces a product with more bells and whistles, that is, a product that offers significantly more value than competitive products currently available, the other side's marketing manager may cut prices as a quick response.

6. If the competitor has a well-publicized new product waiting in the wings, the price on the existing line may be cut so current customers won't stop ordering while they're waiting for the delivery of the new baby.

7. If the competitor's product has experienced widely known problems, prices may be cut temporarily as a way of riding out the storm.

8. If the competition reduces the cost of making or acquiring the product, the marketing manager may pass along that cost reduction to customers in the form of lower prices.

9. If the upstart competitor crowds into the market, the competition may react by cutting prices to protect its market share. In this instance your competitor may be doing you a service. A price cut by existing suppliers raises the cost of entry for new kids on the block. They may decide this cost is prohibitive and back off.

10. If a company in the industry orchestrates an expensive advertising campaign, a competitor without the luxury of such an ad budget may reduce prices as a low-cost response. Offer a deeper discount on your mousetrap and the world will beat a path to your door.

11. If the competitor's senior management is "dressing up" the company for a possible sale, senior management may wish to make the numbers look good by increasing the sales volume. What better way for a temporary volume increase than by lowering prices?

Of course, all of the above reasons are also circumstances in which your company may wish to consider price cuts.

THREE THINGS THAT ARE WRONG WITH PRICE CUTS

1. Price cuts may improve sales, but they also reduce margins and operating profits. The big question every manager must ask is, will this price cut improve sales volume enough to make up for the reduced margin?

2. Those managers whose one response to competitive pressure is to cut prices are considered unimaginative, and even inefficient, by their senior management. In other words, cutting prices is no way to gain the brass's favor.

3. Customers who recently bought the product at higher prices are not to happy to learn it is now available for less. Their investment has been eroded. Customers who purchased just prior to the price cut may even ask for an adjustment.

HOW TO REACT TO A COMPETITIVE PRICE CUT

A salesperson for your company calls you from a pay phone in a customer's lobby. She's angry because she just lost a big order to the competition at a price that is far under any price this competitor previously offered. What do you tell her? First thing, of course, is to verify her information. What proof does she have that the competition offered this price? What is her source of information? Can she identify the product offered, the quantity the customer actually purchased, and the terms of the deal? In many instances, the special price will turn out to be not so special after all.

Let's assume the salesperson's information is reliable and other field salespeople call in with similar stories. This isn't one isolated low-ball incident. The competition has, indeed, cut pricing. Here is what to do now:

1. Assess your own company's situation. If the company is working two shifts to keep up with demand for the product, there's no need to do anything. If the company is looking for more warehouse space to store excess inventory, which now has two inches of dust, you may have to respond.

2. Estimate the impact of the competitive price cut on your company's current sales volume for that product. What will the reduction in sales volume do to operating profit? What would a matching price reduction do to your company's operating profit? Will a matching price cut on your part simply mean that every supplier in the industry is making less profit?

3. Send a "heads-up" to top management if product sales volumes and profit margins appear to be in jeopardy. Give the brass alternative strategies to combat the competitive move. (Rule to win promotions by: Never pose a problem to senior management without offering a solution.)

4. Consider options other than a "me-too" price cut. For example:

- Keep the price the same, but bundle in a supply package for extra value.
- Provide next-day delivery at no extra charge.
- Develop an attractive lease plan.
- Take trade-ins, which are, in effect, disguised discounts.
- Offer extended billing without interest charges. (Better the stuff should gather dust in the customers' warehouses than in yours.)
- Offer free product training.

5. Consider more advertising and closer customer contact to emphasize the value the product offers. Now is the time for hand-holding. Keep the company's customers close.

FIVE SITUATIONS THAT POINT TO STABLE PRICING

It's easier for marketing managers to plan when there's a fair degree of certainty that the competition is not likely to take the profit out of the market by slicing prices to the bone. Every marketing manager would prefer a stable market. Here are signs that point to one:

1. The industry served is mature, market share is fairly well distributed among several companies who serve this industry, sales volumes for each of the suppliers are predictable, and everyone is making a profit. The marketing manager who disturbs this situation with price cuts probably ruins the gravy train for every company involved.

2. The competition has just hired a new marketing manager. New kids on the block are not likely to cut prices right away unless they have been brought in specifically to cure a low sales volume situation. Why don't new fish cut prices? Because senior management has given them the lecture on maintaining profit margins, but they haven't yet had the whipping that comes when sales volumes decline.

3. The competition's plant is running at full capacity and they're selling all they can make. No marketing manager is going to cut prices under these conditions.

4. The cost of manufacture or cost of supply is rising. No one wants to lower prices at a time when production costs are increasing.

5. Several competitors have dropped out of the market, gone on strike, or are having a problem supplying product. Why would anyone want to cut prices at a time when the product may be in short supply?

HOW THE COMPETITION AFFECTS NEW PRODUCT DEVELOPMENT

The competition plays an important role in developing new products and in the marketing manager's determining when these products should be introduced to the market. The kind of role the competition plays depends upon the company's place in the industry.

For "me-too" companies, the marketer allows the industry leader to take the risk of introducing new products, then follows quickly with similar models, perhaps with a few more bells and whistles, a tad faster, and usually at a lower price. This is a second-banana strategy, but it works for companies with limited research or with smaller market shares. These companies are industry leader watchers.

For those companies who are, or strive to be, industry leaders, new models are introduced when the competition begins to be a nuisance by offering lower prices that cut into the leader's market share. Some marketers even keep new products on the back shelf until their market share is threatened. Industry leaders have the advantage of being able to sell "vaporware." That is they can advise, or otherwise hint, to their customers to wait before buying competitive products because they have a new whizbang model steaming upriver as fast as possible.

WHAT TO DO WHEN THE COMPETITION INTRODUCES A NEW PRODUCT

When the competition introduces a new product, the first thing the marketing manager must determine is just what kind of product has arrived. New products fall into two broad categories:

- Evolutionary
- Revolutionary

Evolutionary products

The evolutionary product is one that performs the same functions as previous models, but does them a bit faster, a trifle easier, or at a reduced price. It may feature more benefits than previous models, but its operation is similar to what has gone before.

Products such as these usually don't upset the balance in the marketplace, but when they are announced they do present a problem for the marketing manager selling against them. The new competitive product may offer a better value than anything the company currently has available. If the company doesn't have a similar improvement near completion, the marketing manager can respond to this entry by:

1. *Lowering prices.* Price cuts are unimaginative and reduce margins, but sometimes there is no alternative if market share is to be maintained.
2. *Bundling the existing product* with supplies, peripherals, and so forth to disguise the value difference.
3. *Extending the warranty at no extra charge.* This, again, has the effect of adding value to the product without reducing the price.
4. *Offering leasing or extended financing.* When the customer pays only *x* dollars a month, the value differences between a new and a mature product become hazy.

5. *Use the familiar "vaporware" strategy.* Ask good customers to wait until the company's own new model is ready. Only resort to this tactic if the company actually has such a product under development and near completion.

Revolutionary products

If the competition has just introduced a revolutionary new product that takes a completely new approach to solving industry problems, the marketing manager's dilemma is far more serious. First, good marketing managers should not be caught off guard. They should be plugged into the industry grapevine well enough to be aware of any developments that are likely to shake up the industry.

That aside, what can the marketing manager do when faced with a competitive product that makes the company's line obsolete?

THREE THINGS TO DO WHEN THE COMPETITION INTRODUCES A NEW PRODUCT THAT MAKES YOUR COMPANY'S PRODUCT OBSOLETE

1. Remain calm. The first action to take is to set up an information system that reports back to you on the successes and failures of the new product. Not everything in this world works as advertised. Some apparently wonderful ideas and products had hidden flaws that only surfaced after the product was in general use. If these flaws are serious, the product may fizzle. Early design flaws may slow the implementation of a revolutionary product, but they won't necessarily kill it. For example, the ballpoint pen, introduced just after World War II, enjoyed some initial success as a high-cost, prestige novelty item. That success quickly faded when the "lifetime supply of ink" that marketers advertised had leaked onto thousands of white shirts. Only years later, after the product was improved and the price had fallen dramatically, did the ballpoint pen make the fountain pen obsolete. (The fountain pen has now reversed roles with the ballpoint pen. It is making a comeback as a prestige symbol.)

2. Realize that revolutions take time to capture the hearts and minds of the marketplace. Meanwhile, no matter how wonderful the new process is, the company's product will still find a market among loyal users.

People resist change. Sell as many of the obsolete model as you can while you can.

3. King Canute couldn't hold back the tide and neither can you. If the company's product is now obsolete with no way to match the competitive innovation, establish a time frame for cutting back production. Sure, milk as much sales volume and profit as possible from the line while you can, but don't die the "death of a thousand cuts." It is a very painful way to go.

How the competition affects distribution strategy

Distribution is the method by which companies make their products accessible to end-users. How the competition accomplishes this objective affects every marketing manager's own distribution strategy. For example, "filling up" a channel may deny competition access to that channel. For example, look at companies that sell their products through retailers. Retailers prefer to offer a variety of brands, but they also have shelf-space limitations and constraints on how much they can spend on inventory. The facsimile machine supplier that offers a special deal that "loads up" a retailer with product has essentially shut out the competition for a time because the retailer has no more room for additional products and no money to pay for them.

The physical location of plants and warehouses determines companies' strong or weak geographic presence. The company with facilities only on the east coast will never enjoy strong sales on the west coast. The act of establishing a facility is a commitment that the company intends to compete in that geographic market.

When a powerful competitor seems to have a distribution channel well covered, or has made the cost of entry prohibitive, a marketing manager may decide to use another channel to avoid head-to-head confrontation. Instead of selling its clothes through retail stores, Lands' End chooses to use mail order. Its attractive catalogs are eagerly awaited by thousands of loyal customers.

What to do when you can't match the competition's advertising budget

Do you have a competitor who each year buys all of the half-time advertising spots on the Super Bowl? Don't despair. If the other side's advertising budget far exceeds what is available to you, then you'll just have to be smarter and make your advertising dollar work harder.

One way to get more advertising bang for the buck is to change objectives. For example, the Super Bowl ads are primarily useful for image building. They're designed to give TV viewers the warm fuzzies about the advertiser. There's nothing wrong with that objective—if you can afford it. If you can't, shoot for another goal. For example, spend your ad money on direct mail. Forget about image building and try to get some orders. There's nothing wrong with that objective either. Another method might be to buy many radio spots in a variety of markets. The repetition will give your company name recognition. The point is that when the competition is engaged in an activity that you can't match financially, do something else.

Chapter Eight

FINGERS IN THE WIND: MARKET RESEARCH

Freud, in his famous rhetorical question, asked, "What do women want?"

"That's good to know for starters," the market researcher replies, "but I'm interested in what *everyone* wants and what it will take to get them to buy it."

Market research is just what the name implies: information gathering. Its primary purposes are to uncover opportunities and to reduce risks. Without research the marketplace is a rocky, alien landscape and there's no telling what is lurking on the other side of the next hill. Good research reduces the risks of climbing that hill.

TEN NEED-TO-KNOW THINGS MARKET RESEARCH CAN TELL THE MARKETING MANAGER

1. Market research attempts to answer that most fundamental of all marketing questions: If we make it, will they buy it?
2. Market research offers insights into which product improvements are most likely to meet with customer approval.
3. Market research explains why the competition is eating the company's lunch.
4. Market research suggests the price points at which products should be offered.
5. Market research provides guidelines on which sales channels are likely to be the most productive in moving the company's products.

6. Market research provides "fashion" information on currently popular colors, styles, shapes, trends, and so forth.
7. Market research tells which groups, or kinds of companies or industries, are the most likely candidates for the company's products or services.
8. Market research reveals whether the company's public image is good or poor.
9. Market research exposes those products that have peaked and whose sales volumes are likely to decline.
10. Market research reveals which advertising and promotion programs have been successful and which have been bombs.

HOW LACK OF RESEARCH HURTS START-UPS

One of the biggest reasons start-ups fail is because many entrepreneurs presume they know what the marketplace wants. They see no need to confirm their presumptions before opening for business. The marketplace, however, is unforgiving. It's plain dumb not to test the company's plan of action. The failure rate of start-ups could be drastically reduced with a little basic research.

SIX PEARLS OF WISDOM FOR WOULD-BE ENTREPRENEURS ON THE MARKETING SECTION OF BUSINESS PLANS

Word of advice for would-be entrepreneurs: When writing your business plan, show in the plan that you've done your homework.

1. Devote a great number of pages to describing the potential market your company plans to target.
2. Explain how your product or service fits into that market.
3. Explain how the company intends to attack the market. (Hint: as a new kid on the block, you'll acquire more credibility among would-be investors by targeting an unexploited market niche than by positioning the company head-to-head against well established competitors.)
4. Detail the sales channels the company will use to distribute the product.

5. Acknowledge the competitive pressures the company will face and offer a plan for dealing with that pressure.
6. Outline how the research was conducted that permitted the conclusions the plan reached.

Potential investors will read these market research sections more carefully than any other pages in your plan. The information in this section determines whether investors reach for their wallets or head for the door.

FOUR BASIC QUESTIONS THAT ALL MARKETING MANAGERS NEED TO ASK

No matter the size of the budget, marketing research begins by asking the right questions. Asking the wrong questions can lead to disaster. "Right" questions that apply to any industry include:

1. Who, exactly, are the company's customers, or potential customers?
2. Where are the customers, or potential customers, located?
3. What are the customers buying now?
4. What will the customers buy tomorrow?

Obtain the answers to the above questions and your career as a market research analyst has begun.

GETTING DOWN TO NITTY-GRITTY SPECIFICS

Within the general requirement of learning about customers and their buying habits, the researcher attempts to uncover specifics including:

1. *Competitor research*. What other companies are after in this market, and what are they up to?
2. *New product research*. Is the market ready for our new whizbang?
3. *Pricing research*. How much can we charge for this whizbang without earning a reputation as masked bandits?
4. *Channel research*. How and where should we sell our whizbang?

5. *Advertising research*. Is the money we're spending on TV, radio, newspapers, and magazines promoting this whizbang worth it?
6. *Performance research*. How are we doing as a company vis-à-vis the other guys out there?
7. *Image research*. What does the marketplace think about us?

RESEARCH TECHNIQUES

There are many ways to gather information. Each has its advantages, disadvantages, and attendant costs. The following sections discuss some of the more popular methods.

DEMOGRAPHIC STUDIES

Comedian: My uncle just went bankrupt.
Straight man: That's too bad. What did he do?
Comedian: He owned a "Big and Tall" store.
Straight man: That's usually a good business. Where was his location?
Comedian: Tokyo.

That's a classic case of not studying demographics before beginning an enterprise.

Demographics is the study of where people and companies are located, what they do, their age groups, their incomes and education levels, their ethnic background, and just about everything else about them. Studying demographics is vital to the market researcher.

Demographics is an excellent tool because, among other things, it gives researchers a good handle on prospects' buying habits. For example, people who choose to live in a particular neighborhood are likely to make similar choices in what they buy. The following are two simplistic examples of how demographics can be used to guide marketing efforts:

An area that is zoned for one acre or larger home lots might be a good location for a riding lawn mower dealership. If a great many riding lawn mowers are sold within a small geographic area, not only are more riding mowers likely to be sold there, but this area might also support a landscaping service or a plant nursery.

The area to conduct a direct-mail campaign for a luxury automobile is in an upscale community of high-priced homes. Or to use a ridiculous reverse example, there's no point in mailing four-color brochures on the new sixteen-cylinder Jaguar touring sedan, with a base price of $60,000, to people whose annual income is below $15,000.

Census data: A good place to obtain demographic information

There is a Niagara Falls of useful demographic data available that was developed by the federal government from the decennial census. The data has been analyzed and massaged by firms that specialize in this kind of research. For a price, marketing managers can learn detailed information about the population, including where they live, the kind of cars they drive, where they shop, the food they eat, the clothes they buy, where they send their kids to school, their age and income groups, and much more. Making sense of the data, using it to help the company reduce risk when bringing its products to market, is the difference between the average researcher and the research artist.

SURVEYS

Customer surveys are essentially questionnaires that ask people about their attitudes and opinions. They can cover a wide range of topics. Marketers employ surveys to cut down the risk of introducing new products into a market.

The marketer's starting point for a survey is determining what he or she wants to know. The information sought defines everything else. It's the old systems' rule that output determines input.

Information needs fall into several broad categories. These needs are:

1. What the researcher absolutely, positively needs to know.
2. What the researcher would very much like to know if the information can be gathered as a by-product of the need-to-know material.
3. Any detail data that helps the information come alive and may guide the researcher.
4. Trivial data that may add to the researcher's insight concerning the information gathered.

The three most common survey methods

Surveys are usually conducted one of three ways. These ways are:

1. *Mail surveys.* In this method questionnaires are mailed to a group of individuals. If the researcher is lucky, they are completed and returned.

2. *Telephone interviews.* In this method individuals are called and asked to answer questions over the phone. If the caller is lucky, the respondent doesn't hang up.

3. *Personal interviews.* In this method people are approached on the street, in a shopping mall, at a theater exit, or assembled in a focus group, and asked questions face-to-face.

There are advantages and disadvantages associated with each method. On a per-respondent basis, mail surveys are the least expensive and personal interviews cost the most.

FOCUS GROUPS

In the focus group study, the researcher brings together a small number of individuals, usually from ten to twelve people, and asks them questions about a proposed new product or service. It is a round-table environment and one participant's comments may trigger a response from another. The participants are usually screened in advance or have met some pre-set criteria. For example, an automobile company thinking about introducing a new pickup truck might choose individuals who have purchased such a vehicle in the recent past.

Focus group sessions will last for a few hours. Some last the better part of a day. Participants are usually paid a small sum for their time, or, at the very least, get a swell lunch.

The sessions are conducted by a moderator who leads the group in their discussions. Participants are asked their opinions about a proposed product's styling, color, packaging, features, perceived value, and so forth. The session is often videotaped so the participants' responses, both visual and verbal, can be studied in detail later. In many instances, marketing managers watch the group react from behind one-way glass, though this practice smacks a bit of the police station interrogation.

Six advantages of focus groups

1. They are a relatively inexpensive researching method.

2. They can be put together quickly. The average meeting only lasts several hours. The focus group is one way to gather information fast.

3. The participants' statements and reactions can be visually recorded. This eyeballing is much more meaningful to researchers than merely looking at statistical results on paper.

4. If the participants are carefully chosen, they are fairly representative of the population segment targeted to buy the proposed product or service.

5. The information obtained is more comprehensive than with many other research methods because the moderator's follow-up questions can dig a bit deeper beyond the participants' initial responses.

6. The discussions can be conducted in a central location where they can be observed by marketing managers and other company executives. This makes them popular with advertising agencies who, to demonstrate that they're earning their keep, like to put on dog-and-pony shows for their clients.

Six disadvantages of focus groups

Focus groups are a useful research tool, but they do have their limitations. These limitations include:

1. They're useful for new product introductions, but are often a waste of money for existing product extensions and updates.

2. No matter how carefully participants are chosen, the sampling is necessarily small. The few bodies assembled may not represent the opinions of the vast majority of potential customers.

3. One or two individuals in the group may dominate the discussion, making the sampling even smaller. A good moderator will know how to guard against this.

4. The group can get on the wrong track and the moderator won't be able to bring them back.

5. There are focus group "junkies" who attend just to hear themselves speak, and for the free lunch. Their opinions are worthless.

6. The focus group method is expensive if costs are considered on a per-person-interviewed basis.

THE MAIL SURVEY

The mail survey is the least expensive method for gathering information. In the mail survey, questionnaires are usually mailed to a demographically selected group or groups. Perhaps the group targeted all bought Chevys within the last two years; or perhaps all inquired about, but did not buy, an Alaskan Cruise. There is a common thread that binds the people on the list. A cover letter explains why the questionnaire is important and often tries to tie it to a benefit for the respondent: "We're going to use the information you give us to bring better TV programming to this entire area." Occasionally a gift is offered for the respondent's time. In some instances, the token gift is included with the mailing package.

Three advantages of the mail survey

1. The mail questionnaire is inexpensive compared to other survey methods.

2. Any section of the country can be targeted. The respondent needn't be physically close to those who need the survey information.

3. Large survey samples, which are more accurate, are economically feasible.

Three disadvantages of the mail survey

1. Many people will view the survey form as junk mail and throw it away without responding.

2. The people who do respond may not be typical prospects for the company's products or services, but rather those who want to inflict their opinions on others.

3. There is the possibility only for rudimentary follow-up questions that explore the respondent's opinions.

TELEPHONE SURVEYS

In the telephone survey method, people are called at their homes and asked questions about products or services near and dear to the heart of the researcher. Most calls come in the early evening when the potential respondent is likely to be at home. Again, the people called are culled from a list of people who fit into a category.

Four advantages of the telephone survey

1. The interviewer is in voice-to-voice contact with the respondent. The depth of feeling behind the answers can be discerned.

2. Incisive follow-up questions can be asked, depending upon the respondent's answers.

3. The responses reflect instant feelings, rather than the studied answers possible on a mail-in survey.

4. They cost less than personal interview surveys.

Four disadvantages of the telephone survey

1. Telephone surveys are intrusive in that they invade people's homes. This often leads to resentment and negative feelings about the caller's product or service.

2. The telephone is used so much by high-pressure con artists that many people are suspicious of any stranger who calls them on the phone. They believe the "survey" is the beginning of sales pitch—and they are often right. Many unscrupulous salespeople begin their harangue by announcing that they are conducting some kind of survey.

3. Telephone surveys require skilled questioners. Not enough skilled people are available.

4. Telephone surveys cost more, per person surveyed, than mail-in surveys.

THE PERSONAL-INTERVIEW SURVEY

In the personal-interview survey method, the interviewer is stationed near a heavy foot-traffic area. Often, the survey is done for a nearby merchant. A survey on customers' reactions to K-Mart advertising might be done at an entrance to a K-Mart store. Passersby are approached and asked a few questions. A token gift, say a gift certificate, is sometimes offered in exchange for participation.

Six advantages of personal interviews

1. The principle advantage of the personal interview is that it is face-to-face contact with the respondent.

2. Site choice allows for respondents to be carefully selected. Conducting a survey inside a K-Mart store ensures that only K-Mart shoppers will be interviewed.

3. The interviewer can also visually select those who will be questioned according to sex, age, the way they are dressed, and so forth.

4. The interviewer can attempt to build rapport with the respondent by offering a token gift for taking the time to answer the questionnaire. Once "hooked," there's a high degree of certainty that respondents will answer all the questions.

5. The respondent can look at or handle various items or sample ads, taste test products, and so forth.

6. The surveys themselves are flexible in that a skilled interviewer can ask add-on questions depending upon the respondents' answers.

Five disadvantages of personal interviews

1. Personal interviews have a high cost per interview.

2. Skilled interviewers who can obtain useful information are in short supply.

3. The results can be skewed due to interviewer bias.

4. Many people will shake off the interviewer's request and walk on. That means the "right" people may not get interviewed.

5. Unscrupulous interviewers, who are paid on a per-interview basis, may simply fake interviews to earn more money.

SURVEY SAMPLING

The surveys with which everyone is most familiar are those dealing with voter's attitudes. Predicting the winners of presidential and local elections, and the probable success or failure of various referenda, is a national sport. Survey firms publish weekly reports on the president's popularity and whether the populace is bullish or bearish on the economy. Sometimes the predictions are right on the money and sometimes they are spectacularly wrong.

When survey results are wrong by a wide margin—and there have been some notorious examples—the surveyor's standard excuse is that "the sampling wasn't big enough." In other words, not enough people were asked their opinions. In general, increasing the size of the survey will improve the accuracy of the results—or reduce the margin of error, whichever phrase comes easiest to your lips. Keep in mind, however, that the more people sampled, the higher the cost of the survey. That means researchers must make compromises. They must not only define the information needed, but must also decide how accurate the information must be. If the researcher can live with a 3-percent margin of error, why pay for a survey that ensures 1-percent error rate?

THE SURVEY QUESTIONNAIRE

The art of the survey is in framing the proper questions. Most surveyors believe that open-ended questions ("Why did you decide to shop at this mall today?") are a mistake. The responses to questions such as this are difficult to categorize and correlate. Patterns can't be determined.

Structured questions that ask the respondents to rate things are much more informative: "Which did you like better, Brand A or Brand B?" "On a scale of one to ten, rate this shopping mall compared to others in this area."

Another useful scale rating example is:

> Rate how you liked the movie.
> Liked very much _____
> Liked somewhat _____
> Didn't like _____
> Disliked very much _____

Answering these kinds of questionnaires is very easy for the respondents and provides the researcher with much useful data.

Structured questions that ask respondents to list all the factors that went into a buying decision are also useful if the various alternatives are presented to them. In this type of questionnaire the respondent is asked to check off all the factors that apply.

> List the factors that influenced your computer buying decision:
> Price___ Special promotion___ Store location___ Warranty___
> Ease of use___ System features___ Software bundle___
> Reputation of manufacturer___ Size of monitor___ Other___

This method helps marketers zero in on the factors that are important to buyers.

Another surveying method is to make a statement and ask respondents if they agree or disagree with it.

> Cable television offers better programming than the networks.
> Agree___ Disagree___

This method is a good way to measure attitudes.

SIX COMMON RESEARCHING DIFFICULTIES

The need to know something about the market the company plans to service is clear. Obtaining reliable data on that market, however, is never easy. The researcher must wander through a maze laden with traps. Here are six reasons why this is so:

1. The researcher can ask people what they want or think, but the sneaky, uncooperative rascals don't always tell the truth. Often, people will frame their replies in a way that will make them look good. Ask people what kind of music they prefer, and the answers might lead the naïve researcher to believe there is a crying need for more classical music stations.

2. The researcher can study historical data, but there's no degree of certainty that what went before is any guide to what will happen tomorrow. The past is prologue, but with endless variations.

3. The researcher can test market, but test results won't necessarily be duplicated after a national rollout.

4. In some instances, unscrupulous competitors may try to affect the results on your company's market research. Test market several product variations in a small geographic area and the competition may buy up the model they're confident they can beat in an effort to convince your company to rollout a loser.

5. The researcher can ask industry experts (the Delphi method), but the soothsayers, while willing to offer their wisdom for a price, often have no clue.

6. The researcher can ask the wrong questions, or phrase the questions in the wrong way. In either instance, the information obtained is worse than useless—it can lead the company down the wrong path.

The important thing to learn from all this is that market research can reduce risk, but marketing risks can never be completely eliminated—or there would never be such a thing as product failures. The marketer should use all the available data, but he or she should also rely on past experience, training, and gut feeling.

THE MELTING-POT PROBLEM

One of the biggest problems confronting market researchers, in this country at least, is our diverse population. We are a rich stew of many cultures and ethnic groups. In addition, we have the most mobile population in the world.* European countries are beginning to allow more immigration than in previous years, but their populations are, by and large, still monolithic and stationary. A survey conducted in Sweden, for example, needn't be nearly as comprehensive as one done here to get a handle on national trends.

---

*Impromptu marketing quiz: What industries does mobility benefit? Here's a short list of possibilities to start you thinking: Moving companies; rent-a-car companies; real estate agents; furniture dealers; relocation specialists; mortgage lenders; apartment finders; and home and hardware stores. Think of some others.

Our nation's extraordinary diversity often skews the results of small survey samples because an inordinate number of one ethnic group may have been queried to the exclusion of others. The results may not be meaningful for the general population. Demographics can be used to determine just who is targeted for the survey, but with our high mobility, the demographic information isn't always current.

The solution, of course, is to increase the size of the sample, but that raises the cost. The point is, there is very little national consensus on any issue in this country, no common likes, no unified feelings, and few "me-too" opinions. Researchers must keep the reality firmly in mind when they interpret results.

On research that questions consumer attitudes in general, diverse segments (sub-sample groups) of the population must be surveyed so different attitudes are taken into account.

HOW TO USE THE ANSWERS
TO MARKETING RESEARCH QUESTIONS

The marketing researcher gathers data and uses it for a variety of purposes. These purposes include:

1. As a guide to help the company develop products and services that are likely to become successful.

2. To phase out or discontinue those products and services that are past their prime, or to cancel the development of products that research indicates are likely to be failures.

3. To identify potential problems for the company, the product line, or the market in general. For example, if research reveals the company suffers from a poor image, a public relations campaign to correct that image problem might be initiated.

4. To identify targets of opportunity.

5. To research possible options. The company may be considering several different plans of action. Obtaining accurate information before making direction decisions greatly increases the chances for success for a new product, a new marketing campaign, and even a new company.

Research for Site Location

Sample problem: Where is the best place to open a hat store?
Answer: On a street filled with hat stores.

The logic behind this answer is that prospects seeking to purchase hats will come more often to a street they know to be filled with hat merchants. The potential hat buyers know they will have a greater selection of merchandise within a short distance than anywhere else in town. The stand-alone hat merchant in another part of the city may not have the degree of competition, but neither will that lonely merchant enjoy the same traffic flow. That is the reason why most large cities contain jewelry districts, restaurant rows, antique centers, and other clusters of similar merchants. The suburban mall with its created shopping environment is an extension of this marketing scheme.

Research on the most viable place to locate a business then heavily depends upon the kind of enterprise that business is. Any consumer-oriented business must be located where customers can easily reach it. The closer to the potential customer, the better. To be successful, the ice-cream shop should be located in an area with heavy foot traffic. No bail bondsman ever went wrong by putting his office close to the courthouse. F.W. Woolworth's famous marketing maxim was, "Make it easy for customers to buy." Being where the customers are is that maxim in action.

In many instances, selecting the right business location is just a matter of common sense. The following are some typical examples:

1. Businesses with a crew of outside salespeople should be located near the company's targeted industries and close to highway intersections and through streets so the salespeople can quickly reach their customers.
2. Businesses whose production facilities might have a negative impact on the local environment, say a fertilizer plant, should be situated far from heavily populated areas—thereby saving the company the legal expense of countless class action suits.
3. Businesses that sell their products nationally should be located near transportation hubs so the products can be easily distributed.
4. Businesses that rely on skilled employees should be located near large labor pools of that skill. A classic example is Silicon Valley.

Some of the above location criteria may not appear to be marketing issues, but marketing must always be involved in location decisions. Just try putting a paint factory in an upscale metropolitan area and watch the problems accumulate for public relations and marketing.

WHAT-WENT-WRONG RESEARCH

Often, market research is used to find out why the company's market share has shrunk over the past few years, why the competition has grown stronger, or why certain products have lost their popularity. This type of activity is called *diagnostic research*. Like a physician, the diagnostic researcher is trying to find out why the patient is sick. The illness must be identified before remedies can be prescribed. Some of the things this type of research often reveals includes:

1. There are more competitors out there than previously realized. These companies have some hot new products that offer more value than the company's products. If this one is really news, the marketing manager's head has been stuck in the sand!

2. There are changes in the industry the company serves. Perhaps the industry is going through a rough patch, perhaps the main industry players aren't using the company products in the same quantities or the same manner as they did previously.

3. Your company has internal problems. Many companies forget the first rule of marketing: Make it easy for customers to buy. They develop internal bureaucracies that seem to exist to alienate the customer. Customers faced with resistance just throw up their hands and decide to shop elsewhere.

4. The company has experienced the loss of a sales channel or a decrease in effectiveness of a sales channel. Let's say you're a facsimile machine manufacturer that has traditionally sold its products through a network of independent business machine dealers. This channel has not been able to compete with the mass merchants such as Office Depot and Office Max, and the number of effective dealers has declined dramatically. Any manufacturer who relied on this channel would find that sales had suffered. Moral: don't sail all your shops through one channel.

5. There's been a reduction in expenditures on advertising, promotions, and sales activity. This shouldn't be a revelation even to raw marketing trainees, but when you stop selling hard, sales usually go down.

6. There's something wrong at the factory. If product quality declines or production schedules frequently disappoint good customers, there are consequences.

7. An eager competitor is trying to build market share at any cost. This situation usually doesn't require "research" in that if some other company is cutting prices to the bone and stealing the company's best customers left and right, you'll certainly know about it without conducting a survey. If you don't know about it, please change careers!

8. The product is getting a bit long in the tooth. When this happens, it shouldn't come as a surprise to the marketing researcher. If this information is a shock, you haven't kept tabs on the product's life cycle.

9. The company has lost a key person, or several key personnel. Never underestimate the impact that the loss of one super salesperson, one Crackerjack administrator, one knowledgeable market support person can have on the company's sales.

Diagnosing these problems is relatively easy. Any good marketing manager knows when the company isn't providing the value it once provided. The cure is often more difficult. If a fall-off in sales coincides with a reduction in advertising, the natural solution would appear to be plug in more advertising dollars. Perhaps, however, those advertising dollars were reduced in the first place because of budget constraints. The marketing manager may not be able to simply wave a magic wand and make that lost ad money reappear. What the marketing manager must do is to find ways to use the limited budget more effectively.

Twelve sources for secondary research

When doing market research don't neglect material that has already been published. There is a wealth of data out there, dangling like ripe fruit ready to be plucked. These sources include the following:

1. *Magazine and newspaper articles.* One particularly rich source for relevant material is industry publications.

2. *Newspapers.* Not only do newspapers conduct business studies and collect information, they also preserve this material in their files.

3. *Trade associations.* The industry trade association may conduct surveys that marketing managers would find useful. Often, the price for using the data is merely participating in the survey.

4. *Books.* Most books take at least a year from conception to time of publication, so the information they contain may be a bit stale. Still, they can offer much of value.

5. *Universities.* The business schools of many universities conduct research on business topics that is available to private firms.

6. *Federal government agencies.* The federal government produces studies on everything under the sun. Contact your local SBA, tell them what you want, and you'll be inundated with pamphlets, books, articles, and so forth.

7. *State and local government agencies.* Most states have economic development agencies to assist businesses in their areas. Want to be flooded with business information? Tell a state economic development agency you are contemplating relocating a business to that state.

8. *Chambers of commerce.* The local COC has a good deal of information available about the business climate in the community.

9. *Computer database services.* These are the people who can break down demographic information and tell you where the prospects are hiding.

10. *Libraries.* Libraries house statistical data, lists of businesses, demographic data, and much else that is useful—and it's all free!

11. *TV and radio stations.* Their advertising departments have demographic information available that can be very useful to marketing people.

12. *The internet.* This medium has become a valuable information source. Be careful, however, to document any data received.

How to use secondary research

There is so much information available, the problem becomes sorting through all the data and zeroing in on the stuff that is relevant to the researcher. Here's a step-by-step approach:

1. The marketing researcher must become a reader. Regularly peruse publications such as the *Wall Street Journal, Business Week,* and others for articles that are applicable to the company. Reviewing industry publications should become a priority. Scan through them the minute they arrive.

2. When reading an article or book that has something to offer, the researcher should look at the credits or bibliography for the author's sources. These sources can be accessed for additional material.

3. Don't be afraid to contact the author of an interesting piece. He or she may share additional information with you, or at least provide some sources.

4. Talk to trade association personnel about your company's concerns. They usually reflect the concerns of the entire industry. If no data is available, a study will be funded—which means shared costs.

BUYING RESEARCH

Many companies don't have the time, the know-how, or the in-house staff to conduct appropriate research. There are a number of companies out there happy to do any research you require—for a price. One big advantage in using an outside firm is that they own no ox (no pet projects) that must be spared from goring. Their results should not be biased. When hiring an outside outfit, use a common sense approach:

1. Look for a company that is qualified to handle the job. Ask for references.

2. Don't buy more research than you need. The research firm may try to get you to "trade up."

3. Hire an outfit whom you understand. The more esoteric and technical the language, the faster you should head for the door.

4. Make sure the research outfit is clear on your objectives—and be sure yourself. Fuzzy goals will lead to fuzzy results.

MAKING SENSE OF THE DATA

The following is Ambrose Bierce's example of deductive logic taken from his work, *The Devil's Dictionary:* "If one man can dig a post hole in thirty minutes, then thirty men can dig a post hole in one minute."

The point of Mr. Bierce's bit of absurdity is that possessing all the pertinent data doesn't prevent us from reaching the wrong conclusions. It is easy to accumulate information, but drawing the right conclusions from this information is not so simple. Here's how to ensure that conclusions won't be off base.

1. Researchers must, first of all, be patient. They must keep an open mind during the interpretative phase. One bad habit of many researchers is to reach an early conclusion or start with an assumption, then sift through the material for supporting evidence.

2. Look for consistency. The same kinds of answers from a variety of sources, or from different groups, suggests those answers are valuable.

3. Look for reasons why the data may be skewed. Perhaps the wrong demographic group was surveyed. Perhaps the wrong questions were asked.

4. Cross check. Use different sets of data and then see if the same conclusions can be drawn.

5. Be skeptical of easy solutions to difficult problems. They are very rare indeed.

Research can reduce, but not eliminate, the risk of bringing new products to market. It can tell marketing managers why some products are declining in sales, what makes the competition so tough, where the customers are, and even which products customers are likely to buy in the near future. Research is, however, fallible. It is a tool, and like any tool, its effectiveness depends upon the people using it.

Chapter Nine

MARKET SHARE STRATEGIES

WHAT MARKET SHARE MEANS

Market share means the percentage of products the company sells measured against the total market for that product. If the company manufactures spinning tops and sells five hundred thousand units while the entire industry has sales totaling one million tops, then your company enjoys a 50-percent market share. Not bad—in fact, excellent. You're the top-dog outfit. All the other companies in the business are scrapping to get a piece of the remaining 50 percent.

WHY MARKET SHARE IS IMPORTANT

Market share is important because it is the key to higher profits. Leaders who dominate the market, such as Intel for computer chips and Hewlett Packard for laser printers, not only have the biggest sales volumes, but they control the industry agenda. They ultimately decide the price points at which products will be offered and they decide when the next generation product should be introduced. Think about it: New computer chips are distributed to computer manufacturers when Intel decides the old chips are obsolete.

This control over the agenda is what helps market share leaders make more profit. Higher sales and profits fuel expansion because the company has more money available with which to exploit the market still further.

Market share leaders have the biggest budgets for advertising, special promotions, product research, backup systems, and so forth. In this way the process becomes self-generating. Just as "a rose is a rose is a rose," the market share leader is the market share leader because it is the market share leader.

FIVE WAYS TO BECOME A MARKET SHARE LEADER

Becoming the dominant player in a market is the Holy Grail to many marketers. They will tilt with as many fire-eating dragons as necessary to realize this goal. There are five traditional paths that can be taken to market leadership:

1. *Become the low-cost producer and pass the savings along to customers.* Providing the product or service for a lower price than any competitor will automatically create greater market share. Of course, to become low-cost producer the company must have access to at least one of the following:

a. *Lower cost of manufacture.* Lower manufacturing costs can be realized by buying or developing automated, high-speed equipment that is too expensive for the competition to copy. Developing a patented process the competition can't duplicate is another way to achieve lower manufacturing costs.
b. *Lower material costs.* Energy companies, for example, that also own their own natural gas or petroleum wells, may have lower operating costs than competitors who are forced to buy energy.
c. *Lower labor costs.* One of the reasons for "runaway" companies that put their manufacturing facilities in low-wage countries is the marketer's desire to reduce costs and thereby increase market share.

2. *Superior technology.* Hewlett Packard's laser printers are not the lowest cost units on the market, but they are always state-of-the-art. When the competition almost catches up, Hewlett Packard announces a new model. If the model isn't quite ready to be delivered, so what? Their customers are willing to wait.

3. *Superior marketing.* IBM controls the mainframe computer market, although they have never been considered an industry innovator. They prefer to wait to see if the pioneers (the guys with the arrows in their backs) stumble with brand new market entries. When the other guys define the market opportunity, IBM announces its own entries. Then it relies on a strong marketing staff to overtake the competition.

This "let the other guys do all the experimenting," is a strategy that has worked well for IBM in the mainframe market for fifty years. They stumbled badly, however, when they tried the same approach with the PC market. This market moved too fast for the kind of sober deliberation that IBM prefers. Big Blue was almost left in the dust heap with the other PC also-rans before the company developed a system that cut through their formidable bureaucracy. A belated entrepreneurial approach to the PC market finally allowed them to speed up product development and introduction.

4. *A bigger advertising budget.* Blow your own horn the loudest. The company that advertises more will inevitably increase market share. The problem with this strategy is the market share is achieved at a cost and it can be snatched away if some company is willing to spend more.

5. *Superior financial resources.* This advantage is really a combination of all of the above. The company that is better able to make an investment in an automated plant, tie up commodity contracts, strategically disperse manufacturing facilities throughout the world, hire the best scientists, engineers and marketers, and spend the most on advertising will gain more market share.

DISTRIBUTION CHANNELS EXPLAINED

Distribution is the entire system of delivering products and services to customers. Distributors include retailers, wholesalers, warehouse clubs, mass merchants, discounters, department stores, dealers, agents, and other resellers. They perform a valuable and necessary service. Our networks are responsible for the great diversity of products available to consumers.

One of the reasons the former Soviet Union's conversion to capitalism has been so painful is because, under communism, they had no distribution networks through which goods could flow. There were no wholesalers, no independent dealers, no department stores, outside of the state-sponsored GUM, and certainly no mass merchants. There were no trucking companies, no overnight delivery services, no companies providing communications systems. The lack of this infrastructure for delivering products from manufacturers to consumers complicates the task for anyone wishing to do business in the country.

HOGGING THE DISTRIBUTION CHANNELS

One excellent strategy to increase market share is to tie up the important distribution channels that have traditionally served the industry. Just take them away from the competition. Here's the theory behind this strategy:

1. The resources of any distributor, no matter how well financed, are limited.

2. Shelf space and warehouse space are limited.

3. These limitations mean that distributors can finance and stock only so much inventory.

4. The time they can devote to learning about and selling any one product is also limited.

5. By offering distributors irresistible quantity discounts, long-term contracts, superior service, sales assistance, and other incentives, the company not only increases its sales volume, but it also effectively shuts out the competition from these accounts.

6. Your company prospers while the competition must scramble to find alternate channels.

Homework assignment: What distribution channels does your company use to move its products? Does that same channel also carry your competitors' products? What incentives would you have to offer to these distributors to carry your company's line exclusively?

Seven things marketers do to tie up distribution channels

There is no plain-vanilla strategy for capturing a distribution channel. The task is never easy. Any distributor prefers alternate sources of supply to be able to play one competitor against another. That means the distributor must be given powerful reasons (make that incentives) to opt for an exclusive arrangement. Here are some basic rules that apply to any distribution medium when discussing exclusivity:

1. *Be able to talk their language.* Each distribution channel may appeal to similar prospects and customers, but each reaches these customers in a different way. Their strategies are different and each one makes different demands on their suppliers. Understand how the channel moves product and the basic requirements of the distributors within that channel. For example, if your company wishes to sell art-deco style mirrors through a direct-mail company, the packaging for the product had better be able to endure the bouncing around it will take during the delivery process.

2. *Be aware of the profit-margin expectations of that channel.* Upscale retail merchants, for instance, require an additional 5-percent profit margin than other types of retailers because of their high cost of doing business (store locations in posh areas, liberal return polices, more elaborate decor). Any products they carry must offer this additional 5-percent profit opportunity.

3. *Understand the limits the channel imposes.* If you plan to distribute through traditional department stores, the same model product can't be offered to mass merchants. The department store won't be able to compete with the mass merchants on price. Some suppliers dance around this constraint by offering one model to the upscale department store and another model, with slight cosmetic changes, to discounters. The idea is to make it difficult for customers to do comparison shopping.

4. *Set suggested price points that meet the reseller's margin requirements.* Retail price points are only suggestions, but resellers tend to follow them—unless the product isn't moving well.

5. *Provide the level of support the channel demands.* Selling a technical product? Set up a toll-free help line to give buyers instruction in the use of the equipment.

6. *Create demand for the product or service that the channel can use to stimulate sales.* Creating demand means committing to advertising programs, public relations campaigns, special promotions, and so forth. Every distribution channel wants its selling job to be as easy as possible. If the product has been "presold" by the supplier, there's a much better chance that distributors will want to carry it.

7. *Approach a distribution channel with a complete program.* A sexy product, by itself, isn't enough. A typical program would include showing the distributor the following:

- The company's advertising budget for the product.
- Co-op advertising allowances.
- In-store displays available.
- Marketing support available.
- Warranty policy.
- Toll-free help lines available.
- Defective merchandise and return policy.
- Quantity discounts.
- Other channels used to move the product.
- Packaging. (Can the box be used as an in-store display?)

Be able to discuss these issues before making contact with important distributors. Most will want to examine the program before they'll agree to take a look at the product.

DISTRIBUTION NICHES

One market share strategy used by distributors is to carve out niches for themselves. They'll take aim at a market segment and attempt to dominate it. For example, Home Base and Home Depot have targeted the hardware and do-it-yourself markets. They open up huge stores across the country carrying a wide inventory of products at good prices. Their buying clout commands the best quantity discounts from their suppliers. They, and a few others, are gobbling up a $127-billion-dollar-per-year home hardware industry. The independent hardware stores find it difficult to compete. Ace Hardware survives as a buyer's consortium, but others are fast disappearing. Today's independent hardware store had better be located in a town too small to attract one of the giants.

The same thing is happening in other industries. Large regional banks are currently going through a merger mania to strengthen their distribution of financial services. In a few years, the independent bank will disappear, crushed by regional financial service outlets offering a cornucopia of services.

FIVE WAYS TO KEEP A DISTRIBUTION CHANNEL HAPPY

Once a distribution channel has been established, it's important to keep it contented. The easiest road to distributor contentment is to provide it with a product that flies off the shelves and makes tons of money. The product must be a money-maker for the distributor. Nothing beats this strategy for a happy long-term relationship. There are ways to cement a working arrangement once the product has proven itself. These ways could include:

1. Make it easy for the customer to buy. This strategy works at the wholesale level too. Set up an automatic ordering system that cuts down on to-and-fro time. Consider letting the customer place orders directly into the company's computer.

2. Make sure that inside company people know the account. They should know who the buyers are, what the distributor buys, how often they order, how they prefer to do business, their standard terms, where the stuff gets delivered, and so forth. Having this knowledge will shortcut many problems.

3. Set up a just-in-time delivery system that cuts down on the customer's inventory requirements. This could represent an important cost savings to the distributor.

4. Respond in a positive way to the distributor's internal requirements. Don't let bureaucracy, either yours or your customer's, get in the way of a good working relationship. If they require invoices in sextuplet, and your company has a rigid policy of only supplying them in triplicate, marketers should get their companies to bend. In this instance, the customer's bureaucracy wins.

5. Listen to the distributors' suggestions on the kinds of new products needed to serve the marketplace. They're in the arena every day and their personnel may offer excellent ideas.

Seven possible problems with good distribution channels

There are caveats to the strategy of locking up a sales channel. These caveats include the following:

1. Getting into a good channel is easier said than done. For example, many grocery chains charge their suppliers a "shelf fee" for the privileges of carrying the supplier's products.

2. The movers and shakers within the channel may demand a degree of exclusivity. They won't be willing to make quantity commitments in return.

3. A few big accounts may represent the bulk of the company's business. If one big account goes away, it may be difficult to replace.

4. If the product remains, gathering dust, on the distributors' shelves, expect a call before too long from the distributor asking for an inventory adjustment (markdown), or a demand to send the stuff back. They have enough marketing muscle, and they know it, to force their suppliers to agree to take-backs.

5. Giant distributors often eat small and medium-size distributors alive. You'll be considered snack food. This is because the distributors are capable of taking up so much of the supplier's capacity, the supplier becomes a virtual captive who must comply with each and every demand. The demands are escalated with every negotiation.

6. Sales channels don't last forever. In our tough, competitive marketplace, the inefficient and the obsolete are whistled to the sideline, never more to get back into the game.

7. As the warehouse clubs, price clubs, Wal-Marts, deep discounters, and mass merchants drive independent merchants out of business, their demands to their suppliers have become more and more outrageous.

ELEVEN WARNING SIGNS THAT INDICATE YOUR DISTRIBUTION CHANNEL IS IN POOR SHAPE

Can you get a good night's sleep secure in the knowledge that your distribution channels are in good shape? Will they, for the foreseeable future, support the flow of products you need to maintain the company's market share position? If you're not sure, here are eleven warning signs that suggest a channel is in trouble:

1. Your customers (the resellers) are complaining about new competition. There's a new outfit just down the block with a facility three times the size of a football field and they're just killing your guys. As proof, your customer shows you the competition's fliers with advertised prices that appear impossible to meet: "They're selling to end-users for less than you're charging me!"

2. There's a longer time period between orders from your channel resellers. For example, instead of ordering every month, they're ordering every six or seven weeks. Sell-through has slowed considerably.

3. Resellers begin to ask to return merchandise they can't sell.

4. Resellers ask for price reductions or rebates on goods already purchased to make them more competitive. This practice is known as "inventory balancing." It's a quick fix, but no solution to the larger problem.

5. Resellers no longer purchase for inventory, but only buy goods that have been presold. They're not interested in quantity discounts, baker's dozens, special promotions, or any deal that requires them to buy products for the shelf.

6. More and more of the reseller base requests extended terms of payment. Even then, some of them are late paying their bills. A few default.

7. You hear a few rumors that a few reseller operations are for sale. Reseller personnel ask you if there are jobs available with your organization.

8. There are not enough attendees at the national trade show to get up a pinochle game. Resellers who normally support the show can't afford the travel expense or the time away from their business. A few important exhibitors have pulled out. On the last day of the show, you could fire a cannon down the main aisle without fear of hitting a single reseller.

9. Several prominent resellers, who have been landmark companies, close their doors.

10. The resellers talk about taking on other lines, entering other areas of business, or moving the business elsewhere.

11. Some resellers actually purchase a few items for resale from the competitor that has given them so many headaches. This one is the kiss of death because it demonstrates just how noncompetitive the channel has become.

RAISING THE ANTE

One of the most commonly used ways to acquire market share is to simply buy it. Many companies will lower the price of their products in an effort to capture more customers and even drive the competition out of the market. They will reduce profit margins, or even operate at a loss for a time, to accomplish this objective. The technique is popular with Japanese companies who use profits made in closed home markets to fund "raids" on open markets in the United States and Europe.

As this book is written, Fuji Film is engaged in a campaign to cut into Kodak's market share for camera film. Kodak has been forced to make drastic cuts in personnel to meet the competitive challenge. There's no question that the strategy works: There are no U.S. manufacturers of television sets and VCRs, products that were invented here. It is a strategy, however, that requires deep pockets and patience.

Temporary price reductions raising the ante

Temporary price reductions almost never work to permanently increase market share. They may cause a short upward blip in sales, and that's assuming the competition doesn't match the price cuts. Once prices go back to normal, however, so will sales retreat to their former levels.

The only situation in which a temporary price reduction may work is when a competitor is in financial trouble and can't afford to match the cut, nor can it afford any further erosion in sales. A price reduction could put the competitor out of business. This tactic, however, could be considered a predatory sales practice by Uncle Sam.

Raising the ante by shortening product life cycles

Some companies raise the ante with a relentless introduction of new models, each new entry with more features, larger capacity, higher speeds, or less expensive. Competitors who would rather keep existing models on the market longer to pay for their development costs are left with no alternative, except to follow suit. After a time, they may simply give up and abandon the market.

Another advantage of this strategy is that customers used to seeing new models introduced at short intervals by one supplier tend to wait for the next advancement rather than buy a competitive product.

Raising the ante by providing more

When Domino's Pizza announces extra toppings at no extra charge, they have just raised the ante to Pizza Hut. The latter may counter with free breadsticks or a free six-pack of soda. Providing more for the same price is one way to try to capture more market share.

Problems with raising the ante

In many instances, the effort to achieve market share through lower pricing takes the profit out of the market for all the players. The competition doesn't simply stand still when one company reduces prices. They counter with still lower prices and that leads to more reductions all around. The result is that everyone keeps the same market share, but no one is making any money.

INCREASING MARKET SHARE BY ANTICIPATING DEMAND

Have you noticed that some companies always appear to be ahead of the curve? They are the innovators, and the competition follows their lead. The fact that a few companies are always heading the pack is no accident. They're in front because they have anticipated demand.

Anticipating demand means knowing what the customers will want the day after tomorrow. It begins with market research. This research will want to acquire the following information:

1. Where is the industry the company serves heading?
2. What resources must the company acquire to help our client industries get where they want to go?
3. What value must the next generation of our equipment or service provide?
4. What about the generation after that?
5. Is there any way we can skip generations?
6. What kind of products are our competitors likely to deliver?
7. Is the stuff we're planning any match for future competitive entries?
8. How can our products beat the stuff our competitors are likely to deliver?

The answers sometimes require a crystal ball that unfortunately always has this cloudy section of uncertainty. That means marketers must rely on intuition as well as on what the research seems to indicate.

In the final analysis, anticipating demand is all about steadily increasing the value of what the company offers. Demand follows value.

ACHIEVING DOMINANT MARKET SHARE
BY LOCKING UP VITAL PATENTS

One of the easiest ways to ensure a large market share for a product is to possess important patents that prevent competitors from easily entering that market. Companies who have successfully used this strategy include Pitney-Bowes with the postage meter, Xerox with the electrostatic copier, and Polaroid with the instant camera.

Polaroid and Pitney Bowes maintained their dominant market position even after their patents expired. Their hold on the market was just too strong. Xerox, while still formidable, faltered a bit in the sixties and seventies when high-quality, lower-cost copiers entered the market from Japan. They were guilty of complacency and an expensive distribution system. The company has made an impressive comeback, but they no longer control the market share they once enjoyed.

Moral: Even if the company has an exclusive franchise, complacency is an expensive luxury.

BUY 'EM OUT

Some companies maintain or improve their market share positions by buying out potential competitors before they become too large. Microsoft and Intel are two examples of companies that continually invest in small start-ups with "interesting" technologies.

This strategy also works well when one company wishes to acquire additional sales volume or important customers. It is also useful when the purchased company is strong in geographical areas the company doesn't service or has good name recognition in certain industries. Buying out the competition is also a way to acquire valuable sales or technical personnel.

Problems with buyouts to acquire market share

Buying businesses can also create problems. These problems include the following:

1. The biggest headache may come from Uncle Sam. If the combination of the two companies totally controls the market, the merger may be disputed by the government on the grounds of anti-trust violations.

2. Digesting the acquired outfit may so preoccupy the company, less attention is paid to the market. Never underestimate the problems associated with culture clash.

3. There's no guarantee that those hotshots you wanted on board so badly will stay with the new merged outfit. You can't acquire people in the same way you acquire other company assets.

4. There's also no guarantee that the customers of the acquired company will remain faithful. There's a new ballgame, and they may want to try out new uniforms.

5. That technology you were so anxious to acquire may have warts when seen up close.

ALLIANCES AND LONG-TERM CONTRACTS WITH IMPORTANT CUSTOMERS

Negotiating long-term contracts with important industry customers is an excellent way to maintain or increase market share. The company not only achieves a certain sales volume from these contracts, but the competition is also locked out of that business.

Six things needed to form long-term alliances with important customers

Long-term contracts require commitments that customers may not be willing to make unless the following conditions are met:

1. The company offers the customer an excellent price.
2. The price is adjustable from period to period based on factors such as inflation, cost of raw materials, and quantity taken.
3. The terms are flexible to meet changing demands.
4. The company provides a high level of service.
5. There is a high level of trust on both sides. That means problems are openly discussed and quickly addressed.
6. The supplier sets up a system that makes it easy for the customer to reorder.

Becoming part of the customer's business

Alliances are formed when the supplier becomes an integral part of the customer's business. For example, IBM places a lead salesperson and support personnel at the facilities of their important customers. They are permanently at the customer's site, every hour of every workday. Their checks are cut by IBM, but essentially these people become part of the customer's staff. They have offices, desks, parking places, and passes to the employees' lunchroom. Think of the problems another mainframe computer company would have in selling against this setup!

Alliances are also created when customer and supplier work together in defining the next product generation. The customer who has consulted with the supplier through every phase of product development is certainly a good candidate to buy it when that product finally reaches the market.

HIRING AND KEEPING KEY PERSONNEL

There's no better way to acquire market share than by hiring and keeping the best people.

- Good marketers can provide the strategy needed.
- Good engineers can design the right products.
- Good production managers can ensure the quality and timely delivery of those products.
- Good salespeople can lock up the important customers.
- Good support personnel can do the necessary handholding.

Hiring and keeping good people, however, is more than a matter of paying the best salaries—although that tactic won't hurt. What's needed is a sense of commitment by the organization and assurances that every employee is valuable.

Part Two

THE MISSION OF SALES

Chapter Ten

THE SALES PROCESS EXPLAINED

A WORD ON THE SALES PROFESSION

As a profession, sales has been much maligned. The popular view of a salesperson is a Willy Loman type, sample case in each hand, a stranger to his family and willing to lie his head off to make a sale. Arthur Miller got it wrong. That kind of salesperson exists, but they are in the minority and they are not successful because they are always found out. Salespeople who mislead their prospects and clients are never successful over long periods. That makes ethical conduct the single best sales strategy.

The professional salesperson is a problem solver and an instrument of change. Companies and individuals don't adopt new products, new services, new systems, new anything until the advantages of the "new things" are explained. Overcoming the prospect's natural resistance to change is the sales professional's role.

THE SIX PARTS OF A SALE

One of the enduring clichés of business is that "nothing happens until a sale is made." That cliché is misleading because a whole lot of work takes place before the prospect agrees to buy something and is transformed into a customer. A process goes on as the prospect is "conditioned" into making a buying decision. This process is remarkably similar no matter the product or service being offered. We have refined it to the six following parts:

1. Prospecting
2. Qualifying
3. Uncovering need
4. Finding solutions
5. Making presentations and proposals
6. Closing

Prospecting

Prospecting is the search for customers. This search must be continuous. No company can exist very long without acquiring new customers to replace those lost through attrition. That this endeavor shares a name with the search for precious metals such as gold is appropriate.

Prospecting is the meat and potatoes of the sales process. It is grunt work, life in the trenches, and just plain hard. Much of prospecting is cold calling, which means contacting someone, or some company, who is unknown to the salesperson and asking them if they'd like to buy what the company sells. As you might imagine, it is a process filled with rejection, which is why many salespeople don't enjoy the task.

Salespeople can improve their prospecting odds by targeting those suspects who are more likely to buy. For example, when salespeople solicit charitable or political contributions, they will concentrate on those individuals and companies who have contributed in the past (irreverently known as a "sucker list"). When selling a product, salespeople will concentrate on those companies and industries that have an obvious need for their product. Developing a profile of likely suspects is a good first step when prospecting.

Prospecting can be done in person, via telephone, by mail, or through advertising. The more direct and personal the contact with the suspect, the better the results. Prospecting is a numbers game. The more calls, the better the chance of eventual success.

Of course, not every suspect becomes a prospect and not every prospect becomes a customer. Some sales managers try to demonstrate to their sales people the importance of continual prospecting through showing

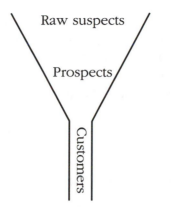

them a funnel. Raw suspects are fed into the mouth of the funnel in large quantities. A few customers trickle out the bottom. The lesson is that the top of the funnel must continually be fed.

Qualifying

Before prospects have displayed interest in the proposition, they are called *suspects*. Qualifying is the stage whereby the salesperson determines if the suspect has a need or desire for the product or service, the means to buy it, and the authority to make a purchasing decision.

Sometimes the need for a product or service is self-evident. Automobile drivers need car insurance because most states require that they carry it. Homeowners need fuel to heat their homes.

Some salespeople, unfortunately, overlook the second factor: whether their contacts have the authority to purchase. They will spend weeks cultivating a contact, only to learn that others must be consulted before an order can be placed.

Suspects are transformed into prospects when:

- They have expressed interest in the product or service.
- A need for the product or service has been determined by the salesperson.
- The salesperson is in contact with a decision-maker.
- The prospect has the ability to pay.

Uncovering need

This is the process whereby salespeople will question the suspect to determine whether there is a possible use for the product. Without a legitimate use, there is little chance of making a sale. Questioning requires good listening skills. Many experts believe that being a good listener is the single most important attribute a salesperson can possess. It is certainly much more important than being a glib talker. In fact, as a desirable sales trait, being glib is very much overrated.

Often, the possible product use will be apparent to the salesperson, but not so obvious to the suspect. That's not important at the information-gathering stage.

Questioning to uncover need can be very simple for products used by most everyone, or it can be lengthy for complicated products, such as sophisticated business systems. Using the earlier example of car insurance, the agent might ask how many miles the prospect drives each month, whether the car is used to drive to work, the purchase price and model of the car, whether there are multiple drivers in the household, and so forth, to determine the kind of policy that best fits the prospect's driving habits.

Uncovering need for a sophisticated business system might require probing questions regarding the size of the business, current procedures, daily volumes of transactions handled, number of employees involved in the operation, problem areas, projected future requirements, and so forth. In these instances, the questioning becomes a "survey."

Surveys often require the suspect to reveal confidential company information, so a degree of confidence must be established before they can take place. To establish confidence, the salesperson must first build credibility with the prospect. Credibility is established through:

- Always keeping promises.
- Demonstrating knowledge about the industry.
- Acquiring knowledge about the prospect company.
- Demonstrating product and application knowledge.

Uncovering need then is the search for problems that cry out for solutions. When no need is established, that is, when the salesperson's product solves no problem for that particular suspect, it is best to simply walk away and search for other prospects. This is a very difficult thing for most salespeople to do because of the time they have invested. Spending more time with the prospect, however, is usually a waste.

Finding solutions

When questioning reveals a need or a problem, the salesperson then fits in a solution that is provided by the company's product or service. The solution for the car driver's insurance needs is the policy the agent carries.

Finding needs and uncovering solutions is used at every level of selling. Although the connection is often obvious, the process takes place unconsciously. Here are a few typical examples:

- The prospect needs transportation. The salesperson offers a car as a solution.
- The homeowner needs protection against fire, storms, and burglary. The insurance agent offers the company's "complete-coverage" policy.
- The company has a paperwork backlog. The copy machine salesperson offers the 200-copies-per-minute, duplexing, sorting, stapling whizbang.

The more information the salesperson obtains about the prospect's needs, the more the proposed solution can be refined and the better the chances for making a sale:

- The car salesperson might realize that prestige is important to the prospect and recommend a luxury model.
- The insurance agent might include an antiques and precious jewelry rider to cover the policy holder's prize possessions.
- The copy salesperson might recommend a lower-speed model for a smaller company with a limited budget.

Budgets are an important part of the solution-finding process. There's no point in recommending more product than the prospect can afford to buy. The office manager with a $5,000 budget for a copy machine doesn't want to see demonstrations of $20,000 models. There are ways, however, around budgetary constraints. The leasing business is founded on pay-as-you-use principles that allow customers to stretch their budgetary dollars.

Making presentations and proposals

At the presentation stage, the salesperson recommends the solution to the prospect. This is where persuasiveness counts. In good presentations the salesperson outlines the problem, as he or she understands it, then proposes an answer to that problem. The prospect's reaction is noted. If it is positive, the equipment might be demonstrated soon after, or a visit made to a satisfied customer's site.

Product demonstrations should show that the product is easy to use, highlight its features, and demonstrate that it solves the prospect's problems. The demonstration should also show or list the benefits of the solution. The benefits, not the features, are what turns prospects into customers.

At this stage, the prospect wants to know how much the "solution" is going to cost. An offering is made whereby the company agrees to provide a product or service at such-and-such a price. Often, the offer is verbal: "I'll sell you this baby for three thousand bucks." The benefits are recited. The company's commitment regarding delivery, follow-on care, and after-sale assistance are also discussed.

When the offer is put in writing it is called a *quotation*. When quotations run on for more than a few pages, they are called *proposals*. The more complete the proposal, and the better it addresses the prospect's genuine needs, the better the chance of its being accepted.

The offering price should never come as a complete surprise to the prospect. During the entire process, the salesperson should make the prospect aware of the price "neighborhood." This is part of qualifying.

Closing

Closing means asking the prospect for the order. Many salespeople don't like this step because it is so final. If the prospect says no, then the deal is dead, their time has been lost, and they have been personally rejected. This reluctance to complete the sales job drives sales managers crazy.

There are many ways to close other than by directly asking for the order. Here are three of the most common:

1. Some salespeople try to get prospects in a positive state of mind by asking a series of "yes" questions (on the theory that when they get to the most important question, the prospect will be conditioned to agree).

2. Some ask their prospects to make decisions on smaller issues that imply the larger purchasing decision has already been made: "Do you want it delivered in red or black?"

3. Some salespeople recite the benefits over and over, as if the reasons to buy are just too powerful to resist.

There are hundreds of other ways to close, but none of them work unless they are used.

Often, the customer will reveal "buying signals" that indicate the salesperson should try to close. These signals might be questions such as "How soon can we get this product delivered?" When the salesperson recognizes a buying signal, the order should be asked for right then and there.

SELLING CYCLES: WHY IT TAKES SO LONG TO LOCK DOWN AN ORDER

Why does it take those lazy, good-for-nothing salespeople so long to close a deal? The answer is something called the "selling cycle," which is the average time it takes from initial contact with a suspect to receiving a signed order. This time differs widely from product to product. Boeing may work with a prospect airline company for five or six years before receiving an order for aircraft. A magazine subscription salesperson going door-to-door will try for a "one-call close," that is, the salesperson will attempt to obtain an order on that first and only contact.

Generally, the more complex and more costly the product, the longer the selling cycle. A new business system, for example, that would have an operational impact on the buying company will have a long selling cycle because the interested company will want to evaluate the potential benefits of the new system versus the cost and the problems normally created by change.

"Big-ticket" products have longer selling cycles simply because they have a greater financial impact on the buying individual or company. The larger the price of the product, the higher up on the organizational chart the salesperson must go to find someone with the approval to buy it. It's much the same with large quantity orders. All sorts of questions must be answered by the prospect before a buying decision can be reached:

- Do we really need this?
- Is the product or service worth the cost?
- Can we afford it?
- Is there money in the budget?
- Could we buy it elsewhere at a lower cost?
- Is there an alternative to buying it at all?

Selling cycles also vary depending upon the size of the prospect. They are generally longer in large companies because multilevel approval is often needed to obtain an order. That's why it's so important for salespeople to determine early on whether their contacts have the authority to make buying decisions.

Sales managers should be aware of the average selling cycles for their products within the industries the company services. This information is useful in sales forecasting and helps the manager defend against unrealistic expectations: If the average selling cycle is ninety days, the manager knows that a salesperson is being overly optimistic if he or she claims an order is pending after two contacts with a prospect within a week.

Information about selling cycles is also helpful in keeping up morale. The salesperson selling a product with a ninety-day cycle shouldn't be discouraged if a sale isn't pending after the first month.

Sales managers and salespeople do everything they can to shorten selling cycles because a shorter cycle means fewer calls and less time spent on a prospect. This permits more time to spent pursuing other accounts. Administrative and production people can assist in this effort to shorten cycles by doing the following:

1. Develop a sense of urgency. The order may be months away, but acting as if it may be just around the corner will help that order happen in a shorter time frame.

2. Engineers, designers, and product managers should answer questions promptly. Let the salesperson know if the prospect can have the product in persimmon. One of the biggest time-devourers is the to-and-fro required when the prospect has questions which the salesperson must refer back to the home office.

3. Sample products and demonstration equipment that have been authorized for the prospect should be provided quickly and in good working order. Check the stuff out before it is sent out. All literature should be sent when and where the salesperson has requested it.

4. Any tests performed at the prospect's request should be carried out promptly and the results reported back to the salesperson responsible for the account. Let the salesperson carry the message back to the prospect.

5. If the prospect ever contacts home office personnel with a question, the contact should be reported back to the salesperson. One of the quickest ways to kill a deal is to take the salesperson out of the communication loop.

6. If a request can't be accommodated immediately, give the salesperson a time-frame that is possible: "It will take me two weeks to get this information for you."

7. Don't second-guess the salesperson, or the prospect. ("Exactly why does your prospect need this information?") This is an irksome question because it suggests that if the right reason isn't forthcoming the information won't be provided.

Close cooperation between the sales staff and internal employees will help shorten selling cycles if both sides have a sense of urgency and believe the other side is acting in good faith.

THE SEVEN BASIC REASONS WHY CUSTOMERS BUY

Why did you buy those shoes last week? Check off the statement that applies:

- Because they looked good on you. (Vanity)
- Because they were marked down from $250 to $195. (False thrift)
- Because the old ones were worn beyond repair. (Genuine need)
- Because you were depressed and buying something that would make you feel better. (Psychological soothing)
- Because a friend just bought a pair of shoes. (Envy)
- Because they go perfectly with a new outfit. (Demonstrating good taste)

Most of the reasons listed above are emotional. That's not surprising, because many marketing people believe that all buying decisions are emotional. The logical reasons come later—to rationalize that burst of emotion. Find out what triggers the emotion, the experts say, and the sale is in the bag.

Here are the basic reasons why people buy:

1. *To make themselves happy.* Think back. Why did you buy that last vacation trip? The conventional wisdom is that riches can't buy happiness, but research shows that rich people are happier than poor people, so maybe the conventional wisdom is wrong.

2. *To demonstrate good taste and inside knowledge.* The designer's emblem on clothes and the "limited edition" sports car cater to this desire.

3. *To be healthy and live forever.* What do you think health food, all-organic vegies, exercise clubs, and mega-mega vitamins are all about?

4. *To be secure and in control.* Where would the insurance companies, the home-security industries, pepper-spray and dead-bolt manufacturers, guard-dog trainers, et al., be without this emotional need?

5. *To look better.* The desire to be beautiful or handsome, while smelling like a rose garden, is the foundation of the fashion industry and the multi-billion-dollar cosmetics industry. It's the reason why the anterooms of plastic surgeons' offices are packed with patients, and why there are hair salons where "Raymonde" offers hundred-dollar perms.

6. *To predict and give order to events.* The desire to control events is the reason why many business purchasing decisions are made. This desire drives people to buy products, systems, or services based on the "logic" of solving perceived problems.

7. *To feel better.* This is not the same as being happy. Some people "take" shopping sprees as feel-better medicine instead of swallowing Valium. (Those who use this remedy often wind up with five-figure credit card bills.)

At first glance, the fourth and sixth reasons would seem to be the only ones which apply to business purchasing decisions, but most of the others do as well. For example, the corporate manager of information services who will only consider IBM as a mainframe supplier, and not even entertain competitive offers, is trying to show off "impeccable taste" and insider knowledge just as much as the sweater buyer who insists on selecting only the Polo logo.

The promise of a better tomorrow: The basis of all selling

Ever wonder why a company's stock declines in value immediately after it announces good news? It's because the marketplace has already discounted the event. Wall Street is waiting for the next rumor of a better tomorrow to send that stock up again.

All selling is based on this promise of a better tomorrow. Want to look like a knockout at tomorrow's dance? Buy this snazzy silk blouse today. Want to keep the car running like a top tomorrow? Fill up on super no-lead today.

Salespeople should take advantage of this desire. A list of benefits is a start in the right direction, but benefits in themselves don't offer a better tomorrow. This promise comes from the benefit of the benefit. Here's an example that helps simplify this concept.

- *Equipment features*: Faster operating speed.
- *Benefit of those features*: Reduces time spent on an operation.
- *Promise of a better tomorrow*: Buyers of this equipment can have more available time for other activities, or can cut back on personnel and save labor costs.

Four emotional reasons why prospects say "no"

One of the comments observers make about the art of hitting a baseball is that, "it's the only activity where the participant can fail seven out of ten times and still be considered a success."

Actually, that kind of ratio would make any salesperson a roaring success. Every salesperson gets far more rejection than acceptance. Prospects say "no" far more than they agree. Just as there are motivators at work when prospects buy, there are emotional reasons why the prospect declines the offer. Here are the most common reasons why prospects say "no," along with their suggested remedies.

1. *Fear of change.* The future is a scary thing, particularly when what will happen is unknown. In this instance the salesperson must find a way to allay that fear. Detail what the company will do to make the product a success. Have the prospect contact happy users.

2. *Inertia.* It's easier to keep on doing what has been done than to change anything. Nothing new must be learned. In this instance, the salesperson must offer compelling reasons for why the prospect should change.

3. *Fear of failure.* If things go wrong, the decision-maker may be blamed. Here is yet another reason why many decision-makers favor doing business with large firms, such as IBM. If a little-known company is chosen and bad things happen, the decision-maker is blamed. If a company such as IBM is chosen and bad things happen, IBM is blamed. The remedy here is that something must be done to make the prospect feel comfortable.

4. *Relationships with existing suppliers.* Trust the devil you know as opposed to the devil you don't know. Many companies are reluctant to change suppliers simply because they have long-term relationships with them. In this instance, the salesperson must present overriding reasons why his or her company can offer a product with more benefits and even greater service than the incumbent.

The fear of change, fear of failure, and inertia manifest themselves when the prospect raises objections to the proposition: "That won't work here." In many cases, objections are ways to rationalize taking no action at all.

FOUR LOGICAL REASONS WHY PROSPECTS SAY "NO"

In many instances the prospect has valid reasons for refusing the proposition. These reasons include the following:

1. *The salesperson hasn't proven the value or the benefits of the offer.* There is no legitimate reason for the prospect to make a change.

2. *The prospect has a legitimate concern about the sales company's ability to perform.* This is a problem that plagues small outfits and one that they must address, particularly when dealing with larger prospects.

3. *Lack of understanding*. The prospect may not really understand the full benefits and scope of the offer. In this instance, the salesperson has done a poor job communicating the deal.

4. *The timing is wrong*. The prospect has other priorities right now that preclude making a buying decision for the salesperson's product. A variation of this one is that there is no money left in the budget.

These reasons can all be attributed to poor salesmanship. Of course the prospect isn't going to buy if the salesperson hasn't proven the value of the proposition or done a good job in communicating the offer. If the prospect has other priorities, that should have been uncovered during the qualifying stage.

SUMMARY

Selling is a complex process that begins with searching for candidates for the company's product or service. This search is known as prospecting and it never ends.

There is a time required between the initial contact with a prospect and when an order is placed. This so-called selling cycle varies from product to product. In general, the more complex and expensive the product, the longer the selling cycle.

Salespeople who are good at their profession build credibility with their prospects, they qualify suspects by searching for need and the ability to pay, they identify decision-makers, they communicate the benefits of the proposition, and they learn the emotional reasons that may motivate prospects to buy.

Chapter Eleven

WHAT GOES ON IN THE SALES DEPARTMENT

THE SALES MANAGER'S JOB

The fantasy: The sales manager entertains clients at three-martini lunches, pockets an additional fifteen to twenty grand a year padding the expense account, travels to exotic cities every week, spends half the work day on the golf course closing deals, then knocks off at two-thirty in the afternoon. That's the myth. If that was the reality, if running a sales department was one long carnival, the profession would be much more crowded.

    The reality: Next to the CEO, the sales manager has the highest-pressure job in the organization, because no company can exist for very long without sales. The manager's responsibility is to bring in business. All other job functions are secondary to that mandate. There must be enough orders coming through the door, week after week, month after month, to reach the overall sales objectives set by the company.

    The amount of business required is determined by senior management. Sales managers often have a voice in setting goals, but, in the end, they must accept whatever figure that senior management passes down. In most situations, this year's number will be bigger than last year's figure, and not so enormous as the one the manager will be saddled with next year. The amount (percentage) of the increase is based on how fast senior management thinks the company can grow. It will almost always be a stretch.

THE TRUTH ABOUT QUOTAS

Sales goals are commonly called "quotas." Quotas are broken down into semi-annual, quarterly, monthly, and even weekly figures. This breakdown helps management know almost on a daily basis if the sales department is on target. It also helps the sales manager determine which salespeople are doing well and which need help.

How quotas are set

Sales managers take the total quota responsibility handed down from senior management and pass out portions of it to members of their sales teams. In effect, the national sales manager assigns every salesperson in a company a bit of his or her burden in achieving this year's goals.

This allotment isn't always done directly. In a large sales organization, the quota assignment process usually "trickles down" the management reporting ladder in the following manner:

Senior management

National sales manager

Regional managers

District managers

Territory salespeople

In very large companies there may also be zone managers, super-regional managers, and maybe even junior salespeople who get a slice of the quota responsibility. In smaller companies, the manager will very likely give quota assignments directly to territory salespeople.

Many large companies are reducing the reporting layers between senior management and territory reps. There are the honchos in the home office and there are the field reps, with no one in between to garble the message. This setup improves field intelligence and shortens the communication link.

Not every territory rep will get the same quota. If the company has ten reps and a goal of ten million dollars, the sales manager doesn't automatically give every rep a one-million-dollar bogey. That's because not every territory has equal potential.

Territory quota assignments are usually based on a combination of the following two factors:

- Last year's sales.
- This year's objectives.

That means if a territory rep did $500,000 in sales last year and company management wants a 10-percent increase in business this year, the rep's new quota is likely to be $550,000, an increase of $50,000.

That may seem unfair in that a salesperson who has an extremely good year is, in effect, penalized for it the following year with a large quota increase. A big increase could have a direct impact on the salesperson's income because it affects the salesperson's ability to make bonuses. Good salespeople, however, find a way to meet their quotas year after year.

There are mitigating circumstances that a sales manager may take into account when assigning quotas. For example, if a large customer that was responsible for 25 percent of a territory's business moved out of the area, the manager may elect to factor that loss of potential into the territory's new quota. The sales manager may be just as likely to tell the territory rep to "find ten small new customers to replace the big one."

New sales people just starting out with the company may not receive as large a quota as experienced reps. Other factors that influence quota assignments include:

- Economic conditions in the territory.
- Economic conditions in the industries the company serves.
- The competitive situation. (The competition may be strong in some geographic areas, and not so active in others.
- The company's planned new product introductions.

It is the national sales manager's job to monitor the efforts of every salesperson in the company to see if they are meeting their quota objectives. In large organizations this monitoring is often done by proxy, that is through regional and district managers. In smaller companies, monitoring is often direct and informal: "How many orders did you book last week, Judith?"

MOTIVATING SALESPEOPLE TO REACH QUOTA OBJECTIVES

The sales manager won't achieve overall objectives unless every salesperson in the company contributes enough business. In every company there are always high achievers and underperformers. Some salespeople will be soaring at 120 percent of quota, while others will be limping along at 80 percent. Good managers will work with the underachievers and let the super-performers just do their thing. Both groups will respond to proper motivation.

The super-performer needs to be motivated to keep on producing, even when objectives have been reached, and the underachiever needs to be motivated to become better. Short-term sales contests in which prizes or cash are awarded are often used as motivators. One of the problems with these contests is that the same super-performers win most of them.

There's an old salesperson's joke about the sales contest in which the winner gets to keep his job. Fear of losing the job is an age-old motivator. Even if not voiced, possible termination for nonperformance is always an unspoken reality. Salespeople, particularly veterans, are allowed a bad patch in most companies, but those whose numbers are consistently below quota are eventually replaced. Sales managers can't afford to do anything else. They will be questioned by senior management if an ineffective salesperson is retained for too long. That's because every territory must make a contribution if the company is to achieve its overall sales objectives.

The most effective motivators are good compensation, continual training, encouragement, and support that give salespeople the tools and confidence necessary to do their jobs effectively.

Bonuses

Many companies use bonuses to motivate their salespeople. The bonus is an amount, over and above salary and commission, awarded when the salesperson reaches or exceeds the sales figure set by the company. Often, the bonus is graduated so that salespeople who are at 100 percent before the end of the qualifying period will keep on working hard. Here's the way this works:

Semi-annual Bonus Schedule

Quota performance	Bonus
100% of quota	$5,000
125% of quota	$6,500
150% of quota	$7,500
200% of quota	$20,000

Note that the $20,000 figure represents a higher escalation than the others, because doubling quota assignment is truly remarkable and deserves a larger percentage reward.

The bonuses are usually adjusted each period to reflect increases in quota. In this way the amounts paid out are controlled by the sales manager.

The problem with this arrangement is that salespeople who reach quota three or four years in a row begin to regard the bonus as part of their regular income. As the company keeps raising the target, inevitably a time will come when quota is not reached. Others in the organizations with much lower quotas will receive their bonuses, but the super-performer will not. This leads to low morale because the salesperson begins to feel deprived, a victim of his or her success.

THE SALES MANAGER AS A CONDUIT

Like any supervisor, the sales manager is an interface between senior management and the field sales force. The manager becomes a two-way communication link, passing down the requirements (sales goals) of senior management and passing the results upstairs. The larger the company, the more time spent by sales managers supervising the activities of others as opposed to direct selling.

Fifteen typical duties required of most sales managers

To achieve company quota objectives, the sales manager's job is broken down into a variety of tasks. These activities are:

1. Forecasting sales.
2. Hiring salespeople.
3. Training salespeople.
4. Assigning territories and set quotas.
5. Motivating salespeople.
6. Running sales meetings.
7. Running trade shows and conventions.
8. Supervising the activities of the sales force.
9. Providing senior management with field intelligence.
10. Negotiating contracts with large customers.
11. Setting sales policies.
12. Controlling expenses.
13. Making product suggestions.
14. Solving problems (soothing customers).
15. Linking senior management and the sales force.

That is a long laundry list of activities, and the typical sales manager's time, of necessity, is segmented between them. There's no time for that mythical three-martini lunch.

FORECASTING

A sales forecast is the prediction of the sales volume anticipated over a specific period of time, or predictions of future events. Forecasts are necessary so the company will know how to set up production schedules, what quantities of raw materials and finished parts to buy, how many employees will be needed, how much money will be needed to run the operation, and so forth. Forecasts are frequently broken down by:

- Dollars.
- Units.
- Time frame (week, month, quarter, year).
- Product lines.
- Models.
- Number of orders.
- Territories (salespeople).
- Regions.
- Districts.

- Customers.
- Sales channels.
- A devil's brew of all of the above.

Sales managers make their forecasts based on the following four factors:

- The forecasts provided by field salespeople.
- Past history.
- The company's plans regarding new products, available promotion dollars, and so forth.
- What senior management wants to hear.

Managers and salespeople alike don't enjoy forecasting, because it requires them to make educated guesses about future events and then committing their time and efforts to make these guesses come true.

Yearly forecasts

The sales manager is required to be part fortune teller by making a yearly forecast of sales figures. Senior management will require the following information:

- Total sales anticipated for a full twelve months.
- A month-by-month breakdown of sales.
- Which products will be sold.
- Who will buy these products.

The sales manager's problem is, how to come up with accurate figures. A year is a very long period. How can the sales manager possibly know in January what will be sold next November? Historical data is often used as a starting point. Sales results for the past several years, including the rate of growth or decline, offer a good hint for what is likely to happen next year. Here's how sales managers get started putting together a historical pattern:

1. They go to the files and pull out the sales figures for the past five years. The percentage of increase or decrease for that period is noted. If the company has enjoyed a steady 10-percent increase in sales for five years in a row, it's fairly safe to forecast a ten-percent increase again this year.

2. They make charts comparing the sales volume accomplished month-by-month for each of the five years. Past results help spot seasonal business variations. If sales always decline during certain months of the year, the chart will show it. Chances are, these same months will be lean this year too. This kind of data makes the forecaster's job easier.

History also provides a dose of reality. If the company is shooting for a 25-percent increase in sales this year, but no past year has ever exceeded 10 percent, this year's target may not be realistic.

Sales managers often require territory reps to make yearly forecasts for their areas, including the name of the customers who are expected to buy. They use these predictions in preparing the total forecast. The territory reps' forecasts help define exactly where the business will be coming from.

A dose of reality regarding yearly forecasts

For career reasons, the yearly sales forecast made by the sales manager had better be in line with the total dollar figure senior management wants the sales department to achieve. Some argument is allowed, but the sales manager who tells senior management the job can't be done is the manager who should have his or her résumé out on the street.

Most managers can and do use the same "hammer" on their territory reps. The reps are allowed to dispute the "bogeys" they are given, but when the arguments are completed, they must agree that the quotas can be made.

Weekly, monthly, and quarterly forecasts

The weekly, monthly, and quarterly forecasts are near-term predictions of business. They should be more accurate than yearly projections simply because they are closer to the prospect's time of decision. Historical data can also be used in preparing these forecasts. The customer who traditionally orders a dozen gross of a particular product every quarter can be expected to keep the same pattern next year.

Sales managers will want the territory reps to be specific when making these predictions. More information is wanted than merely dollar amount sales projections. A typical forecast form may look like the following:

WEEKLY SALES FORECAST

Salesperson _____Territory _____

Order Amount	Product	Quantity	Customer name	Closing date
Totals				

HOW MANAGERS USE FORECASTS MADE BY TERRITORY REPS

The experienced sales manager does more than merely add the forecasts made by territory reps into a grand total and present that number to senior management. The manager will know that some reps will be optimistic in their forecasts, while others tend to be extremely conservative. The manager also knows more about company plans, budgets, planned new products, the competitive situation, and economic condition of the industry than do the territory reps. These factors will be weighed when the sales manager sends the forecast numbers to the brass upstairs.

Forecasts by territory reps also help the manager spot potential problems. When the same accounts appear on a rep's forecasts for week on end, the manager knows something is wrong. Perhaps the territory rep making the forecast can't accurately interpret a prospect's intentions, or that rep has no legitimate prospects to list. In either case, the manager should have a talk with the rep.

PRICING AND PRODUCING A PROFIT

The sales manager's primary responsibility is for booking a certain dollar amount of business. These sales must be made at prices that are profitable for the company. One of the most often repeated truths of selling is, "If the company is losing a dollar on every unit sold, you can't make it up on volume."

Marketing will usually set original pricing parameters, but the sales manager will have some discretion in allowing discounts. Here are the reasons why a sales manager might offer lower pricing:

- To make deals with large or prestigious customers.
- To obtain quantity orders or to lock up customers for long periods.
- To match competitive discounts.
- To offer temporary reductions to stimulate sales.

Price reductions will often result in sales volume increases. The problem is that margins and profits then decrease. The manager must be careful not to use discretionary discount authority too often. Enough orders must be booked at full margins to compensate for those orders for which the price has been reduced. The ways to maintain this control are the following:

1. Insist on prior management approval before territory reps can offer nonstandard discounts.

2. Supervise the territory reps to make sure they are soliciting a sufficient number of small customers who will order at full margins.

3. Turn down marginally profitable business. This is a toughie. Turning down orders is one of the most difficult things for territory reps and sales managers to do.

4. Supervise the territory reps to make sure they are spending enough time selling high-margin products.

SELLING THE FULL PRODUCT LINE

Sales managers are also responsible for making sure that the company's full product line is being sold. There's no point in keeping a product if the sales team can't, or won't, sell it. Territory reps are likely to concentrate on those products which are easiest to sell, or those products which provide the highest commission rates on sales. They tend to ignore those products with longer selling cycles or those products that aren't as glamorous.

There are several ways to motivate salespeople to sell slower moving items. These ways are:

1. Attach a higher commission rate to some slow-moving items.

2. Tie any bonuses to selling the complete line. The salesperson who is closing in on a bonus based on volume will make sure to devote time to slow-moving items.

3. Run contests with prizes or cash given for moving certain items in the line.

If the sales team really dislikes talking about a product, find out the reasons why this is so. Perhaps the item is a dog and should be removed from the line.

SELLING AT THE RIGHT MARGINS

Some companies give their sales managers access to information concerning the actual costs for products. The managers are then told the minimum margins that must be obtained on any order. They are allowed to set prices at anything above the minimum. Nonetheless, they are still expected to maintain desired overall profit margins.

RECRUITMENT

Recruitment means finding and hiring new salespeople. For the sales manager, this endeavor is a never-ending task. In many companies, the sales manager will spend as much time searching, interviewing, and hiring as on any other job-related activity. Here's why so much time spent looking for new bodies:

1. People are continually needed to handle any vacant territories. An empty territory is a lost opportunity.

2. The manager may wish to try new faces in those territories that aren't producing the desired sales volumes.

3. Some salespeople who are good performers will voluntarily leave the company. "The grass may be greener on the next hill, but it's just as tough to cut," said Little Richard.

4. Replacements are needed for salespeople who are promoted to management or transferred.

5. As companies expand, they decrease the size of their sales territories to get tighter coverage. That requires more bodies.

Hiring new salespeople requires care and planning. Mistakes are expensive. When a new rep is added to the payroll, the company risks money on salary, expenses, and training. There is no guarantee that the person will succeed. Worst of all, a territory may be mismanaged for a time before the mistake is corrected. Sales are lost.

Judging sales talent

Getting good people is difficult because judging sales talent is an art, not a science. Contrary to popular conception, there's no such thing as a sales "personality." The shy, introverted listener may be exactly the kind of person needed to move some products. A salesperson may be successful with one firm and fail with another in the same industry. This uncertainty makes every hiring decision a crap shoot.

Eight sources for new salespeople

When a territory becomes vacant, managers typically place help wanted ads in local publications or they hire headhunters. Some sales managers don't wait for a job vacancy to occur. They are continually on the look-out for talent. Here's where most of them look:

1. *Within their own organizations.* Managers are wise to keep alert for energetic customer support personnel, tech aids, service people, and others who might like to advance into sales. Promoting from within always builds morale in a corporation. It makes everyone believe that upward mobility is possible.

2. *Among salespeople who call on the company.* Have you ever noticed that the sales manager is usually the easiest person to see in the organization? It isn't just because of professional courtesy. The manager may be measuring the salespeople who call on the company to determine if they might be good candidates for hire.

3. *At trade shows, conventions, and other industry functions.* Some managers spend much of their time at other suppliers' booths trying to get a handle on possible employment candidates.

4. *At seminars.* Salespeople who attend seminars are usually trying to improve their professional skills. What better place to recruit?

5. *From the competition.* If a particular salesperson has been giving the company fits, many sales managers will try to hire that salesperson.

6. *From customer referrals.* When a good customer praises a salesperson from another company, some managers will take note of the name and attempt to arrange a meeting. At the very least, that salesperson would be effective with one account.

7. *From peers.* When sales managers get together at the local watering hole, at industry affairs, on the train ride home, or in customer waiting rooms, the names of effective salespeople may be mentioned. The recruitment-minded sales manager takes note.

8. *From retreads.* Former sales representatives are often good candidates for rehire. Don't discount a candidate simply because he or she once worked for the company. People leave for a variety of reasons that have nothing to do with their abilities.

Managers who scout the above sources and maintain files of likely candidates for hire are prepared when territories become vacant. They often don't have to resort to costly newspaper ads or expensive employment fees to find qualified people.

WHY SALESPEOPLE CHANGE JOBS SO OFTEN

One commonly held perception about salespeople is accurate. They change jobs more frequently than other professions. The single biggest reason why they move about so much is simply because they can. Selling is a transferable skill. It's just plain easy to get a selling job, particularly for those with successful track records. When the grass looks greener, when a rival sales manager dangles a carrot, when another company introduces a hot new product or offers a juicier commission schedule, some salespeople will jump ship.

Another reason salespeople leave companies is that they become victims of their own success. They will string together four of five very successful years, their quotas escalating each year, until they are saddled with a bogey that seems unreachable. Rather than risk failure, they will move on to another company.*

How others in the organization can help the sales manager recruit good people

An effective sales team helps everyone in the organization. That's why all departments should take an interest in the sales operation. Managers in other departments should pass along the names of the salespeople they see from other companies who appear to be professionals. They should also be willing to allow their own employees to move up into sales. When the sales department posts job openings, other managers should recommend those personnel who might be qualified.

What others can do to help retain good people

It's easier, and cheaper, to retain good salespeople than it is to find, hire, and train new ones. Good salespeople are more likely to remain with organizations in which they don't have to wade through mud to get their jobs done. That means the departments in the company which directly interact with salespeople should cooperate with them whenever possible. Here's how:

1. Help salespeople cut through the company's bureaucracy. Focus on result, not form.

---

*These defections often come as a shock to the sales manager who is losing one of the company's stars. Managers can avoid this shock by giving a star performer a light quota increase every few years, so bigger and bigger mountains mustn't constantly be scaled.

2. Answer questions regarding order status, inventory levels, customer credit ratings, equipment specifications, special pricing, and production schedules promptly and courteously.

3. Don't take the salesperson out of the loop when speaking directly with customers, but report back any contacts or inquiries.

4. Remember that everyone in the organization is there because the sales department brings in orders.

SUPERVISION

Management is the effort to control time, money, or people. The sales manager gets a crack at handling all three. Of these, people management is the most important skill.

People management includes the following:

- Hiring.
- Training.
- Coaching.
- Monitoring.
- Setting goals.
- Motivating.
- Counseling.
- Firing, when necessary.

Secrets of supervising a field sales force

The field sales manager is like the juggler who keeps many balls in the air while standing on one leg on a galloping horse. The manager must supervise the efforts of a sales staff with diverse personalities.

A rep in New York City may have a territory of four city blocks while one covering the Western plains may have four states. Their customer bases will be different, their quotas will be different, and their selling styles will be different. The New York rep may be considered a failure if the territory produces a lousy two million bucks in sales, while the Wyoming rep deserves Star Club membership by writing two hundred thousand dollars in business.

Some reps may be old pros with more than twenty years of experience while others will be raw recruits who tremble in front of prospects.

There is a three-pronged secret for supervising this kind (the typical kind) of sales crew. It is:

1. Each salesperson must be treated as an individual. The circumstances in the rep's territory are distinct from the circumstances in any other territory.

2. A reporting system must be established that gives the sales manager accurate and timely knowledge as to what is going on in the rep's territory.

3. The manager should spend at least 75 percent of the time working with, and talking to, salespeople, their prospects, and customers and less than 25 percent of the time on paperwork. No sales manager can get an accurate picture of what is happening in the field from reports alone.

THE ROLE OF THE CALL REPORT IN SUPERVISION

The manager can't be on every call with every territory rep. He or she can't even be absolutely sure that the rep is out there making calls at all. The problem is how to make sure that every rep in every territory is doing the best job possible. In most cases, supervision is on a long-distance basis. The best alternative for learning what the rep has accomplished that day is the infamous call report. (Infamous because salespeople hate to fill them out.)

A typical call report will contain the following minimum information:

1. Name of the prospect company.
2. Name of the contact.
3. When the call was made.
4. What was discussed.
5. The result of the call.
6. Planned future action.

The sales manager going through this kind of report learns how many accounts the territory rep called on in any specific time period and what happened during those calls.

CALL REPORT

Salesperson _____ Territory #_____

Date	Company	Contact	Time Call Started	Type of Call	Result	Future Action

Weekly Summary   **Call types**

Calls made_____   A-Cold call

Demos _____   B-Survey

Surveys _____   C-Demo

Proposals _____   D-Proposal

Orders _____   E-Call back

Orders $$ Value _____   F-Service

_____   G-Order

The reports are easy to check for veracity. The manager can simply call an account to "follow up" on the subjects that were discussed. If the contact has no clue, then the manager knows the rep is being "creative."

Call reports are also useful for training purposes because they tell the manager how effective the rep has been in arranging demos and surveys, making proposals, closing orders, and so forth. If the same accounts appear on one rep's call report for week after week, the manager knows the rep is in a rut, not spending enough time searching for new prospects, or just plain not working.

Narrative call reports

In some industries the sales manager will opt for a "narrative" call report which requires the rep to explain, in detail, exactly what happened on every sales call. These reports are used most frequently for major accounts and big-ticket sales in which the product may have a long selling cycle. Narrative reports can be very informative in explaining prospect status, but they take time to fill out—and more time to read. If the field sales force is large, much valuable management time will be spent wading through them. Often, significant information can be ignored because of the sheer volume of stuff to read.

A final word on call reports

Call reports give managers a handle on the daily activities and accomplishments of their field sales crews. There could not be effective supervision without them. Sales managers must remember, however, that their primary role is helping the field rep to make quota. Monitoring activity is a by-product of this goal. It is not the primary objective.

THE ROLE OF THE FORECAST IN SUPERVISION

Sales managers require their territory reps to make weekly, monthly, and longer forecasts on sales because these forecasts are an effective supervision tool. Here are just some of the things the manager can learn by reading the territory reps' forecasts:

1. The rep who consistently forecasts deals that never happen may not be able to close effectively, or hasn't done a good job communicating the proposition.

2. The rep who continually forecasts only existing customers is not spending enough time searching for new business.

3. The rep who forecasts only a few blockbuster deals may be swinging for the fences and not spending enough time seeking small and medium-size prospects.

4. The rep who forecasts a good mix of new business and existing customer orders of various sizes is doing a good job and deserves a commendation.

5. The rep who consistently forecasts numbers that are below the quota assignment desperately needs help, or retraining, or perhaps isn't suitable for the position.

Field sales forecasts give the manager other useful information. For example, if every member of the field sales force forecasts low-quantity sales for a particular product in the line, that product may be in trouble. If every rep forecasts very large sales quantities for a product, even beyond expectations, perhaps the company should expand its production plans. In these ways, the forecast serves as an early warning system.

WHY SALESPEOPLE SOMETIMES APPEAR UNDISCIPLINED

Employees with other job responsibilities sometimes become annoyed or irritated with salespeople for what appears to be their cavalier attitude toward company rules and regulations. Salespeople, given a decision they disagree with on a credit line for a customer or a production delivery date, will sometimes go over the head of the decision-maker and appeal it to a higher-up. Salespeople seem unconcerned about protocol and often encourage other employees to bend or even break company rules to get something accomplished for a client.

This is not an apology for discourteous behavior, which should never be tolerated; the reason salespeople behave this way is because they play two roles. These roles are:

- To represent the company to the customer.
- To represent the customer to the company.

This second role is just as important as the first to the salesperson's, and to the company's, success. The truly professional salesperson fights on behalf of the customer for the best terms and pricing, favored delivery schedules, adjustments when mistakes are made, and so forth.

When companies enjoy long-lasting relationships with specific customers, it is often because a salesperson was an aggressive advocate for that customer. This advocacy sometimes appears to put the salesperson in direct conflict with company policies, but it is really in the company's long-term interests. Customers who are strongly represented this way remain customers.

There is still another reason why salespeople behave the way they do: If they are to be successful, they cannot be respectful of the other guy's bureaucratic rules and regulations. They fight through the prospect's barriers to reach decision-makers. This irreverent attitude inevitably spills over when salespeople are dealing with their own company's employees. Salespeople faced with a negative answer from a prospect are encouraged by their management to seek a higher authority to try to have the decision reversed. When they use the same tactic back at the home office, they're merely doing what they have been trained to do.

TERRITORY ASSIGNMENTS

Territories are the geographic boundaries in which company salespeople are authorized to hunt for business. When a territory is exclusive, the assigned salesperson will receive credit for any business coming out of that area, even if the order is mailed or called in by a person or company who has never met the territory rep. This arrangement gives the rep a feeling that the company is dealing fairly. It also allows the sales manager to set specific quotas.

The rep will be given a quota for the territory based on:

- Last year's actual business.
- The business potential in the area measured by the population, number of companies, industry concentration, and so forth.
- This year's company goals.

When setting up territories, most sales managers want to create boundaries that give every salesperson an equal shot at potential business. That's why in many companies one salesperson will have a territory of twelve city blocks in Manhattan and another, with a similar quota, will cover several upper-Midwestern states.

Natural geographic boundaries and administrative considerations are also taken into account when setting up territories. For example, it's simpler to end a territory at a state or county line, or to define a region by a natural boundary such as the Mississippi River. That's why one territory rep in the company may be covering Kansas City, Kansas while another covers Kansas City, Missouri.

Territories and calling efficiency

Assigning territories becomes more complicated when sales managers try to factor in calling efficiency. Compact territories are always a good idea because the territory reps can spend more time in front of prospects and less time to-and-fro. It might be more efficient for a rep based out of Portland, Oregon to call on accounts in Vancouver, Washington, just over the state line, than it would for a rep based in Seattle to travel 170 miles to cover the area.

Why it's impossible to set up territories that are entirely fair

When the requirement for calling efficiency is added, territory boundaries inevitably change. This, in turn, creates imbalances in business potential. One rep gets half the Fortune 500, while another's biggest prospect is a Salvation Army thrift shop.

Another thing that leads to territory imbalances is the effectiveness of the reps handling the areas. One energetic, efficient rep will inevitably acquire more customers than a mediocre rep handling an adjacent territory. That seems fair, reward based on effort and all that, but what happens when both reps move on? The sales manager must now assign these territories to new reps. One territory is a plum, while the other one more closely resembles a dried-up prune. In these situations the manager will often use the plum territory as a step-up for a rep who has performed well with a less promising territory.

A single or a few big customers in a territory can also create an imbalance. If you're selling steel to the automotive industry, it sure is nice to be assigned Detroit, Michigan. In some situations, sales managers will designate certain customers as "house accounts" because the volume of business they produce would give an unfair advantage to the salespeople who handled them.*

No matter how well the sales manager tries to equalize territories for business potential and calling efficiency, imbalances will always occur. They can never be entirely corrected. What is important for morale is that the sales manager tries to be fair when establishing territories and setting quotas for those territories.

---

*Accounts, no matter how big, should never be taken away from the salesperson who established them. This practice is highway robbery and it's terrible for morale. Once the salesperson has moved on, been given a promotion, or been handed another assignment, however, there's often a good reason to turn very large customers into house accounts. The action may even improve morale because the sales force realizes that one or two reps won't have an unearned advantage.

The problem of "cursed" territories and what to do about them

Some territories just seem cursed. They go through a parade of reps, one after another, and never produce at quota no matter how small the quota assignment is set. The root cause is usually because a series of inefficient reps have handled the territory. They have "turned off" potential customers. Another possibility that explains a "cursed" territory is the presence of a very strong competitor who has locked up all the area's plum customers.

Here's how managers traditionally try to solve the problem of the cursed territory:

1. They hire or transfer a very experienced rep for the area.
2. They assign this rep a low quota so even a minimum performance will look good. This way the rep won't be discouraged.
3. They work with the rep to develop an attack plan for the territory. In fact, they spend a lot of time in the territory themselves so they learn, first hand, what the problems are.
4. They throw more advertising money, promotional dollars, co-op funds, and so forth, into the area.

CONTAINING EXPENSES

The expense account is a way to compensate the traveling rep for direct out-of-pocket costs associated with his or her trip on behalf of the company. A full expense account normally covers the following items:

- Travel expenses, including air fare.
- Meals.
- Hotel or motel charges.
- Car rental or mileage.
- Incidental expenses, including tips, baggage handling, and transfer fees.

All of the above largess seems as if the salesperson gets to fly to exotic cities, entertain clients, stay at posh hotels, all at company expense. The reality is that, in most companies, expenses are so tightly controlled that the rep often loses a bit of money when traveling.

Expense accounts are put into place for a very good reason: Travel is very costly today; one trip could eat up several thousand dollars, and reps who are required to visit different cities on behalf of their companies would have to be paid much higher commission rates if they weren't compensated for their expenses. The reps also wouldn't travel as often if they were footing the bill, which means accounts wouldn't receive the kind of coverage they deserve. Companies use expense reimbursement because it is the most cost-effective way to get business.

The five most common ways to control expenses

Setting up expense budgets, and making sure that the department operates within that budget, is part of the sales manager's responsibility. In some companies this function is considered almost as important as bringing in quota. Most sales managers set up systems to control the expenses of their sales force. The following are the most popular methods:

1. *Using company-authorized travel agencies.* In this method the company requires their salespeople to use a particular travel agent to make all airline, room, and car-rental reservations. This ensures that the rep won't be traveling first class, staying at the Ritz Carlton, or driving a Mercedes when traveling. Travel expenses incurred without going through the agent are not reimbursed.

2. *Per diem.* In this method the salesperson will be reimbursed a set amount for every day on the road. Some companies will allow a lump sum, while others break down the per diem between room and meals. A typical schedule might call for the following amounts:

Room . . . . $75.00 per day
Breakfast . . . . $ 7.00
Lunch . . . . $ 8.00
Dinner. $25.00

These become the maximum amount allowed, and the salesperson is still expected to submit verifying receipts. The advantage of this system is that it requires sales reps to budget when traveling. The disadvantage is that when the sales rep travels to expensive cities, such as San Francisco or New York, the per diem amounts won't cover actual out-of-pocket costs.

3. *Flat sum per month*. In this arrangement the salesperson is given an expense allowance, say $500 per month, and is expected to pay all expenses from this figure. The advantage of this system is that the sales manager can budget travel expenses to the exact penny. The disadvantage is that the salesperson has some incentive not to travel. Any unspent expense money can be pocketed.

4. *Yearly expense budget*. Under this arrangement the sales rep is given a yearly travel budget based on the territory's needs and is expected to stay within that figure. The advantage of this system is that the sales rep is free to travel as opportunity dictates, making many trips one month, staying close to the home office the next. The disadvantage is that some salespeople who don't plan well will use up the complete budget by the end of August.

5. *Yearly expense budget with bonus tie-in*. Some companies will give their traveling reps a bonus for expense money that isn't spent. First, a reasonable budget is set for the territory based on coverage needs. Then, a sliding scale is developed that permits the salesperson to pick up a few bucks for the allowance that isn't used. Here's how the yearly bonus scale might work:

	Bonus
Within budget	$1,000
Spent only 90% of budget	$2,500
Spent only 80% of budget	$5,000

This system works best to control big spenders who might otherwise be out of control.

How others in the organization can help the sales manager contain expenses

Other departments can help the sales manager control expenses by giving the manager requested information on a timely basis. A big expense item for any sales organization is the follow-up and call-backs required when salespeople lack the right information needed to close a deal or reassure a customer.

The myth of the three-martini lunch

Go to lunch at a posh restaurant with an important client, knock down two, three, four drinks, sign a blockbuster contract, then go back to the office or head home to nurse a hangover: That's how some employees think salespeople spend most of their time.

It's true: Some business is conducted over a lunch table. One common (and effective) sales strategy is to get the prospect out of the office and away from interruptions. A restaurant is neutral territory, and both parties can be comfortable while discussing the proposition. In most instances, however, there isn't much drinking. Both parties want to remain sharp, particularly if negotiations are involved. Besides, Uncle Sam now looks unkindly at those kind of expense-account entries.

The lunch that closes a big deal is usually the culmination of a lot of work by the sales rep and careful investigation on the part of the prospect. Both parties have done their homework long before they sit down to break bread together. The lunch itself doesn't play a part in closing the deal. Nobody hands over a six- or seven-figure order simply because a sales rep picks up the luncheon check. To believe that is true is to believe in fairies.

The truth is that entertainment expenses are tightly controlled in most companies. Often, prior approval is needed for every entertainment expense. Sorry, but the champagne simply doesn't flow.

The ten top things every sales manager has to know

To do the job required by top management, every sales manager absolutely, positively must know the following things:

1. *What top management wants.* The sales manager needs to have specific goals defined. The target can't keep shifting from period to period.

2. *What the budget is for doing the job.* The manager must know how much money top management is prepared to spend to reach desired goals.

3. *How many employees the manager will be able to use to reach assigned goals.* The number of employees allowed on the payroll dictates the approach the manager will take to selling the product or service. For example, if the sales staff must be limited to one person, the manager may decide to appoint independent reps to handle remote areas.

4. *The resources the company will place at the manager's disposal.* What is the budget for advertising? What kind of brochures will be printed? These questions, and others like them, must be resolved with marketing.

5. *The company's production capacity.* How much product can be made every month? How big is the warehouse? What is the size of inventory?

6. *The cost of making the product and bringing it to market.* Profit margins cannot be determined until costs are defined.

7. *Desired profit margins.* Has the company operated at this margin in years past? (This is a reality check question.)

8. *The strengths and weaknesses of the sales force.* Which territories are the strongest? Where are the weak links? Which salespeople are ready to be promoted? Which require more training? Which salespeople may need to be replaced?

9. *Where the prospects and customers are located.* Most industries tend to concentrate in one or two geographic areas. For example, petroleum companies are located in every part of the United States, but companies serving this industry had better have strong representation in Houston, Texas.

10. *The programs needed to secure existing customers and acquire new ones.*

The above seems like a fairly tame list, but what is surprising is that not everyone in the organization will cooperate with the sales manager in acquiring this information. For example, in some companies, the exact costs to produce a product may be a closely guarded secret. Sales managers will produce their best results in an open atmosphere where information between departments is freely exchanged.

Chapter Twelve

WHAT GOES ON
IN OUTSIDE SALES

THE TERRITORY REP

The territory representative is the backbone of any outbound (outside) sales force. The rep is the point of contact, the individual whom most customers, prospects, and suspects associate with the company. For many, the rep *is* the company. An important part of the rep's job is to convey a positive image of the organization.

The territory rep's role

The rep's job is to manage an assigned geographical area called a territory. This means the rep searches for business within specific boundaries. These boundaries could be limited to several blocks in a major metropolitan area, or could extend to a half dozen far-western states. Normally, the larger the company the tighter the coverage.

Orders are expected to come in a relatively steady stream from a mix of existing and new customers. The amount (dollar volume) of business required is the rep's quota assignment. This amount is normally broken down by month, so reps are faced with a new challenge with the turn of every calendar page.

The rep has a number of other duties, including:

1. Serving as the company's advance scout, providing information about local market conditions, about the competition, or about anything else that goes on in the area.

2. Delivering products and/or servicing equipment that may be located in the territory. (In some instances.)

3. Resolving problems with customers.

REPORTING STRUCTURE

In most large companies reps report to a district or regional manager who monitors their activities. These managers often will work with the reps on important deals and track their progress toward meeting quota.

In some instances reps will maintain desk space in a company sales office where they are expected to report on a periodic basis. In other instances reps will work directly out of their homes. Those companies which require reps to report to an office feel the need to closely monitor their actions. A sales office is also useful for the rep's telephone work, holding meetings, offering demonstration facilities, and providing support services. On the negative side, the sales office provides a "sanctuary" for reps who really should be out in the field in front of prospects.

Those companies that prefer reps to work out of their homes feel that their reps will spend more time in the field. They also save money on office space. On the negative side, their reps' activities cannot be so closely supervised, their reps must scramble for normal support services, such as copying and typing, and because reps seldom see one another, there is no camaraderie.

THE SEARCH FOR NEW BUSINESS

The rep's primary responsibility is to make quota. Making good on this responsibility covers a multitude of sins, but if the rep achieves quota only by receiving orders from existing customers, management won't be happy with the results.

Most sales managers insist that territory reps bring in a mix of old and new business. Consistently adding new customers is important because some customers are inevitably lost every year for a variety of reasons. No company can stay in business for very long without acquiring new accounts to replace the ones that are lost.

Keeping existing customers happy is important, but acquiring new customers is the hardest part of the rep's task. Most companies, and individuals, are quite content with the way things are right now. This resistance to change is called inertia. It is a natural feeling that must be overcome to be successful in sales. The rep becomes an instrument of change by convincing the prospect things will be even better if an order is placed with the rep's company.

THE SALES PROCESS

Selling is much more than asking people to buy something. For most products it is a step-by-step process that can be broken down into the following basic parts:

- Prospecting.
- Building credibility.
- Qualifying.
- Finding problems or need.
- Presenting solutions.
- Closing.

PROSPECTING

The search for new customers is called prospecting. It is the meat and potatoes of the sales process. Nothing is more important—nothing. Finding customers through prospecting is the key to the rep's personal sales success, the success of the sales manager, and the growth of the company.

Prospecting is grunt work. It is life in the trenches: repetitious, grueling, filled with rejection, and just plain hard. For new salespeople, prospecting can be bewildering and demoralizing. Prospects rarely react to an initial sales pitch with an open mind. The sales prospector is awash in a sea of blank stares, "no thanks," and "if we need anything, we'll call you." Perhaps the cold reception given salespeople is the reason why the process is known as "cold calling."

Prospecting is a numbers game. The more suspects seen, the more prospects will be developed, the more demonstrations and proposals will be made, the more orders will be closed. Some managers even encourage their reps to keep a tally of their "no" responses, on the theory that every "no" brings the rep closer to a "yes."

Cold calling

For the outside rep, cold calling means knocking on doors, or walking into a suspect's office, or calling on a phone, and asking for a few minutes in which to talk about a product or service. In most instances the request is denied. Remember, most people are comfortable with the way things are right now.

The inability to cope with continual rejection is the principal reason why there are so many early dropouts among salespeople. Newly hired salespeople often leave after a few weeks or a month in the trenches. Not that veteran performers enjoy the process—they're just reconciled to it. Cold calling is the single most disliked activity on a salesperson's agenda because it incorporates:

1. *Fear of the unknown*: Who knows what lies beyond the next door?
2. *Fear of failure*: They're not going to like me or what I have to offer!
3. *That old standby, fear of rejection*: No matter how well I present my case, they're going to say "no" and throw me out the door.

Reducing the odds for rejection

Experienced reps reduce the rejection odds by advance preparation:

1. They learn the names and/or titles of the person in the contacted company who is responsible for buying or using the product.

2. They seek out decision-makers and actual product users, not just purchasing agents. In most companies, the purchasing department doesn't initiate anything. It merely executes the wishes of product users, though purchasing agents may try to negotiate a better deal.

3. Many reps use a "hook" to get an appointment: "Give me five minutes and I'll tell you how we can cut your energy bill in half."

4. Some reps use a strategy of simple persistence. If the rep makes repeated efforts to gain an appointment, the prospect may finally reach the conclusion that the rep has something important to offer.

Although these strategies will reduce the rejection odds, the rep will still hear no considerably more often than yes.

ESTABLISHING CREDENTIALS AND CREDIBILITY

When an interview is granted, the rep usually has only a short "window" in which to excite the suspect's interest in the proposition. A rep won't be granted much time at an initial interview. One of the first things the salesperson must do in those few minutes is to establish the company's credentials. The most common way to do this is to mention other satisfied customers. If these customers are in the same industry or locality as the prospect, so much the better. Almost everyone has been exposed to this sales tactic: "We're putting in a new driveway for your neighbor down the street."

It's important for reps to also establish their personal credibility. People today are cynical about salespeople and simply don't believe what most of them say. It doesn't matter how smoothly the sales message is delivered. If it isn't believed, the rep has failed. Credibility is established in the following manner:

1. By displaying personal knowledge of the product, its applications, and the industries in which the product is used.
2. By demonstrating reliability by following through on all promises, implied or expressed.
3. By always behaving in an ethical manner: never knocking the competition and being truthful at all times.

In front of the prospect: Having an objective

Good sales reps will establish an objective before beginning a call. They know the result they want to achieve from that call. That result isn't always an order. For some products with long selling cycles, premature closing before all the proper spadework has been done will only help to kill the deal.

The call objective should involve some action that moves the prospect closer to a buying decision. For a product with a long-term selling cycle the objective of a call might be only one of the following:

- To arrange a survey.
- To arrange for the prospect to visit a satisfied customer.
- To demonstrate equipment.
- To set off a few trial balloons.
- To make a quotation or proposal.
- To try to close.

In front of the prospect: Listening

One skill necessary to a rep's sales success is being a good listener. Listening reveals what is important to the prospect. Many experts believe that reps should spend 80 percent of their time in front of a prospect listening and only 20 percent talking.

In front of the prospect: Five popular selling styles

How the rep performs "on stage," that is, his or her ability to capture the interest of prospects once granted an interview, determines success or failure. Delivering the sales message is the art and craft of the profession.

There is no single best way to sell. What works for one person would fail for another. There are, however, five popular techniques that many salespeople find effective.

1. *Selling through product knowledge.* These reps are technically proficient. They know their products' features, applications, benefits, bells and whistles, how the product differs from the competition, pricing, which industries find it useful, how to demonstrate, and so forth.

2. *Selling through extraordinary service.* Some reps take special care of their customers. They baby them, check on inventory levels, go to bat for them with the company, handle minor repairs, personally handle the returns on defective products, help the customer resolve problems, and do anything else necessary to keep them happy.

3. *Selling through establishing relationships.* These reps become the friends and confidants of their customers. They take them to lunch and the ballgame, they attend their customers' company picnics, they send them greeting cards on personal occasions. Once these ingratiators become established with an account it takes dynamite to blast them out.

4. *Selling through persuasion.* These reps are masters of the emotional sell. They learn the prospect's hot buttons—and just when and how hard to push them. They know the power of words, they understand timing, and they always ask for the order.

5. *Selling through offering a better way.* These reps offer their prospects a system that will cut operating costs by 40 percent, improve the rate of return on a direct-mail piece, increase the life span of a production machine, lower labor costs, move goods across the country in half the time, double warehouse space, and so forth. They sell through an appeal to the prospect's logic.

Many reps use a combination of these methods. They all work—when they are combined with sincerity.

MULTILEVEL SELLING

When selling to large companies, the rep must maintain contacts with many different levels and departments within the prospect's organization. In a typical big company the rep may speak with:

- The product's actual users.
- The decision-maker (the person who is responsible for the budget).
- Other departments that could be affected by a decision to buy the rep's product or service.
- The purchasing department.
- The prospect's financial officer, controller, or legal department (for really large orders).

In addition, some companies make important decisions by committee. That means everyone on the committee must be "romanced." Slighting anyone in the chain could result in the deal being lost.

Often, the rep becomes an information conduit for the prospect, telling one department or level what another is planning. This role must be handled with sensitivity. The rep must be careful not to become involved in the prospect's territorial disputes.

The rep and the rabbi

When working on big orders or with good customers, some reps try to establish what amounts to a personal relationship with a decision-maker at the contact company. The rep can't always be present when the deal is discussed by members of the prospect's organization. The idea is to find someone who will become the rep's "rabbi," informing him of his own organization's priorities and acting as a surrogate in the rep's absence.

THE REP'S RELATIONSHIP
WITH PURCHASING DEPARTMENTS

In a few companies, such as Sears Roebuck, the purchasing department is extremely powerful. Its role is natural because buying products at the right price, and in the right quantities, is key to the success of that gigantic merchandising organization.

In most companies, however, purchasing merely executes the wishes of other departments. In an automobile maker, purchasing doesn't have the need, or the budget, for high-end analytical software that measures metal stress, but the engineering department does. Purchasing may place the order for such software, but it will be at the request of engineering and it will be charged against engineering's budget.

Requests for products come through to purchasing in the form of requisitions. It is purchasing's function to make sure they are buying the product at the right price from a reliable supplier. They take care to negotiate the best deal; they don't specify what is wanted.

Large companies' purchasing departments will have buyers who specialize in procuring certain kinds of equipment. There may be a buyer for office equipment, another for production hardware, still another for raw materials.

One advantage to calling on purchasing is that it is usually the easiest department with which to gain an appointment. After all, it is their job to see salespeople. Buyers like to talk to salespeople who can educate them about product and industry developments.

The problem is that these calls are frequently fruitless. Unless the purchasing department already has a requisition from engineering, they don't know that there is a need for metal stress measurement software. When they do get the requisition, it will perhaps contain specification requirements which only one company can meet. The order is placed with the software company that bypassed purchasing and went directly to the end-user.

Bypassing purchasing, however, can be hazardous because, while they don't requisition products, buyers can delay and even derail deals if they feel they have been left out of the loop. The best tactic for reps is to make courtesy calls on purchasing when visiting end-users and decision-makers. When purchasing is kept informed, requisitions are quickly turned into orders.

CONDUCTING SURVEYS

One of the most effective selling methods is through conducting surveys. In a typical survey, the rep reviews the prospect's current method of doing things to see if improvements could be made through using the company's product or services. One advantage of a survey is that it allows the rep to speak to actual users to dig out problems. Surveys also allow reps to quantify things using numbers supplied by the prospect: "You're using ten thousand grommets a month at a cost of forty cents per grommet.")

The right to conduct a survey must be earned. No organization wants an outsider poking around its operation unless there is reason to believe that something of benefit will be found. One common way reps "sell" surveys is by pointing to the success similar organizations have enjoyed by switching to the rep's product or service.

A typical survey will try to uncover the following information:

- The prospect's current method of operation.
- The time involved to conduct that operation.
- The cost involved in the operation.
- The number of people needed to handle the operation.
- The quantities involved.
- The space required for the operation.
- The prospect's priorities.

Once gathered, this information becomes the bedrock for a proposal. The rep can decide which area of the prospect's operation to attack via the proposal. The idea is to find an area that can be improved: "Through our just-in-time delivery system, we can cut your inventory and space requirements by thirty percent!" To get the kind of attention that leads to an order, the proposal must also address the prospect's priorities.

THE DEMONSTRATION

If new equipment will be proposed, it usually must be demonstrated to the prospect. Demonstrations are staged presentations. They are tailored toward two groups within the prospect's organization:

1. The actual product users or operators who must be convinced that the product is easy to use or will make their jobs easier.

2. The decision-makers who must be convinced that the product solves a problem and can be delivered within budget. Demonstrations will contain the following parts:

- An opening or greeting.
- Setting the stage (explaining what will be seen).
- Showing the product features (the bells and whistles part).
- Explaining the significance of what was seen (the benefits of the bells and whistles).
- Answering questions and objections.

Demonstrations will usually focus on equipment features. The best demonstrations will show how these features translate into benefits for the prospect.

It's wise for the rep to try to limit the attendees at a demonstration to those who will actually be using the equipment and the decision-maker. The larger the group, the greater the chance it may become unmanageable.

Experienced reps prepare for demonstrations well in advance. Here's how:

1. They have all the material required (including extension cords) for the presentation.

2. They know what they want to show. It isn't always necessary to demonstrate every equipment feature. In some instances, demonstrating a feature that isn't useful to the prospect will only deflect attention from the main issues.

3. They maintain control of the situation.

4. They know what the prospect's hot buttons are and they manage to press all of them.

5. They avoid technical jargon.

6. They're prepared for objections.

7. They have a goal.

Most demonstrations take place in one of three environments:

- At the prospect's facilities.
- In the rep's office.
- At an existing customer's site.

The most impressive demos, when they can be arranged, are done at user sites. There is nothing more effective than a satisfied customer to help cement a deal. Smart reps will stand aside while the proud user demonstrates the product and allow the prospect to speak confidentially with the user after the demonstration is completed.

Demonstrations done at the prospect's site, or in the rep's office, are more effective when the prospect's materials are used. These materials should be tested long before the demonstration is arranged.

Offers

An offer frequently follows a presentation. When an offer is made the rep agrees to provide a product or service for a specific price. There are four kinds of offers:

1. The verbal offer.
2. The written quotation.
3. The proposal.
4. The estimate (often used in construction work).

How are all those numbers developed for quotations and proposals? In most companies, reps will carry price books that define the price that can be offered depending upon the quantity purchased. Today, this information may also be available to reps from their laptop computers. In addition, the company may offer special pricing for a short time when management wishes to promote a product.

In most instances, reps do not have the authority to deviate from established pricing. They cannot offer discounts that do not appear in the price book. The reps can, however, explain a special situation to management in the effort to get a better price to land a deal. The bigger the deal, the better the chance management will trim pricing.

In some industries, salespeople may be given pricing parameters. The reps can offer prices within a range specified by management, but their commission percentage will depend upon the final sales price.

THE VERBAL OFFER

"I can deliver a dozen of these motors at fifty dollars each." The verbal offer is often used with existing customers in which the two sides trust one another, or in small, informal transactions. They can be done in person or over the telephone. Frequently, the prospect may initiate a request for a price which results in the offer. In some instances an agreement will be reached after a verbal offer, but follow-up paperwork, such as a purchase order, is needed to get things rolling.

THE QUOTATION

The quotation puts the offer in writing. Good quotations should include all pertinent details about the deal. They will usually include a description of product, the price, the quantity, the financial terms, any warranty, and the time of delivery.

Large companies usually require quotations before they will issue purchase orders. In many instances, they will request quotations from competing companies to make sure they are getting the best deal. This is often disturbing to the rep who has worked for weeks, or maybe months, to

---

SAMPLE QUOTATION

Ms. Very Big Buyer
ABC Industries
Main Springs, New Mexico

Dear Ms. Big Buyer:

We are happy to present our offer on your company's requirement for steel sprockets.

144, our model 18Z stainless steel "1" sprocket: $7.15 ea.

If you would consider increasing your order to our next quantity break at 200, we could reduce this price to $6.75 per piece.

We can ship the complete batch in five days after receipt of order. Our terms are 2 percent 10 days, net thirty, FOB delivered. All of our products carry a one-year warranty.

Ms. Big Buyer, if you have questions regarding this quotation, please call me.

Joe Seller

---

uncover the problem at the prospect's company and to provide a solution, but it is the way business operates.

PROPOSALS

A proposal is a formal offer, written in detail by the rep to the prospect. It is by far the most comprehensive offer to sell something. Proposals are often used with system-related products, with large-quantity deals, and when attempting to sell products or services to new prospects.

A good proposal will include the following:

1. The opening: the reason why the prospect should keep on reading.
2. A statement of the problem or situation the proposal addresses.
3. A statement of goal.
4. A statement of the goal's benefits.
5. A description of the solution.

6. A statement of the price for the solution.
7. A statement of the cost savings the solution would bring.
8. A summary of other benefits the solution would bring.
9. Details involving delivery schedules, payment terms, and so forth.
10. The selling company's guarantees, warranties, commitments, and so forth.
11. A short summary of what the proposal includes (for those "bottom-line" decision-makers at the prospective company).

Proposal limitations

One thing that should *not* be included in a proposal is any statement or claim that can be challenged. For example, it's a bad idea to inflate current operating costs beyond the prospect's own estimates. If one thing seems wrong, every statement in the proposal will be regarded suspiciously. Smart reps resolve any disputes regarding numbers before making a formal presentation.

Boilerplate proposals

If proposal preparation seems formidable, it's important to remember that not all proposals are written from scratch. Many companies use boilerplate proposals in which standard pages or paragraphs can be interchanged according to requirements. Even handcrafted proposals may contain some boilerplate pages. (Lawyers do the same thing with contracts.)

Presenting proposals

It's a mistake to send or drop off a proposal to a prospect without comment. Proposals should be presented in person so the questions may be asked and the prospect's reaction can be determined. Presenting proposals is a nervous time for most reps. The prospect's reaction to the material determines whether a deal is possible. The presentation should involve more than merely reading the written material.

In many instances, proposals must be presented in front of a group or committee. This situation usually means many unconvinced people on one side throwing out questions or offering objections, and only one person on the other side to field them. On important presentations, many reps will bring along another salesperson or a field manager just to even the odds a bit. Smart presenters can also lower the odds by doing the following:

1. They speak with conviction. They really believe that what they're presenting is a good deal for the prospect.

2. They limit the size of the group attending the presentation. Of course, it's important the prospect's decision-makers attend.

3. They use visual displays, charts, graphs, transparencies, slides, tapes, and other methods to make sure the message is clear.

4. They reach agreement on important points in the presentation before going on to others.

5. They make small concessions on points that can be amended without damage to the proposition.

6. They follow up the presentation with a question-and-answer period.

7. They finish the presentation with a call for future action. All those books on closing techniques to the contrary, they may not ask for the order at this point. The bigger the deal, the more time the prospect will want to ponder it.

BUYING SIGNALS

Knowing exactly when to ask for the order is as mysterious as knowing when to kiss a girl for the first time. It's an art, not a science. Fortunately, prospects send out signals when they're agreeable to the proposition. Here are the standard signals that should send sales reps searching for the order pad:

1. The prospect nods and agrees with everything the rep says.

2. The prospect asks questions related to details about the sale or events that will occur after the order has been signed.

3. The prospect tries to negotiate a slightly better deal than the one offered.

4. The prospect seems happy to see the rep and perhaps even takes her along to meet the big boss.

5. The prospect admits that all objections to the proposition have been met.

When any one of these things occurs, experienced reps will immediately try to close the order.

CLOSING

Many reps are afraid to come right out and ask for the order. It is a reluctance that drives their managers nuts. One reason for this hesitation is fear of rejection. If the prospect says no, all work up to this point is for naught. Still, there is a time to try to close the deal. This time is:

- When the prospect's need has been identified.
- When the value of the offer has been established.
- When the prospect has been persuaded to want the product or service.

There are as many ways to close as there are pebbles on a beach. There is none more effective than a direct request for the order, such as: "Ms. Jones, I'd like the opportunity to serve your company. Can I write up the order?" This short, sweet request will increase any sales rep's closing ratio.

PURCHASE ORDERS

In retail sales, the rep will ask the buyer to sign an order form. In industrial sales, the buying company will issue a purchase order. The difference in the two forms is in the disclaimers. The seller's order form will protect the seller and the buyer's purchase order will protect the buyer. It's important for reps to read purchase orders carefully before accepting them. It doesn't matter what the quotation or proposal says. The terms and conditions of the deal will be what's written on the buyer's purchase order.

REFERRALS

A referral is made when a satisfied customer gives the territory rep the names of other companies or individuals who might be interested in the product. They are one of the most important sources for new business.

Smart territory reps ask their customers for referrals. Often, this is done right after closing an order. This is the honeymoon period and the new customer is anxious to please.

There are two primary types of referrals:

1. Local referrals are those from individuals and businesses in the area. The idea a local referral promotes is that if an outfit down the street uses the product, it must be good.

2. Industry referrals are those from other companies in the same industry as the prospect. They are powerful because companies within an industry often conduct business in a similar manner.

CALLING ON ESTABLISHED CUSTOMERS

Established customers are the best accounts. They have already used the product, and if they have been customers for a few years, they are obviously satisfied with it. Established customers are also the best source for new business. They know the company to be a reliable supplier and are more likely to try new products or to expand the use of existing products to different departments.

Spending time servicing current customers and keeping them happy is essential to growing a territory, a branch, a region, or the company. The rep who gets new business, but at the same time ignores the existing customer base, is, at best, running in place. This is a poor strategy because it's much easier to retain an existing account than it is to find a new one.

EIGHT WAYS REPS KEEP CUSTOMERS HAPPY

Competent reps know that the competition doesn't steal accounts through better prices or superior products. Accounts are lost through neglect. Here are eight ways reps keep customers happy:

1. They call on customers frequently. These calls must be made in person. The occasional phone call to ask for an order is an invitation to the competition.

2. They assist the customer is making the best use of the company's product. Reps make suggestions. They sell to other departments in the customer's organization. They learn the customer's applications. They talk about innovations.

3. They are the customer's advocate within their own companies. They explain the customer's side during disputes. They fight for a share of scarce inventory on behalf of the customer. They work to resolve problems related to warranty claims, damaged goods, lost shipments, returns, credit disputes, and so forth.

4. They learn the customer's business. The more they know about the customer's industry and method of operation, the better they can be of service.

5. They are candid about any problems. If the company will be late shipping a product, or if a particular product the customer is planning to buy has a spotty performance record, they keep the customer informed. As Henry Kissinger put it, "What must be revealed eventually should be revealed immediately."

6. They follow through—on orders, on deliveries, on product performance, on the customer's satisfaction, and on future requirements.

7. They make their contacts at the customer organization look like heroes. If the contact needs something for her boss, a special delivery to meet a deadline, a report, information in a hurry, they get it done.

8. They work with every department within the customer's organization in which the product has an impact. They do what is necessary to keep the product users happy.

FILLING OUT FORMS

Most salespeople hate to do paperwork. It is a necessary evil if the company is to keep apprised of the rep's activities. Sales managers must be careful, however, not to require their staff members to spend their golden selling hours filling out forms. The average territory rep has the following paperwork requirements:

1. Weekly planning or itinerary sheets. These state where the rep plans to be and what accounts will be visited during the following week.

2. Daily or weekly call reports. These report actual calls that were made. Managers then compare the planning sheet to the call report to see if the rep is following the work plan.

3. Weekly, monthly, and quarterly sales projections. These list the accounts that will place orders and what the orders will be for.

4. Expense accounts (if the company reimburses expenses).

Getting these reports on a timely basis is often like pulling teeth. Some managers will not reimburse expense accounts unless they are accompanied by a call report covering the same period. Samples of most of these forms are illustrated in other chapters.

Customer profile sheets

Most companies also require reps to keep customer profile sheets. These are one of the most important sales records in the company. A basic profile sheet contains such data as the customer name, address, phone number, key contacts, number of employees, products purchased, dollar volumes of past orders, buying rhythms, and future plans. These profile sheets are useful to the territory rep handling the account, and they are vital to the company in the event the rep ever leaves for greener pastures. (See example on p. 265.)

This form is a semi-permanent record that is only updated as the information changes. For example, the form would be updated when a key contact left and was replaced by someone else.

When working a territory, the rep should carry a similar, but slightly different customer account record. This form should include entry spaces to record calls made on the customer, sales by period, and specifics on products purchased by the customer. This form is updated after each call on the account.

The territory rep and the competition

One of a territory rep's responsibilities is to provide information to the home office about competitive activity. Competition is economic war. The more information available about the other side, the better the chances to take countermeasures. Here are the basic things management wants territory reps to find out about those rotten SOBs who are destroying the market.

1. What the other side makes or provides that is directly competing with company products.

CUSTOMER PROFILE

Account Name _____

Address _____

City and State _____

Phone number_____ Ext. _____

E-mail _____ Fax _____

Key contacts   Title

_____   _____

_____   _____

_____   _____

Annual revenues _____   No. Employees _____

No. Locations _____   Type Business _____

Credit rating_____   Normal Terms _____

Orders in $$:   1998_____   1997_____   1996_____

Products purchased _____

_____

Applications _____

_____

Competitive equipment used _____

Salesperson _____ Branch # _____

Comments _____

_____

_____

_____

2. Which competitive products are the most difficult to sell against, and why this is so.

3. The company products that seem to offer an advantage over the competing line.

4. The competition's pricing policies (this information is particularly important).

Reps uncover this information primarily through their daily rounds in calling on their customers and prospects. The competition will also be calling on these same accounts. Friendly contacts will let the rep know when the competition offers anything significant.

Most customers will also let the rep know if a deal is lost because of price: "Acme beat you guys by twenty-five percent." When the rep verifies this information and relays it to the home office, it helps the company prepare to be more competitive next time.

HOW TERRITORY REPS USE WORK PLANS TO GET MORE CALLS OUT OF EVERY DAY

The cost of making a single industrial-type sales personal sales call has soared to about $400. This heavy cost makes it imperative for territory reps to manage their time and activities to squeeze the most calls out of any single day.

The first step toward managing a territory is to develop a working plan. An intelligent plan can milk an extra call or two out of every day. That adds up to an extra 250 to 500 calls per year. A good work plan contains the following ingredients:

1. The next day's activities are planned the evening before.

2. The plan will include specific calls with specific objectives.

3. The territory rep will plan to be in the territory, ready to make the first call, *before* the beginning of the work day. That's one reason why sales managers often assign territories to people who live in or near them.

4. The plan sets up calls in geographic proximity to one another.

SAMPLE WORK PLAN

(Developed the evening before.)

7:30–8:00	Coffee shop near prospect's office. Cup of coffee while polishing today's plan.
8:05–9:15	Appointment to conduct systems survey at Leed Gasket company's order entry dept. Objective: find bottleneck in order entry procedure.
9:15–9:30	See purchasing agent at Leed Gasket. Inform her of survey. Objective: Get purchasing on my side.
9:30–9:45	Canvass businesses in immediate vicinity of Leed Gasket.
9:55–10:15	Drive to next appointment.
10:15–10:30	Call office for messages. Make appointments for tomorrow.
10:30–11:15	First meeting with Flood Plumbing. Initial presentation of the product line and probing session. Objective: Try to sell a survey.
11:15–12:00	Canvass area in immediate vicinity of Flood Plumbing.
12:00–12:15	Drive to Home User's Wholesale, a current customer.
12:15–1:00	Lunch with Ed Perfetti, senior buyer, in company cafeteria. Discuss month's special promotion in effort to obtain order.
1:00–1:20	Meet with Roger Newly, Home User's administrative manager, to discuss improving system. Objective: Get Newly to think about upgrading Home User's system.
1:20–1:40	Drive to next appointment at Lassiter Labs.
1:40–2:00	Bring in and set up demo equipment at Lassiter Labs.
2:00–3:30	Conduct demo before Guy Lewis, decision-maker, and Gloria Allen, system user. Objective: Get commitment on order.
3:30–4:00	Phone office for messages. Make telephone appointments. Conduct telephone canvassing.
4:00–4:10	Drive to next appointment with Larry Meeks, president of Meeks Lumber, a small customer.
4:15–4:30	Meeting with Meeks. Objective: Resolve problem customer is experiencing with our billing department.
5:00–5:30	Coffee shop. Make notes on needed actions. Work on call and expense reports.
5:35	Drive home. Take wife to dinner.

5. Preplanned appointments are mixed with cold calls and drop-ins in the same neighborhood.

6. The salesperson carries everything needed on the call, including literature, price book, business cards, customer profile sheets, address and phone book, demo equipment, and so forth. There's no need to leave the territory during the day to find something.

7. Whenever possible, the salesperson tries to arrange a working lunch with a client or prospect, even if this lunch takes place in a company cafeteria or fast-food outlet. The idea is not so much to entertain as it to make the most use out of every minute in the day.

8. The rep calls the home office at least twice a day for messages. During these calls the rep uses the home office staff whenever possible to send prospects literature, check on inventory status, or do anything else to bring an order closer to reality.

9. The rep avoids make-work projects that send him or her completely across the territory to deliver a spare part, a piece of literature, put out a fire, or otherwise spend five minutes with a customer.

10. The rep makes notes after every call as a reminder of any needed future action. The actions required are followed up promptly.

A typical day in the work life of a territory rep

Contrary to popular belief, most territory reps do not leave the house at 9:30 in the morning, make a few calls, have a swell lunch in a posh restaurant, phone the home office, and then take off for the golf course, or the mall, shortly after 2:00 P.M. The successful reps plan full days that require juggling many different activities.

This rep's very full day included an initial presentation to a new prospect, a systems survey, a demonstration, a discussion with an existing customer on upgrading equipment, an attempt to resolve a problem, and several attempts to close orders. The schedule is very tight, but the rep included time for prospecting, which is always necessary.

Chapter Thirteen

WHAT GOES ON IN INSIDE SALES

ORDER TAKERS, ORDER EDITORS, AND ORDER EXPEDITERS: WHAT THEY DO

Orders don't flow in a seamless channel. Sales organizations could not exist without an army of internal personnel to handle a variety of tasks involved with order processing, inside selling, and customer service. Many of these tasks require customer contact. The larger the sales staff, the more infrastructure is needed. Here's a description of what the bodies inside a sales organization do and how their efforts assist in the sales process.

TELEPHONE ORDER TAKERS

Order takers field incoming phone calls from customers and prospects. These calls may be prompted from advertising the company has placed in various media, such as newspapers, magazines, and television. For companies such as Lands' End, the calls are prompted from catalogs that the company has mailed to their customers.

In the order-taker environment, the caller is already predisposed to buy something. The advertising piece or the catalog created the desire. It is the order taker's job to convert that desire into an actual sale. This is done by ensuring the prospect that the process is very simple, if not foolproof, and that the company stands by its products.

When speaking with a caller, the order taker must obtain the following information:

1. The merchandise or product the customer wishes to order. If the items are clothing, sizes, colors, styles, and so forth must be identified.

2. The address where the customer wishes the merchandise delivered.

3. The method of shipment the customer prefers. For most companies, the charges will be extra if the customer chooses express delivery.

4. The method of payment. Today, the payment method for phone orders will primarily be by credit card. The order taker will give the customer the total due on the order, then record the customer's credit card number and later verify that the cardholder is in good standing with the credit issuer.

The order taker may check inventory to make sure the items ordered are in stock. Approximate shipping dates will be given to the caller. Alternate items may be suggested for out-of-stock merchandise. The order taker may also recommend certain specials or merchandise combinations to raise the dollar value of the order.

The requirements for the job are a clear speaking voice, accuracy, keyboarding skills, knowledge of the product line, good communication skills, courtesy, and the ability to operate a computer terminal.

Order takers are not considered highly skilled or "salespeople" in the traditional sense because the customers have already decided to buy something before making the call. In most instances, order takers' incomes will be heavily weighted toward hourly salaries rather than commissions. They are production workers and may receive incentives based on their efficiency in handling calls. They can also receive bonuses. For example, they may receive spiffs for recommending items on which the company has too much inventory.

Inbound telephone salespeople

A step above order takers in a sales hierarchy are inbound telephone salespeople. These individuals field inquiries from prospects who, in most instances, have not finalized their buying decisions but who are seriously interested learning more about the product. The telephone salesperson serves as a consultant to the caller offering suggestions and making recommendations that may lead to a sale. Because the caller is not committed, more persuasive skills are necessary than with an order taker's position.

Examples in the inbound category are telephone salespeople for mail-order computer companies, such as Dell and Gateway, and cruise "consultants" for companies such as Princess Cruise Lines.

In both of these instances, the caller usually wants more information before making a buying decision. The prospect calling the computer company wants information about bells and whistles, cost of the system, warranties, and so forth: "With that system you really should buy more RAM." The prospect calling the cruise consultant wants information on ports of call, length of cruise, the ship's amenities, and the costs for various cabins: "Formal attire is optional, but you'll feel more comfortable in a long gown."

Orders can be high ticket, up to $25,000 and more, but the ratio of closing isn't nearly as high as it is in a straight order-taking environment.

Inbound sales positions require all the attributes of a good order taker, plus even more detailed knowledge about the company's product line. These positions also require patience and the ability to close on the telephone. The inbound salesperson is trained to ask for the order.

In these positions, income is usually based on a combination of hourly salary, commission, and bonuses, with more than half of their income slanted toward commissions. In some instances, the inbound telephone salesperson will work entirely on commission plus bonus.

TELEPHONE SOLICITORS

The telephone solicitor makes calls to suspects at random, or operates from lists of likely prospects. Their job is the most difficult of all those engaged in telephone selling because, in most cases, they are cold calling. That is, they are contacting people who have not previously indicated an interest in the product or service.* The rejection rate for this kind of activity is very high. (The first job requirement is a thick skin.) Someone using the telephone can

---

*The one exception is companies who use telephone solicitors to contact existing customers regarding possible supply reorders. A copy machine distributor, for example, might use telephone solicitors to contact their customers regarding toner and paper reorders.

reach twenty to thirty people per hour until they connect with someone interested in the proposition.

Companies use telephone solicitors when the price tag for the products they offer can no longer support an outside sales staff. Newspapers and magazines, for example, often use telephone solicitors to sell subscriptions. Banks use telephone solicitors to "sell" credit cards.

In many instances telephone solicitors work from prepared scripts. The scripts often have branches which the solicitors follow, depending upon the prospect's responses. If the respondent doesn't want the subscription because he "can't afford it," the solicitor will suggest an easy payment plan. If the respondent "leaves the house too early in the morning to read the paper," the solicitor will suggest buying the weekend package. The trick is to provide an answer for any objection.

Unfortunately, telephone solicitors also are associated with sharp practices. Dubious investments, low-quality products, fake contests, time-shares, and out-and-out swindles are sold by cheap hustlers out of "boiler rooms." They give the entire industry a bad name. It is certainly dumb to buy an investment from an anonymous voice on the telephone, or to send money to someone who has just announced that you've won a new Cadillac.

Telephone solicitors must be persistent, persuasive, and versatile with the ability to improvise as the situation requires. They must also be excellent closers. The solicitor has one chance, usually consisting of just several minutes, to make the sale. The professionals can make excellent incomes, usually based primarily on commissions.

Telephone appointment makers

The appointment makers call prospects to arrange times when the prospects will meet with outbound sales representatives. They sell nothing themselves, except this "date" to meet with someone from the company. They are often used to set up appointments for heavy-hitter sales types offering big-ticket items and where the sales pitch is likely to require an extended period of time. The theory is that the heavy-hitter's time would be diluted by initial prospecting when it could be better spent in face-to-face meetings with qualified prospects. Companies using this kind of prospecting method include in-home encyclopedia outfits.

A wrinkle on this approach is the appointment maker who attempts to make a date for the respondent to attend a meeting, a lunch, or a dinner where a sales pitch will be made to a captive group. Companies who use this approach include HMOs, time-share outfits, "living will" lawyers, and various investment deals.

The telephone appointment maker usually works for an hourly salary and collects a small percentage, or a small bonus, if the appointment that is set up results in a sale.

INTERNAL PERSONNEL

There are personnel in the sales department who serve as a conduit between the sales force and other departments in the organization. They usually report to the sales manager or the director of marketing. The functions of these internal personnel is important because they ensure that the instructions received from the outside sales force are understood, that the order received is within the company's parameters, that the customer gets what has been ordered, and that the order is processed on a timely basis.

ORDER EDITORS

The order editor's first responsibility is to keep mistakes from happening. An order editor reviews orders submitted by salespeople and customers to make sure that the order is acceptable and that everything adds up. For example:

1. They will check the price, depending on product and quantity, shown on the order to make sure it is correct.

2. If the order includes both hardware and supplies, they will make sure that the two are compatible. ("That cartridge won't work with that model printer.")

3. They will make sure that customer purchase orders don't contain the wrong discounts, or terms and conditions that are unacceptable to the company.

4. They will rewrite a salesperson's sloppily scribbled order to make it legible.

5. For companies that manufacture products, they will rewrite the order in the format that production prefers.

6. When they have questions on orders, for example, if the part number requested cannot be deciphered, they will contact the salesperson or the customer, for verification.

7. They may return orders submitted with incorrect pricing, questionable model numbers, and obvious mistakes. Or, they may call the salesperson and, in some cases, the ordering company.

8. Order editors also check on inventory and customers' credit status. They generally perform a number of valuable services for an outbound sales force. The good ones even make suggestions that make the company's products more useful: "You can use the model 300 bit with that drill, but the model 350 is better suited for cement."

The job requires an eye for detail, intimate knowledge of the company's product line, knowledge of other departments, the ability to operate under pressure, and a great deal of patience. Order editors have to deal with all those idiots in the field who cannot fill out an order form.

ORDER EXPEDITERS

The order editor and order expediter are sometimes, but not always, the same person. When orders come into a company, they flow through a normal procedure moving from one department to another until they finally get out the door. A typical procedure in many companies finds orders moving through departments in the following sequence:

1. *Order editing*, to make sure everything on the order is correct.

2. *Credit*, to make sure the company has a reasonable chance of getting paid.

3. *Production*, to set up a schedule, if the product is to be manufactured.

4. *Order picking,* or warehousing, to collect the items to be shipped.

5. *Shipping*, to get the product out the door.

Expediters determine how long orders remain in the house until they are shipped. If the product is to be manufactured, they consult with production to get a date when it will get to the production line and a completion date. They work with credit and other departments to make sure orders don't get hung up in somebody's "in" box. They check on inventory. They also work with field salespeople to give them estimated shipping dates and to inform them about problems: "Credit won't approve this one. Your customer is ninety days overdue on his last order." The good ones know how to improve normal delivery times if a rush schedule means more business for the company.

A typical exchange between an outside salesperson and an order expediter

Salesperson: Acme is interested in fifty thousand units of our corrugated sidewall panel. How long before we can deliver?

Expediter: In that quantity? We're looking at eight weeks minimum!

Salesperson: No good. Acme needs the stuff in five weeks, and they have a supplier in the wings who claims he can meet their schedule.

Expediter: So why don't they buy from him?

Salesperson: They like our price and quality better. My personal charm and good looks have something to do with it too.

Expediter: They can't use all 50,000 units at one time. What if we delivered twenty-five thousand pieces in five weeks and the balance three weeks later?

Salesperson: I think they would go for that.

Expediter: Let me confirm that schedule with production. Get back to me in an hour and I'll tell you if you can go ahead with the offer.

Order expediters are often involved in this kind of negotiation, matching the demands of the marketplace with reality and the limitations of making everything rush-rush. The expediter brings a semblance of sanity to the table by sometimes questioning the reasons for a customer's demand.

Order expediters will also check on the status of an order for outside sales reps who may be pressured by customers for faster delivery. When the company is going to be late on a promised delivery, the expediter may give the salesperson advance warning, or authorize an express shipping service to placate the customer.

The requirements for the job are the same as for order editors—with the additional needed skill of being able to be in several places at one time.

CUSTOMER SERVICE REPS

Customer service reps handle problems and questions that come from people who have purchased the company's product. Often, these problems relate to the product's operation. For example, GE maintains a twenty-four-hour HELP line for customers who have purchased GE appliances and need advice on how they work. Software companies, such as Microsoft, use HELP lines for customers who need assistance running programs.

Service reps fall into two general categories:

1. Those reps who field customer calls on the telephone.
2. Those reps who visit customer facilities.

Both groups need to be extremely well versed in the company's product line. They must be able explain things simply and to "walk" customers through a product's operation. They must be tactful because these reps are often dealing with people who are irritated because they can't make the product do what they expected it to do.

Service reps who visit customer offices and stores often serve as demonstrators and trainers, actually showing users and retail salespeople "hands-on" how the product operates. They are sometimes used for in-store promotions to help retailers sell more of the company's products. Their work frees up sales reps from the detail activities related to servicing customers.

Both telephone and outbound support personnel are usually salaried or hourly employees with no commission arrangement. They may be eligible for bonuses. Service reps who visit customer facilities may report to a regional or district sales manager who will direct exactly where she wishes them to spend their time.

There is an incredible shortage of qualified telephone customer service reps. It is one of the fastest growing job categories in the country, as more and more companies turn to the telephone to handle many of the tasks formerly handled by outside reps.

IN-HOUSE MARKETING SUPPORT

In-house marketing support personnel handle a variety of duties which assist outside sales reps in doing their jobs. For example, a support person may be in charge of sales literature, sending copies on request to sales force members or prospects and making sure that there are ample copies in inventory.

Marketing support people will usually handle inquiries that come into the company as a result of various advertising programs. These leads will be distributed to the appropriate sales force team member. In some instances, the support rep will track leads to see how many actually result in sales, thereby checking on the efficacy of the advertising media that produced the lead.

Support personnel also pick up competitive literature at trade shows, assist at trade show booths, maintain files on the competition, support sales reps who are conducting surveys, demonstrations and proposals, and generally assist the sales effort.

The job requires energy, enthusiasm, organization, an acquaintance with other departments, and a basic knowledge of the company product line.

HOW LEADS ARE HANDLED

A sales lead is nothing more than a suspicion that an organization, or person, may be interested in the company's product. It will remain a suspicion, and little else, until the lead is acted upon. Leads fall into several categories. These are:

1. *Unsolicited inquiries.* In these instances, prospects have called, written, or stopped by the company's facilities to get more information. These are the best leads because they are prompted by the prospect's desire to learn more about the product or the company. When properly handled, a good percentage of these leads will turn into sales.

2. *Solicited inquiries.* These are inquiries that come as a result of the company's advertising in various media, or from direct-mail and telephone campaigns. These leads are also valuable, but, in many instances, those making the inquiries are curiosity seekers. Some are merely "literature collectors," who, for reasons known only to themselves, maintain files of brochures on various products. Still, many of these leads will result in sales if they are worked.

3. *Customer referrals*. These are suggestions from satisfied customers about other organizations who may be candidates for the company's products. They are an excellent source for prospects and should be closely worked.

4. *"Pointers."* These are suggestions from company employees, friends, or interested parties who point and say, "Why don't you call on XYZ Corporation? I think they could use the product." They are the least effective lead source because so little thought goes into them. Pointers, however, should also be investigated. Any sales lead is more promising than cold calling because it is a known starting point.

"Bingo" cards

Most trade magazines will contain a postcard somewhere within its pages. (They often flutter to the floor when the magazine is opened.) This postcard will be printed with a series of two digit numbers that represent the various ads in the magazine.

These are the infamous "bingo" cards. Readers who are interested in receiving more information about any of the products featured in the magazine's ads may circle the appropriate number and mail the postcard. The magazine receives the cards, sorts them, and forwards the inquiries to its advertisers as proof that their advertising is effective. The company receiving the bingo card will usually handle it in one of two ways:

1. They will send the lead a letter with the information requested. If the product is sold through retail outlets, this is the usual form of response.

2. They will forward the lead to a territory rep who is expected to follow up with a phone call, a letter, or a visit. This is the usual form of response if the company sells an industrial-type product.

Many companies will track the leads to see how many result in sales. Tracking is also used to find out how effective territory reps are in following up on leads.

SALES LEADS AND OTHER DEPARTMENTS

In many organizations people calling the company with an inquiry will reach other departments. For example, someone with a question about a product specification may reach the engineering department. It's important that these inquiries be recorded and passed along to the sales department so they can be followed up.

Complaints should also be passed along to the sales department. Don't keep a salesperson uninformed about an unhappy customer.

Why a delayed response drives the sales department crazy

Salespeople often request information from other departments in the company. These requests are made on behalf of their customers and prospects. The typical things they want to know include:

1. Inventory status on various products.
2. Production schedules.
3. How long before back-ordered items will be shipped.
4. Whether custom changes can be made to products: "Can we reverse the assembly housing and paint it black?"
5. Whether the products can perform in ways not suggested by the specifications or literature: "My customer wants to use this in the Arctic. Will the plastic tubing become brittle and snap off at a hundred degrees below zero?"

The questions, which can appear endless, may seem to be an intrusion on the department's work, but they are an indication of interest in the company by a prospect or customer. In some instances the answers to these questions will result in sales, in others absolutely nothing happens. The salesperson will sometimes be a pest because she demands a response "right now." What is really going on is that the sales rep wants to establish a reputation as a reliable resource of information for the prospect. When answers are delayed by departments because they have other fish to fry, it is the salesperson who appears to be disinterested in servicing the client.

The salesperson's image suffers. The company never gets close to a potential sale.

No matter how much of a nuisance they appear to be, information requests should be handled in a timely manner. The best way to handle queries from sales is the following:

1. Get all the details on what the sales department wants to know.
2. Ask questions to clarify.
3. Make suggestions on alternates when this is practical.
4. Avoid the it's-not-my-job syndrome.
5. Avoid the it-only-comes-in-white syndrome. The bigger the opportunity, the more willing the company should be to please the customer. We are in the age of customization.
6. If the answer isn't known, give the sales department a date when it will be forthcoming. They'll be more patient if they can tell their client that the company is actively investigating the issue.
7. Don't become jaded when several special rush projects requested by salespeople don't result in sales. Doing work on speculation is part of selling.

WHY THE SALES DEPARTMENT OCCASIONALLY TAKES BACK GOOD MERCHANDISE

The profit picture for most companies would sparkle a lot brighter if the sales department never agreed to take back perfectly good merchandise. So why do they do it? Why not simply order the trucks to run in one direction, from the company's warehouse to the customer's facility? The answer is simple: companies take back merchandise to remain on good terms with their customers. The company that refuses to take back goods may never get another order.

This policy is particularly important for companies that sell their products through distributors, retailers, and mass merchants. Today, distributors of goods have an edge over producers. Their financial and marketing muscle gives them a significant negotiating advantage over their suppliers. They control the market and suppliers had better dance to their tune.

If, for example, a company making widgets has Wal-Mart for a customer, they enjoy the tremendous merchandising power of that organization. Orders from Wal-Mart probably take up much of the widget company's production capacity. If Wal-Mart wishes to return a large number of widgets because they aren't selling well, the widget company may have no choice except to agree. Wal-Mart is too important a distribution channel to make angry.

There is, however, one alternative to taking merchandise back. The supplier can agree to "inventory balancing," which essentially means marking down the cost of merchandise so the retailer can put it on sale and move it out fast.

SETTING UP A COMMUNICATION LINK
WITH THE SALES DEPARTMENT

Sales departments can be annoying to others in the company because everything, it seems, has to be done on a rush-rush basis. The information they need, however, is important, and assisting them in making sales can only help the entire organization. Here's a good way to establish a good communication link between sales and other departments.

1. Remember that the sales department is not in an adversary relationship with other departments. The two of you are on the same side.

2. There's no need to become a fetch-and-carry lackey for every outside salesperson in the company. Establish a personal relationship with someone in sales management who becomes your point of contact.

3. Funnel information through your point of contact.

4. Don't hide behind your phone and e-mail. Be available. Don't hide behind the company's bureaucracy either. Be responsive.

5. Get back to people even when you don't have the information they requested right now. When there's a delay, tell them the reason why and give a new time estimate.

6. Live up to promises.

Chapter Fourteen

COMPENSATION PLANS EXPLAINED

Do salespeople earn too much? One of the feelings that many other employees have about the sales department is that the rascals are vastly overpaid. There's often a suspicion that few of the salespeople in the organization may even be pulling down six figures! Based on the work they do, these high wages (mostly rumored) just don't seem right. Myths aside, how much do salespeople actually make and why are they compensated the way they are? The following is an explanation of how most organizations compensate their salespeople and why, in some instances, a few individuals in sales can make more money than others in the company, even department managers with vastly more responsibility.

Sales compensation plans are developed to motivate the sales force to produce more sales and make more profit for the company. Why the need to motivate salespeople when other employees aren't similarly rewarded for their efforts? One of the reasons is because the salesperson's accomplishments, or lack of them, are so easy to measure. It's hard for a manager to know exactly how many documents a clerk in the department filed last week, but the sales manager knows, to the penny, how much business a salesperson brought in.

One experienced salesman I know writes "Today I am a bum," on every Monday sheet of his daily calendar. That message of self-deprecation appears fifty-two times. It means that last week's results cut no ice for the future. Those orders have been booked. This week is a new challenge. The pressure of performance is never-ending.

Because salespeople are paid on results, their incomes vary widely. One salesperson may be making twice as much, and even more, than another working out of the same office and responsible for an adjacent territory. A salesperson's income can even vary widely from year to year. That salesperson who earned $100,000 last year may struggle to make $30,000 the following year.

One way or another, all salespeople are paid a percentage of the orders they bring in. Typical compensation arrangements are:

- Straight commission.
- Draw against commission.
- Salary.
- Salary plus commission.
- Salary plus commission plus bonus.

The methods of compensation may vary, but they are all related to the contribution the salesperson makes to company sales and profits.

HOW STRAIGHT COMMISSION WORKS AND WHY IT'S EITHER FEAST OR FAMINE

Under a straight commission arrangement, sales reps receive no salary. Zero. Instead, they are paid a percentage of the dollar value of every order they bring in. The percentage can vary from item to item. Many companies pay their reps a higher commission percentage for high-margin products and a lower rate for popular sellers that don't bring in as much profit. Some companies pay a higher commission rate on new business as opposed to repeat orders. The different commission rates are designed to influence sales reps to channel their efforts in particular directions.

New business is harder to get than repeat business, so a greater reward is offered for it. The company benefits when higher-margin products are sold, so the compensation plan allows the salesperson to share in that benefit.

Companies pay out earned commission at different times. Most pay out at one of these times:

- Upon the company's acceptance of the order.
- When the order is shipped.
- When the customer pays for the goods.

The common thread behind these payment arrangements is that the company doesn't lay out a dime until results are achieved. In essence, the salesperson is advancing the company his or her labor. In many instances, the rep will not receive any fringe benefits such as medical insurance and participation in a pension plan.

Most straight-commission reps also pay their own expenses, so they are actually out of pocket until a sale is made. For some products with long sales cycles, reps may go several weeks, or even months, without any income. Some of the help wanted ads for straight-commission reps will include the caveat: "Must be able to support yourself for *x*-number of weeks." The straight-commission rep then is a testament to optimism and self-confidence.

So why do salespeople opt to work on a straight-commission arrangement? It's because this kind of compensation plan can be more lucrative for competent salespeople than any other. The commission rate is usually higher than with other compensation plans. Successful salespeople earn more. Those who are unsuccessful earn less. Most of the salespeople making six figures are working on a straight-commission plan. They deserve this high reward because of the uncertainty. They take the big risks—which is why this arrangement is considered feast or famine.

Companies adopt straight-commission compensation plans, even though they may pay out more, as a way to establish and maintain a sales force without incurring advance expenses. They pay out nothing until an order comes through the door. The downside is that these companies have less control over their sales forces. The sales rep is really an independent agent, not tied to the company by a salary structure.

For obvious reasons, it's difficult to obtain a good commissioned rep in a virgin territory where much missionary work must be done before any business will be forthcoming. The rep who is sharp enough to get the job done is also sharp enough to realize that lean times may be ahead before there is any income. Still another problem is that good reps suffering through a long dry spell are likely to drop out of the company because they can't finance themselves anymore.

Draw-against-commission plans

Draw-against-commission plans are really straight-commission arrangements, with the wrinkle that the company advances the salesperson a certain amount of money on the anticipation of future earnings from commissioned sales. In essence, the salesperson borrows the money from the company. It is not a salary and must be repaid. The amount of the draw is deducted from the salesperson's commission check. If the commission check doesn't cover the draw, the salesperson has a negative balance which accumulates from commission period to commission period.

Why draw-against-commission salespeople often leave the company

Draw-against-commission is a good way to give salespeople walking around money while their deals simmer and percolate. The problem with these plans is that they can demoralize and demotivate the sales force. They often lead to large employee turnover. If a salesperson does not bring in enough orders to make the amount of the draw, he or she owes money to the company. The salesperson going through a bad patch can accumulate a large debt that future sales won't wipe out.

If the salesperson sees that accumulated debt is too large, he or she may simply resign. Although the money is theoretically owed, very few companies try, with any real resolve, to collect draw-against-commission debts from ex-employees. They may write a nasty dunning letter or two, but few will take legal action. Attorneys' fees would be high and sympathetic judges may not follow the exact letter of the law.

How some companies reduce the negative impact of draw-against-commission plans

Draw-against-commission arrangements also create a dilemma with recently hired salespeople. Because they're just starting out with the company, it may take some time before these new fish produce any business. They're in the hole from the very beginning. Some companies adjust for this problem by giving their new salespeople a 90- to 120-day grace period. Any debts owed are wiped out after this period and the salesperson starts again from scratch. This gives the salesperson enough time to get deals percolating. If the salesperson is an immediate success and has a positive balance over the grace period, so much the better.

Salespeople, however, are not stupid. Those who owe large amounts on their draw are likely to hoard orders near the end of the grace period. Why submit an order that will only go to reduce a debt that will be wiped out anyway?

Why salary-plus-commission is the most popular compensation method

The way most companies compensate their salespeople is through a combination of salary plus commission. Under this arrangement, salespeople receive a base salary that is not charged against future earnings. They also receive a commission on sales. Sometimes commissions are paid on all orders. In other instances, the salesperson must achieve a certain dollar volume before commissions are paid.

Generally, the commission percentage in salary-plus-commission plans is less than for straight-commission plans. That's because the salesperson is taking less risk. The base salary is always there, offering a bit of security even when sales aren't forthcoming.

The advantage to the company of the salary-plus-commission arrangement is it has more control over the sales force. They are direct employees and their activities can be closely managed. They can be required to fill out reports and attend sales meetings. The sales force is more stable because staff members have a certain income guaranteed. Customers see a continuity of service and support.

This arrangement also motivates staff members to work hard because of the commission portion of the plan. The company can steer their salespeople toward certain high-margin products by offering higher commission schedules on these items.

The disadvantage of this kind of plan is that some salespeople may be satisfied with their salaries and not sufficiently motivated to seek extra income via commission. It may take time to weed these individuals out of the company.

How bonuses work and why they are offered to salespeople

Many compensation plans offer bonuses. A bonus is an extra sum of money, beyond salary and commission, paid to a salesperson for achieving a specific objective. That objective varies depending upon what management wishes to accomplish. The following are typical objectives:

- Achieving certain sales volumes for a specific period.
- Making certain profits, or achieving certain profit margins, for a specific period.

- Moving certain products.
- Achieving certain levels of new business.

Bonuses differ from sales contests in that they usually cover a longer period of time. A bonus period may cover the entire year. Some bonus arrangements are broken down into six-month periods so that those salespeople who fall hopelessly behind in the beginning have a new incentive at the halfway mark. Some bonuses offer a sliding scale, with more money paid for higher achievement.

Bonuses are used by companies to motivate their salespeople to perform better than they did the previous year and to give them a long-term focus. Essentially, the bonus sets a new performance standard every year. No matter how well the salesperson did last year, this year must be better to earn a bonus. The bar is always set higher.

A Typical Bonus Arrangement			
	100% quota	*110% quota*	*120% quota*
Six months	$1,000	$2,500	$5,000
Year	$2,500	$5,000	$10,000

Under this bonus plan, a salesperson who had a miserable first six months would have a chance to make bonus money by recovering in the second half.

Managers like bonuses because they are easy to control via setting quotas. Salespeople like bonuses because they represent a chance to make extra income. They become something to shoot for.

The problem with bonus plans is that salespeople who have earned them for several years in a row begin to consider them as part of their regular income. When the bar is set too high one year, they become demotivated by what they regard as an impossible task.

STRAIGHT SALARY: WHY IT'S AN UNSATISFACTORY METHOD FOR COMPENSATING SALESPEOPLE

Why can't salespeople be compensated just like other employees? Wouldn't it would be fairer and create less intramural jealousy if salespeople started with a salary and received annual raises depending upon their performance? This kind of arrangement would eliminate those occasional bonanzas in which one or two salespeople received much more income than other employees on the same grade level.

Some companies use straight salaries to compensate their salespeople, but this kind of arrangement doesn't work with most product lines. Here's why: The company wants to sell more goods at a greater profit. The best way to achieve this objective is to offer salespeople some sort of incentive arrangement. The more they sell, the more they make. Money may not be the top priority on everyone's list, but it is number one with most salespeople.

To get salespeople to sell more, they must be stimulated to do things that make them uncomfortable. For example, they must make a great number of cold calls and that means facing rejection every day. Cold calling is a lot harder than visiting existing customers. In both instances the salesperson is working. In both instances, the salesperson is getting orders. Obtaining new customers, however, is key to the growth of the company.

WHEN STRAIGHT SALARY IS A GOOD COMPENSATION ARRANGEMENT

Straight-salary compensation plans do have their place. They are useful in the following circumstances:

1. Straight-salary compensation is useful when the company's products have an extremely long sales cycle. Nobody can afford to live on straight commission if the product takes two years to sell.

2. Straight salary also works when the product carries a very high price tag. No company is going to give a salesperson 20 percent of a three-million-dollar deal.

3. Straight salary is often used in competitive bid situations in which the profit margins are so very low, there's no room for commission.

4. Straight salary is often used to compensate salespeople for their efforts in handling house accounts on which no commission is paid.

THE PURPOSE OF SALES CONTESTS

Sales contests are used to boost sales and profits over a specific period of time. Sometimes contests are used to get the staff's attention when a new product is introduced. The idea is to get a short burst of extra effort from the sales staff over a limited period.

Contests can be run involving the entire product line to stimulate sales during a typically slow period, or they can be used as an incentive to move more of a high-margin product. Contests can be run for the entire company, or they can be used to stimulate activity for a local office. They can last three months, or a single week.

Contest prizes can be anything from trips to merchandise to cold, hard cash. In some contests the winners earn "points" which can be used to purchase items from catalogs supplied by sales promotion outfits that specialize in incentive awards. Luggage, cashmere sweaters, Kansas City steaks, and so forth, can be ordered through these companies.

Contests are good morale boosters because members of the sales force feel they have the opportunity to earn something extra. The prizes provide concrete recognition of the salesperson's performance. It's nice to come home one evening and brag to the spouse that, "I aced everybody this month. We're going to Bermuda for a few days."

Contests also have their limitations. When they're run for short periods, and properly promoted by management, they can help give sales a temporary boost. When contests go on forever, they simply become another form of compensation and salespeople become jaded.

How sales contests are run

Sales contests are designed to meet specific objectives. To take advantage of the salesperson's natural competitive nature, contests often pit individual salespeople against one another. Contests may also be run that pit one branch office, one district, or one region of the company against another. Winners get awards and bragging rights. Losers get to grumble about how the rules were unfair.

If management wishes to promote a new product, they may design a contest that gives awards to the person, or office, that brings in the most orders for that product over a specific period of time. That stimulates the sales force to concentrate on the new product. The product gets heavy coverage and a few people in the company win a prize. Not a bad deal for the company!

One of the easiest contests to design and administer is the short-term contest for the local office. Let's say the branch manager wants to prove that more demonstrations will lead to more sales. The manager devises a contest that gives $250 cash to the person on the sales crew who does the most demos over the next week. The rules of the contest stipulate the sales don't matter, demos do. If the sales team is large, first, second, and third prizes might be awarded. This will keep everyone participating for the full week.

Each day a record of the verified demos done by every member of the sales team is posted on the bulletin board. Daily leaders are announced. The manager offers everyone encouragement. At the following week's regular sales meeting, there is a short ceremony where the winner is announced and handed a check for $250. Every member of the sales team who did better than the normal number of demos is congratulated because more sales will surely result. The manager "tracks" the demos over the next several weeks and points out to staff members how they result in sales. The point is proven for a relatively small expenditure.

The most frequently used sales contests are those that focus on total sales volume, or percentage of sales over quota. Those contests that use percentages of quota are more equitable because sales territories are not equal in volume, potential, or maturity. Frequently, predetermined goals are given as bogeys, with everyone who exceeds certain dollar figures or percentages of quota counted as winners.

Longer contests of this type can run for a month, a quarter, even six months. Anything longer loses the interest of the contestants, except for those near the top. Even a six-month contest is a bit of a stretch. Some managers, however, prefer longer-term contests because the prizes can be more sumptuous.

STAR CLUBS

"Star clubs" are known by a variety of names, but their purpose is all the same: to recognize and reward the company's top salespeople. In most companies, only one out of five salespeople will qualify for the star club. They are the elite, the salespeople who, over a full year, sold the highest percentage over their quota assignment.

Most companies make their star club a big deal. Those who qualify will be flown, along with their spouses, to an exotic resort for a long weekend. Top company brass will attend. There will be banquets, picnics on coral reefs, rubbing elbows with senior management, and long drinking bouts. The opinions of star club members will solicited regarding the product line, company problems, and the competition. A formal meeting or two will be held so the company can write off the expenses. The main thing a good star club accomplishes is that it makes the attendees try even harder next year because they want to come back.

MICROMANAGING COMPENSATION PLANS

Some managers become so concerned about salespeople making too much income in relationship to others in the company that they develop plans that stifle rather than stimulate incentive. They put caps on earnings, or cut off commissions after a certain dollar volume of sales is reached. They reduce commission schedules on popular products. They turn very large customers into house accounts. They raise quota assignments so bonuses can't be reached. They cut territories. These income-limiting devices work against the concept of incentive-based compensation.

Caps on earnings

Some companies put a cap, or a maximum limit, on what members of their sales teams can earn. When a cap is in place, no matter how many orders are placed, regardless of the dollar volumes or profit margins of those orders, members of the sales staff can earn so much and not a penny more.

The companies that use caps rationalize them on the basis that it keeps earnings for salespeople in line with what others in the organization with similar responsibilities make. It eliminates jealousy toward sales team members. Companies that think this way are usually highly bureaucratic and concerned that one salesperson's sensational year could throw their compensation plans out of whack. Companies that place their employees in "grades," as does the U.S. Civil Service, are more likely to cap the earnings of their sales team members. It stems from a philosophy that compensation should be based on responsibility and the number of people managed, rather than specific accomplishment.

The problem with caps is that they are a powerful disincentive to stop working once the earnings limit has been reached. They also "motivate" sales team members to play games. For example, a salesperson who has reached the income limit near the end of the year is likely to hold back any new orders until the following year.

Caps also create morale problems. The salesperson who brings in order after order and is not compensated for them will feel cheated, no matter the explanation.

House accounts

A house account is one on which the company pays no commission for goods sold. They are usually high-volume customers with special needs, or one given special pricing that leaves no room for commission payments. Contacts with these accounts are usually handled by management.

Salespeople hate house accounts because they represent a large opportunity they are forbidden to go near. Many field managers hate them as well, because their sales volume is often excluded from the district's or region's totals.

SUMMARY

Compensation plans for salespeople are a management tool. There is no single best compensation method. Straight commission might work best for one company, salary plus a small commission might be the best answer for another. The best compensation plans are designed to motivate sales team members to try harder and to channel their efforts in specific directions. They are simple and they are fair.

The poor compensation plans are overly concerned about what one or two people on the sales staff could earn with a fantastic year. They become the opposite of what is intended—demotivators.

Chapter Fifteen

SALES MEETINGS, TRAINING, AND TRADE SHOWS

THE PURPOSE AND CONTENT OF SALES MEETINGS

Sales meetings are an integral part of a salesperson's normal work routine. Some meetings are boring, while others help the manager accomplish specific objectives. At their worst, a manager stands behind a podium and bullies everyone present to turn in more orders. Everyone with a long career in sales has attended this kind of meeting. The manager isn't accomplishing much because all he's doing is taking people out of the field where they could be trying to sell something.

The best meetings provide the sales staff with valuable information and insights that help them do a better job. Good meetings are a two-way street. The manager also gets feedback from the sales staff on the kind of support they need to succeed.

The frequency of sales meetings varies according to the circumstances and the sales manager's style. Some managers hold sales meetings every week. Others convene meetings less frequently. In a few companies, sales meetings are held early every morning as sort of a sales crew shape-up. In this last instance, the meeting is primarily held to make sure that everyone on the sales staff is present and ready to work. They are an indication that management doesn't trust the sales staff.

Online and video conferencing meetings are recent phenomena. These electronic get-togethers help companies with scattered sales forces to keep in touch with the troops.

Sales meetings are called for a variety of purposes. These purposes include:

1. *To inform the sales crew about changes.* New products, new company policies, contests, pricing changes, competitive activity, and targets of opportunities are all highlighted during these meetings.

2. *To motivate sales crew members to do better.* Many of these meetings are like an evangelical happening. The manager preaches the gospel to the faithful. Unfortunately, the fervor wears off quickly once the sales crew is back in the field.

3. *To educate and train the sales crew.* Some meetings will primarily consist of training sessions on new products, ideas on product applications, ways to demonstrate products, or discussions with product managers. Sales training meetings may focus on sales techniques. For example, a sales training meeting might include information on how to close a deal. Role-playing sessions might simulate real-life situations.

4. *To review recent activity.* In many sales meetings, crew members are asked by the manager to summarize their successes and failures since the last meeting and to forecast what is likely to happen in the near future. The sales manager uses the information gathered in these sessions to make forecasts and to evaluate the effectiveness of the sales staff. The manager may also offer assistance in closing big deals and will often make suggestions when deals are stalled.

5. *To reward achievement.* A few sales meetings are really award sessions in which superior performance is recognized and awards are given. These meetings are also considered motivational.

6. *To build camaraderie.* Getting everyone together periodically at one time and in one place builds team spirit.

7. *To discuss common problems.* Common obstacles to the sale, and ways to handle them, are often discussed at sales meetings. Competitive activity is reviewed, industry concerns are discussed, and suggestions are made.

8. *To handle emergencies.* If, for example, a glitch develops in a well-distributed product, a special sales meeting may be called on how to handle it.

What shouldn't be discussed at sales meetings—but often is

If the manager allows it, some meetings will turn into griping sessions. One salesperson will voice a complaint. Others will make their own "contributions." Soon, there's a chorus of unhappy voices. Griping sessions are infectious; they contaminate everyone present. Many salespeople will take any opportunity to complain about company policies, about the competition, about pricing, about delivery schedules, about product quality, and everything else under the sun. Complaining transfers blame for poor performance.

The manager should always be open to discussing legitimate problems. Wise managers handle griping by suggesting to the complainer: "We're eating into everyone's time. Let's discuss this privately."

Typical sales meeting environments

Sales meetings are held in a variety of venues. The most popular places are the following:

1. *In branch sales offices.* Branch managers often call small, informal meetings which everyone on the sales staff is required to attend. These meetings are often held on Monday mornings or Friday afternoons. The agenda is haphazard but usually related to local sales activity. Specific customers, pending deals, and prospects may be reviewed.

2. *In hotel conference rooms.* Some managers rent hotel space for even ordinary sales meetings because they don't want their staff members distracted by phone calls, paperwork, and office personnel. All good hotels can provide conference rooms and appropriate paraphernalia, such as slide and overhead projectors. The hotel conference room is often a better meeting choice when salespeople who will be attending are traveling from other cities. The hotel can provide accommodations and food service for the travelers, as well as the conference facilities.

3. *In home offices.* Meetings at the company's home office are often restricted to district or regional managers. They may be held as frequently as every quarter, or as seldom as once a year. These meetings are often planning sessions in which the company's course over the next fiscal period is charted. The attractive feature about the home office meeting is that it allows salespeople to meet with headquarters personnel.

4. *At resorts*. These are the meeting spots that salespeople like best. They are usually held no more than once a year to reward excellent performance. They are more play than work. Just enough business is discussed to qualify for expense write-offs.

A typical meeting agenda

Salespeople do not stand around at meetings and brag about big deals. Real work gets done and the hours can be long. Here is the agenda for a typical sales meeting:

SAMPLE SALES MEETING AGENDA

Time	Activity
7:30-8:00	Coffee and rolls
8:00-8:15	Welcome, Frank Jones, regional sales manager
8:15-9:00	Review last quarter's performance, R. Smith, branch manager
9:00-10:00	Outline this quarter's objectives, Bill Brown
10:00-10:15	Coffee break
10:15-11:00	Competitive activity review, Lucille Watson, marketing support
11:00-12:00	New product introduction, Jim Carlson, product manager
12:00-1:00	Lunch
1:00-1:30	Credit policy changes, Ethel Macy, credit manager
1:30-2:00	Order processing review, Lana Kinsey, head of order processing
2:00-3:00	Leasing to increase sales, Sondra Beasly, leasing representative, AT&T Leasing
3:00-3:15	Afternoon break
3:15-6:00	Hands-on training, new "Alpha" System product. All participate. Training conducted by Ed Ringer, director of training
6:00-7:00	Dinner in LeBaron Room
7:00-9:00	New compensation plan, Frank Jones
9:00-10:00	Free discussion, all participate

The sample agenda shows the attendees will be putting in a very full day. Most sales meetings run long, so this one may not be over until midnight. The afternoon schedule includes a hands-on training session because the wise manager recognizes that it's difficult for salespeople to sit and listen to speakers all day long.

Note that compensation, a subject dear to every salesperson's heart, is held until next to last. This strategic placement ensures an attentive audience all day long. Also note that the free-form discussion is absolutely last on the program. This is the section at which griping is technically allowed: "If you have a problem, Linda, bring it up during the discussion period." By placing a free-form discussion last, the manager hopes that everyone will be too tired to gripe for long.

SALES TRAINING

The purpose of sales training is to prepare salespeople to perform effectively. No matter how well a company may support its sales staff, each staff member is essentially alone when in front of a prospect or customer. Salespeople must be familiar with all aspects of their jobs. The "natural-born" salesperson is more myth than reality. Few are born with the ability to sell. Sales skills must be learned, and heaven help the company that allows its sales force to learn them haphazardly.

Sales training philosophies

Companies approach the problem of sales training in different ways. Larger companies may employ professional trainers as part of their sales departments. The advantage of this approach is that the company's own method of selling may be taught. In fact, some companies prefer to hire only people without prior sales experience so there are no bad habits to unlearn. The disadvantage is that it is expensive to maintain trainers as a permanent part of the staff.

Some companies send their new hires to outside sales schools. The advantage is that the training is still professional, but the cost incurred is on an as-needed basis. The disadvantage is that the training may be too general and not specifically related to the company's product line.

Small companies with no training capabilities will often hire only experienced salespeople who require little schooling. The advantage is that no training expense is required. The disadvantage is that experienced salespeople will command higher salaries and the prior experience they have may not be relevant to the company's product line.

How sales training is conducted

Sales training itself is conducted in several different ways. These include the following:

1. Formalized training conducted in classrooms. Many companies use this type of training with new sales hires before sending them out into the field. The training sessions are conducted by professionals. A class may include up to twenty or thirty students. These sessions may last for several weeks and will often include the following subjects:

- Basic product knowledge.
- Product applications.
- Sales techniques.
- Demonstration techniques.
- Proposal writing.
- Pricing.
- Company history.
- Ordering procedures.
- Competitive information.

The students are evaluated by the trainers on their ability to absorb the material, their personalities, and their attitude. Not everyone passes.

2. Formalized training conducted in the field with professional trainers. Many large companies use full-time trainers to conduct field training. These are "graduate" training sessions that often follow classroom training. The lessons of the classroom are tested in the marketplace.

Frequently, the training takes place in what will be the trainee's assigned territory. The trainer accompanies the trainee on actual sales calls. The two may take turns assuming the lead role before prospects and customers. The trainer will try to schedule a broad spectrum of a territory rep's normal responsibilities, including:

- Cold calling on suspects.
- Territory familiarization.
- Territory management.
- Calling on existing customers.
- Conducting surveys.
- Making demonstrations and proposals.

- Following up on leads.
- Closing orders.

The trainee learns by watching the trainer work. When the trainee assumes the lead role, the trainer becomes a coach who critiques the calls.

3. The most common training method, particularly for small companies, is the situation in which a branch or regional sales manager will spend one or two days in the field with the trainee. This kind of training leaves much to be desired. The manager is not a professional trainer, so the focus is usually on obtaining immediate business rather than on educating the trainee. Often, the manager will handle every call. When the trainee does assume the lead role, the manager will often take over at the first sign of difficulty. The manager may also get caught up in other branch business, giving even less time to the training mission.

4. Many companies will schedule training sessions for their salespeople when new products are introduced. These sessions are often conducted by product managers and marketing support reps. Their goal is to familiarize sales staff members with the new items. Product features, specifications, applications, pricing, competitive products, planned promotions and hands-on demonstration practice are usually emphasized in this kind of training.

5. Some companies will regularly schedule follow-up training sessions for all their staff members, regardless of how experienced or successful they are. These sessions are designed to keep their people current on sales techniques and the product lineup. In many instances, the training sessions are conducted by outside companies, colleges and universities.

6. Some companies send their salespeople to seminars. These are given by organizations such as the American Management Association. They are run by professionals with many years of sales and marketing experience. Most are well run and pack a lot of information and practical how-to technique in short, information-packed sessions. The seminars can be expensive, costing anywhere from $500 to $5,000, but they are a bargain when compared with the time and effort of putting together a program. Many of the seminars are scheduled during weekends, so no valuable sales time is lost.

Always investigate the sales seminars agenda. Some are merely motivational meetings. They are run by sales evangelists who deliver an inspirational, almost religious message of salvation through selling. They fire up people with enthusiasm, but the emotional "fix" wears off quickly once the meeting is over.

Sales training for small companies

Small companies with little training capability can take advantage of courses run by groups such as the American Management Association. They can also subscribe to sales journals and bulletins such as the kind put out by the Dartnell Corporation. These monthly bulletins usually run about four pages. They offer practical tips and suggestions on selling.

Local universities and colleges are additional training resources that can be tapped by small companies. Most offer evening courses in sales and marketing. Paying the tuition for salespeople to take these courses is an inexpensive way to develop seasoned sales personnel.

Local libraries have shelves filled with books on selling and sales training. The sales manager of a small company might play the role of instructor and assign reading material to every person on the sales team. The material could be discussed after the golden selling hours are over.

Finally, the sales manager of a small company can be the best resource for ongoing field training. He or she can make every joint call a training experience. The manager can use questions, observations, and coaching to develop a professional staff. When discussing sales problems, the manager can guide the person to the right solution rather than just dictate an answer.

The two "nevers" in sales training

There are two nevers to remember about sales training. The first is that salespeople can never be overtrained. The second is that sales training never ends.

THOSE WILD AND WICKED TRADE SHOWS AND CONVENTIONS

Trade shows and conventions are annual affairs in which companies within an industry gather together to display their products. They go back to the Middle Ages when merchants assembled in town squares on festival days to sell their goods and to this day they remain an effective way to market products.

Every major industry has its own trade show. Shows like COMDEX for the computer industry and the Consumer's Electronics Show give manufacturers the opportunity to showcase their products before thousands of potential buyers. They are major events and some companies account for up to 50 percent of their sales volume from trade show participation.

Trade shows are often sponsored by the industry trade association. Major players in that industry are expected to participate. Those companies that fail to participate do so at their peril. Rumors begin to circulate about that company being in trouble.

To encourage wide attendance, trade shows are often held in desirable destinations, such as Las Vegas or San Francisco. The promoters will book nationally known figures as guest speakers. Seminars will be conducted on subjects of industry concern. The promoters will guarantee that a certain number of hotel rooms will be filled and receive special rates in return.

Trade shows mean good business for hotels, restaurants, and shops, so many cities compete for trade show bookings. The first requirement is a large convention center to accommodate large audiences.

The way trade shows work is that exhibitors rent booth space from show promoters. The amount charged for booth space will be related to the show's attendance and its importance to the industry. National shows that attract important industry buyers, such as the Consumer's Electronic Show, cost the earth.

Space rental is only the beginning of the expense for participants. The booth itself must lure trade show visitors inside. In that regard it competes with every other exhibitor's booth. So the exhibitor must pay to have an attractive booth built. Some booths are elaborate affairs that cost up to seven figures. There's an entire industry that does nothing except design and construct trade show booths. One of the constraints in show booth design is that they must be able to be "knocked down" and stored until the next show. Entertainers, attractive models, and minor celebrities are hired to further attract visitors.

The exhibitor must also provide transportation, hotel rooms, and other expenses for the salespeople and support reps who will be working the booth. Shipping costs for the equipment to be displayed, sales literature, booth setup, and so forth account for more than just incidental expenses. All the trades people who handle things like electrical connections are union employees.

Many exhibitors also entertain during trade shows. The entertainment part is how trade shows and conventions acquired their reputation as wild affairs. A few exhibitors will host huge cocktail parties, luncheons, or dinners in the ballrooms of first-class hotels. They'll hire big-name bands. Important clients are privately entertained; many are taken to posh restaurants. Some exhibitors maintain hospitality suites where customers and prospects can expect free-flowing liquor and munchies at almost any hour. Exhibitors may take their good customers on excursions to see local points of interest. Often, the amount spent on entertainment is directly related to the exhibitor's position in the industry. The market share leader is expected to put on the biggest bash.

With all these expenses, and others that are less direct, why do companies exhibit at trade shows? What can they expect to get in return for money spent? There is one overriding reason for this cash layout: Trade shows are an effective marketing medium. The purpose of a trade show is to generate leads, and good ones accomplish that purpose. The leads are highly qualified. Many will result in sales. Some companies generate up to half their annual sales volume through trade shows and conventions.

Despite the high cost to participate in a national trade show, the cost per contact can be surprisingly low. In a well-attended trade show, the cost per contact can be low as fifteen dollars. The cost for a sales rep to make a direct call on a prospect varies by industry, but it can be as high as four hundred dollars. That's quite a contrast in value for achieving a similar result. Some managers expect a ten-to-one return for every dollar spent on a trade show. It is this concentration of customers and prospects in one place that makes trade shows an attractive marketing tool.

WHAT HAPPENS INSIDE A TRADE SHOW BOOTH

A typical trade show booth is set up to attractively display the company's products. It is open on all sides so there is no obstruction to visitors wandering through. Salespeople are located at various stations within the booth. There aren't too many salespeople to discourage visitors from coming into the interior. If a celebrity or entertainer has been hired, he or she will be plainly visible.

Visitors to the booth will come in various categories. They include:

1. Good customers stopping by to say hello.
2. Customers with a complaint.
3. Prospects interested in seeing a product they have heard about.

4. Industry mavens interested in anything that is new.
5. Prospects interested in a demonstration.
6. Customers and prospects with an appointment to talk to a salesperson or the brass about a pending deal.
7. The competition, snooping.
8. Curiosity seekers and literature gatherers.
9. Students. (Some commercial trade shows will only permit attendees from inside the industry or limit students to one particular day.)

Salespeople working the booth should be trying to make as many product demonstrations as possible. These demos may be shorter than usual because quantity of exposure is paramount. The prospect's name, company affiliation, and other pertinent data should be recorded. If the prospect appears to be in the market for something ("I'm going to buy five hundred desktop computers for my company within the next sixty days"), that lead should immediately be routed to the appropriate salesperson or manager. Most trade shows provide name badges for attendees so visitors are easy to identify. Most shows also provide data capture devices (for a fee of course) so the information on the badges is easy to record.

Some booths maintain reception desks where sales literature is dispensed and leads are recorded. Many booths have private rooms in the back with telephones and fax machines. New products and prototypes that aren't quite ready for the market may be kept under wraps in these rooms to show to a few special customers.

Technicians should be standing by in case of equipment breakdown. If equipment does break down, it should be repaired out of sight, or after the show closes. Nothing looks worse than repairs going on during show hours. There should be a booth manager who develops a booth work schedule so every salesperson and support rep knows exactly what times he or she is on the floor. This schedule is also useful if a customer stops by and asks for a particular salesperson.

Some companies develop special pricing or "show specials" for the duration of the convention so the salespeople can actually take some orders. Often, the equipment displayed at the show is sold to a dealer or distributor at a discount on the last day.

The competition will inevitably stop by the booth. They should be treated courteously, but you should also expect the same courtesy when visiting their booth. Exchange literature on products that are currently available, but keep tight-lipped about products under development, customer lists, or any proprietary information.

The whole idea of the trade show is to expose as many prospects as possible to the company's products and to develop leads. Good leads are the desired product of the trade show. They should be treated like gold.

Why non-sales types should occasionally "work" the booth

The sales and marketing departments will frequently invite other company personnel, such as department managers in credit, production, and engineering, to visit during a trade show. It's a good opportunity for one and all to see how the company line stacks up vis-à-vis the competition. A trade show is also a place to learn, first hand, about industry concerns and to get a feel for market conditions. These non-sales employees should consider spending a few hours actually working in the booth alongside the salespeople assigned to that task. This time can be profitably spent because:

1. The booth is the marketplace in microcosm. Every condition salespeople experience in the marketplace will be repeated there in a few days.

2. They will learn about the problems and concerns of customers. It is one thing to have the sales staff report that customers are unhappy about a product deficiency and another to hear complaints about that deficiency twenty times in one hour from a steady stream of customers.

3. They will learn about the hot buttons that turn prospects into customers.

4. They will hear what customers and prospects want in the next generation of products.

In summary, they will learn what the sales team has been telling them for months.

How non-sales types can interact with customers and prospects at a trade show

Trade shows represent an excellent opportunity for employees in other departments to learn about the marketplace. They are particularly valuable for the following departments:

1. *Credit department.* Credit managers can meet with good customers to talk about expanding their credit limits or to explain company credit policy. They can also talk to those customers who are marginal credit risks on what is needed to improve their credit standing, and can meet with companies whose accounts are in arrears. Discussions can be held on bringing those accounts up to date. Finally, a credit manager can be available to work out the financial arrangements on potential big deals.

2. *Engineering department.* Many product users will be attending the show. Talking to these users will give the engineering department a good handle on needed product improvements and the bells and whistles desired by users on the next generation of products.

When prototypes are shown to selected customers, the engineering department can quickly gauge their reactions while there is still time to make changes. Further, observing the competitive product line may give engineers valuable ideas on how the company's product can be improved.

3. *Production department.* The people in production can also get valuable information from trade show participation by listening to customer complaints about the product's quality. If many customers report a particular part is breaking down, the need for corrective action becomes apparent.

TRADE SHOW SUMMARY

Industry trade shows and conventions can be very expensive. They are, however, the best and most economical way to meet face-to-face with many prospects and customers in a short period of time. Trade shows are not only a valuable sales and marketing tool, they can be useful to other company departments as well.

Chapter Sixteen

THE CARE AND FEEDING OF CUSTOMERS

Customers are the company's treasures. They should be guarded and protected just as jealously as gold and silver or precious gems. Almost every company pays lip service to this concept: "Our customers are our most important asset." Unfortunately, many companies act as if they don't believe their own propaganda. This is the way they behave:

1. Their marketing and sales energies are primarily devoted to attracting new customers rather than preserving and nurturing the ones they already have.

2. Their advertising dollars and promotional campaigns are directed toward people and companies who have never used their products.

3. Their salespeople spend the majority of their time calling on and developing new prospects rather than ensuring that loyal customers remain satisfied.

4. Their management strategies concentrate on entering new markets.

These activities aren't wrong. Finding new customers is vital to the growth of any company, but they are not as important as taking good care, make that *excellent* care, of the organization's existing customer base. The salesperson who chases a new prospect with a $20,000 order potential, but ignores an existing customer who consistently produces $100,000 a year in business is more than foolish. He or she is engaged in career suicide.

EIGHT REASONS WHY REPEAT BUSINESS IS VITAL TO ANY COMPANY'S SURVIVAL

1. Mature sales territories will produce a combination of new and repeat business. In most instances, repeat business will produce the greater sales volume. The company counts on this repeat business when setting up sales targets for a new fiscal period. If most existing customers aren't retained, the plan fails.

2. Customers arc difficult to acquire. Each customer signed up represents all the failures, all the cold calling, all the prospecting, all the rejections that occurred before success was achieved. Companies who ignore their customers risk throwing this work away.

3. No company can grow without keeping a large percentage of its existing customer base. The company that finds new customers but loses old ones is like one of those gerbils running endlessly inside a wheel: Much energy is wasted going nowhere. The company may be building a tower, but towers require a solid foundation. The existing customer base is that foundation. Each customer lost is like a brick removed from the base. If enough bricks are removed, the tower crumbles.

4. For most companies, existing customers are the best source for new business. Customers already have confidence in their reliable vendors and the products these vendors offer. They are more open when new applications are discussed. That's why time spent with customers is never wasted.

5. The company that consistently loses a large percentage of its customers develops a bad reputation in the marketplace. The word gets out: "Oh, we tried Acme. They made a lot of promises, but we never saw them much after the order was signed."

6. The company that has a good reputation among its customers will acquire additional customers through word of mouth. One of the best prospecting methods is to develop a reputation for service and keeping promises.

7. Loyal customers are the best source for candid appraisals of the product line. They will tell the company which features are most useful, when the competition appears to be mounting a real challenge, and what is needed on the next generation of equipment to make it more useful.

8. Maintaining customers denies them to the competition. This prevents the competition from growing stronger. Keeping customers and acquiring new ones is the way to increase market share. When ignoring a good account, even one that appears well satisfied and "locked in," salespeople should remember that their good customers are the competition's appetizing targets. The competition isn't ignoring them.

How much time should be spent with customers

There is no mathematical formula that defines the amount of time that should be spent servicing existing customers. That will depend on the needs of the customer. Many salespeople allocate their time depending upon the number of customers they have on the books and the amount of business these customers produce.

In companies offering big-ticket items, such as IBM, a salesperson may be assigned to cover a single very large account. In some instances, these large accounts produce millions of dollars in yearly business. The salesperson may have an office or desk located on the customer's premises. The focus will be on protecting existing contracts, but the account rep is expected to write new business through upgrading equipment and finding different applications for the company's products.

One key to the amount of time needed to service an account is whether the customer is satisfied with the coverage. When customers feel ignored, they're likely to stray. Accounts won't usually acknowledge that they feel ignored—until they start doing business with the competition.

Six things to cover on calls
to existing customers

So how can salespeople know if they're spending enough time servicing their customers? They should take customer service out of the context of hours spent and put it in terms of things that need to get done. Enough time should be spent with customers to make sure that the following things are accomplished:

1. The salesperson should make sure that the customer is well satisfied with the product. This means the salesperson should not only call on management, but time should be spent with the customer's employees who actually use the product. The point-of-use is where complaints usually begin.

2. The salesperson should make sure the customer has no logistical complaints. Administrative problems cannot be ignored. An incorrect invoice, a return credit that didn't get processed, or a back order that didn't get shipped when promised all can be sources of irritation that override the customer's satisfaction with the product. The salesperson has a role as the customer's ombudsman who handles these minor problems.

Handling problems for customers requires more involvement than simply referring them to somebody on the administrative staff, and then running off to chase a rainbow. It means following up and staying with the problem until there is a resolution. Remember, the problem becomes truly serious when the customer feels the need to complain a second time.

3. The salesperson should make sure to establish a personal relationship with a decision-maker on the customer's staff. Both sides benefit from this kind of relationship because it permits candor and "horse trading."

4. The salesperson should make sure the competition hasn't made inroads. If the customer represents a substantial amount of business, of course the competition will come calling. Sniping is to be expected. The important question to be answered is, Is the customer listening to what the competition has to say? The customer will reveal interest in a competitive product or company in a variety of ways, for example, "A salesman for Consolidated told me their product is thirty percent more energy efficient than yours. Is that true?"

5. The salesperson should make sure that the customer is informed about other applications for the product. This means conversations with other departments, new investigations and surveys, demonstrations, and proposals. In other words, the salesperson should be engaged in the kind of activity related to developing and selling a new prospect. The difference is that prospects who are currently customers are easier to sell because they already know the company can deliver on its promises.

6. The salesperson should take care to learn the customer's management hierarchy and method of doing business. If the contact at the customer company needs approval from upstairs to place an order, the salesperson should help obtain that approval.

WHY THE FIRST ORDER TO A NEW CUSTOMER IS THE MOST IMPORTANT ORDER

Many salespeople feel their job is completed when the prospect signs on the dotted line and is magically transformed into a customer. Those with this attitude often wonder why so many of the outfits they worked so hard to sign up never place repeat orders.

The continuing relationship between two organizations often depends upon how the first order is handled. The new customer may have signed an order form or issued a purchase order, but the vendor company is still on trial as far as they're concerned, until the goods have been delivered and pronounced satisfactory by the users.

It's up to the salesperson to make sure this satisfaction occurs. The work begins when the order is signed. This is a critical moment. The salesperson's behavior over the next few minutes can determine whether the order is likely to be a one-shot deal, never to be repeated, or if a long-term relationship has just been established. Here's what should happen:

1. The salesperson should go over the terms of the agreement. The commitments made by both parties should be clearly understood.

2. The salesperson should tell the new customer what will happen next: "I've checked inventory and we have the items in stock. You're a new customer, so this order will take about a week to process. It should be shipped from our Las Vegas warehouse by truck about next Tuesday or Wednesday."

3. The salesperson should find a reason to return in the near future to take some action related to the order: "I'll come back tomorrow and check with your warehouse people to see if they want this stuff delivered on pallets." This immediate follow-up on a minor detail assures the new customer that he or she won't be abandoned just because the deal has been consummated.

4. The salesperson should go over the nitty-gritty details to make sure that the order is correct. This procedure is particularly important if the customer uses its own purchase order form. Here's a sample check list:

- Are the prices right?
- Are the quantities and model numbers confirmed?

- Are the "ship to" and "bill to" addresses right?
- Who is paying for freight? Are the right FOB terms listed?
- Has the customer listed the proper prompt payment discount? (This one is very important to check. Many purchasing departments will try to sneak larger discounts than the company allows.)
- Has all the necessary paperwork been submitted along with the order?
- If the new customer is applying for credit, does the credit application include all the data required for the credit department to make a decision?

5. The salesperson should thank the customer for the order and get out. There should be no celebration, at least not in the customer's office, as if a victory has been won. The customer will begin to wonder if a mistake was made. It is okay, however, to look pleased.

What should happen after an order for a new customer is submitted

Salespeople who submit orders to the company for new customers and immediately run off to attend to other business are giving hostages to fortune. Most mistakes happen on first orders because there is no past record of business between the two organizations. Everything has to be entered for the first time. Here's what the salesperson can do to reduce the number of mistakes:

1. The salesperson should keep a copy of the order for reference. If there are questions related to the order the salesperson can refer to the copy rather than relying on memory. Verbal orders should never be accepted from new customers. They are prescriptions for disaster.

2. The salesperson should learn enough about the company's internal procedures to know the path the order will follow. The department or person responsible for order entry should be called. Here's a standard checklist:

- Was the order received?
- Is the pricing okay?
- Is the product available?
- Has the edited order been forwarded to credit?
- What is the estimated time of delivery?
- Are there any foreseeable problems?

Some companies use order acknowledgments, with copies of the entered order sent to the salesperson and the customer. They are excellent for catching any mistakes in interpretation before they have a chance to do any damage. We recommend this procedure, particularly for custom-made products.

3. If there are any changes from what the salesperson has told the new customer, for example, shipping will take two weeks rather than one, the new information should be relayed to the customer immediately. Follow Henry Kissinger's advice: "What must be revealed eventually should be revealed immediately."

4. The salesperson should check with the company periodically to make sure the order is on schedule.

What should happen when an order for a new customer is shipped

First, the salesperson should be on top of the situation and know when an order to a new customer is shipped. After the order leaves the plant or warehouse, the salesperson should take the following steps:

1. The salesperson should call the customer and supply the shipping data: "Good news, Mrs. Jones. Your order went out from our warehouse via Acme Freight this morning. The waybill number is 111222."

2. The salesperson should check with the customer to make sure the order is delivered on schedule. If it's late, an inquiry should be made with the freight company.

3. When the order has been delivered, the salesperson should check with the customer to make sure that everything is satisfactory. That means a visit to the customer's site and speaking with both the decision-maker and the actual users. If instruction or training is needed for the product, that should be scheduled according to the customer's request.

4. Any complaints or problems should be attended to immediately. If, for example, the product arrived damaged, a return for credit should be processed even before the customer requests it.

This procedure is the best way to ensure that a new customer will become a repeat customer.

The never-ending battle between sales and credit: Why they're both on the side of the angels

When orders for new customers are delayed, the usual reason is because they are tied up in the credit department. This is a natural bottleneck. The company has no history of doing business with the new customer and it's up to the credit department to make sure that payment will be made. No order is really complete until the company has been paid for its merchandise.

What frustrates salespeople is that credit managers are slow in granting credit to new accounts, insisting first on what seems to be an inordinate amount of paperwork related to the new customer. The common complaint by salespeople is that new customers are regarded by the credit department as criminal suspects.

What frustrates credit managers is that salespeople seldom provide enough information on which to make an intelligent credit decision. They submit incomplete credit applications, don't include profit-and-loss statements, ignore bank and trade references, and insist on approval and shipment to strangers of thousands of dollars in merchandise within twenty-four hours.

The result is that salespeople clamor that orders be released and credit managers stand firm until trade and bank references can be checked.

The intramural struggle is intensified because that first order shipped to a new customer often sets the tone for the entire relationship. Sales managers and sales crew members are anxious to prove that the company provides good, responsive service. That's difficult to do when that first order is hung up in credit.

The solution is easy. The new customer is an unknown quantity. Salespeople must give the credit department the information they need to make a rational decision. If the new customer turns out to be a deadbeat, the credit department, not the sales department gets called on the carpet by the company's chief financial officer.

Seven facts the credit department wants to know about a new customer

Smart salespeople make the credit department's job easier. Here's the kind of information that will make credit applications sail through credit.

1. Credit wants a *completed* credit application. "Does that hold true for General Motors?" the salesperson sarcastically asks. Why not? Salespeople should not be embarrassed to ask even a Fortune 1000 firm for credit data. Large corporations have boilerplate hand-out sheets for vendors that should satisfy the most cautious credit manager.

2. Credit wants a copy of the customer's balance sheet. A small outfit whose balance sheet is not available because it's "being updated right now by our accountant" is suspect. Even accounts in this situation can be given credit if other data is available. The salesperson should ask for a copy of the last period's balance sheet. The name of the customer's accountant should also be passed along to the credit manager. It's very helpful for salespeople to learn how to read balance sheets. When it's obvious that credit won't be granted, the salesperson should ask for cash or check with the order. The account may appear to be offended, but companies who have bad credit know it.

3. The credit department wants the name of the new customer's bank. Banks provide a reliable guide to the customer's financial stability.

4. The credit department wants the names of trade references. Payment histories are important. Other trade creditors can provide this information.

5. The credit department wants to know how long the customer has been in business. A start-up company is suspect because it has no credit history.

6. The credit department wants to know the size of the initial order. Most credit managers are unwilling to provide a huge amount of credit for a new customer's first crack out of the box. They'd rather wait see how the payment pattern develops.

7. The credit department wants to know if anyone from the company has actually visited the customer's premises. Eyeballing the new customer's location is important because fraud is becoming a significant problem in business. Phantom companies order goods which are delivered to drop locations where they disappear.

Give this information to credit and decisions will be made much faster.

One "fact" that doesn't cut any ice with credit

One bit of information that doesn't cut any ice with credit is the customer's claim that "I have a million-dollar line of credit with Acme." When this information is passed along, the credit manager will just dismiss it.

The manager isn't being a jerk. For one thing, there's no guarantee the account actually has a million-dollar line of credit with another vendor. For another, the reason that customer is so anxious to do business with your company may be because that line of credit has been exhausted. Accounts that owe other companies large amounts of money aren't good credit risks.

HOW TO GET CREDIT APPROVAL ON A REALLY BIG DEAL

Salespeople who close blockbuster deals representing big bucks are often frustrated by the amount of time the order spends in credit before it is approved. If delivery is on a tight deadline, these delays can be critical and could get the deal canceled.

This problem can be eliminated with a little advance planning on the part of the salesperson. Big deals don't happen overnight. They take time to percolate. During the negotiation stage, the salesperson can prepare credit that a blockbuster order is pending. Credit information for the potential customer can be submitted in advance. If there's likely to be a problem, credit terms can be part of the negotiation: "For an order this size, we'll need twenty percent in advance." When the order does happen, everyone knows what comes next.

HOW REPEAT ORDERS SHOULD BE HANDLED

Many salespeople don't use the same amount of care when processing and checking up on repeat orders as they do with new accounts. This is just plain foolish, because repeat business will usually represent the major portion of their income. It should be carefully protected. Here is how:

1. The salesperson should avoid verbal orders. If the customer is really in a rush for the product, they can expedite the purchase order through their system or take the time to sign the salesperson's order pad.

2. The details on the order should be carefully checked. The company may have been shipping to one address for years, but one order will suddenly indicate shipment to a different warehouse or location.

3. The salesperson should still check on when the order will be shipped. The customer should be informed of any possible delays.

4. The salesperson should occasionally check to see if the product's users are still satisfied. The customer's personnel moves can quickly change a situation. A supporter can be replaced by an enemy. A customer staff member may need to be retrained.

5. The salespeople should not take the customer, or any order the customer places, for granted. Servicing existing accounts well is the real key to growth.

FOUR THINGS TO DO WHEN A CUSTOMER CONTACTS A NON-SALES TYPE

Long-term customers eventually become familiar with people in the home office. They may learn the names of employees in the credit department, in engineering, in order processing, and in shipping, among others. It is often easier for the customer to contact one of these individuals rather then try to get in touch with the sales rep, who may be in the field making calls.

Problems can develop with these contacts because the office employees may not know the full extent of agreements made between the salesperson and the customer. For example, a credit clerk looking at the customer's credit limit may assume that an order is on hold, pending payment of an outstanding balance, when the sales rep has made arrangements with the credit manager to raise the customer's line of credit. To keep problems of this sort at a minimum (they never can be completely eliminated) home office people should do the following:

1. Refer as many calls as possible back to the salesperson handling the account. It's the salesperson's job to be the go-between. The customer may be impatient for an answer, but a few hours rarely make any difference.

2. Don't offer information that hasn't been requested. It may be necessary to tell a customer that an order is on hold. Explaining that the reason for the delay is because the company's assembly line has just shut down is the salesperson's responsibility.

3. Report any conversations with customers back to the salesperson. Let the salesperson know when the customer has placed an order directly with the office, if the customer has reported a problem with the product, or if a question has been asked of engineering.

4. Never become angry with a customer no matter the provocation. The customer may have a legitimate reason to be angry with the company.

Chapter Seventeen

SELLING TO MAJOR ACCOUNTS AND GOVERNMENT AGENCIES

Major accounts are the big leagues, the Fortune 1000 companies, the giants of industry. Sales to these companies mean bigger orders, juicier commission checks, and a more prestigious customer list. Even credit managers prefer doing business with major accounts because these customers always pay their bills.

Obviously, most companies would like to have major accounts as customers, but they're not easy to sell. For one thing, the competition is fierce. Call on any major corporation and the lobby will be crowded with sales types. For another, big companies recognize their buying clout. They make heavy demands on their suppliers, and they're cautious about entering new relationships. Once satisfied with a vendor, however, they are usually loyal as long as that vendor continues to perform.

NINE THINGS MAJOR ACCOUNTS EXPECT FROM THEIR SUPPLIERS

Despite the fierce competition, major accounts can be sold by vendors who deliver what they want—and what they want isn't all that surprising. The following is a short list:

1. What major accounts value most in a supplier is reliability. Price is always important, but it is usually secondary to the supplier's history of delivering good products on schedule.

2. Major accounts prefer doing business with other companies in their own class. They may set up special programs to encourage small business vendors, but big purchases will usually be awarded to other large companies.

3. Major accounts have their own agendas. They know the projects they wish to address and the problems they'd like to solve. They want suppliers who are tuned to this same wavelength. A great cost-saving idea pitched to a major account may not excite them because their energies are directed elsewhere.

4. Major accounts trust the devil they know as opposed to the devil they don't know. The incumbent is always in a strong position with Fortune 1000 companies. If the supplier has been used successfully before, there's little risk for the decision-maker in using that supplier again. That supplier is a known factor.

5. Major accounts are impressed by industry name recognition. Managers from major corporations prefer doing business with those companies who have solid reputations within the industry.

6. Major accounts value financial stability. A strong balance sheet always helps when soliciting the high and mighty. They want to do business with companies who are going to be around tomorrow, next month, and next year.

7. Major accounts require their vendors to possess the ability to service or maintain the product on a national basis. Large corporations often do business in many locations. They prefer vendors who can provide the same level of service in New York City and Boise, Idaho.

8. Major accounts demand fair pricing in line with the quantity purchased. They won't normally negotiate pricing that cuts all profits out of a deal, but their purchasing departments will insist that their pricing be at least as good as others who buy in those quantities. But heaven help the vendor if the major account discovers that another customer has received more favorable terms.

9. Major accounts revere no-problem relationships. This writer once sold point-of-sale equipment to Sears. The contract was a good one and it was renewed year after year. At one negotiating session, the senior purchasing agent told me, "The reason you guys keep getting the business is that I never hear any complaints."

Any commercial customer wants to hear the above from their suppliers. Establish a no-complaint relationship and keep your major account customer.

DEVELOPING A BIG-LEAGUE ATTITUDE WHEN SELLING TO MAJOR ACCOUNTS

The actual selling job to major accounts requires a different approach than with other types of customers. Forget about razzle-dazzle, high-pressure methods and the one-call close. These tactics are counterproductive in almost all major account situations. The following are tactics that will work:

1. The first requirement in major account selling is patience. Don't expect too much too soon. This patience must be reflected by everyone in the organization from the executives at the top to the people on the firing line. The manager who asks where the orders are after a salesperson has made two or three calls to a major account just doesn't understand the process.

2. Major account selling is multilevel. The salesperson must be prepared to call on many different departments and speak to both managers and product users in these departments.

3. Product knowledge is important when calling on major accounts. The salespeople who are successful with major accounts become information sources for the account. They understand their company's products and their products' applications as they relate to the customer. Industry knowledge and industry success are also important. If the company's products are used by other organizations in the same industry as the major account, they are likely to be more interested.

4. Major accounts insist on a level of service consistent with their volume of business. They want problems to be handled immediately. They expect their account reps to drop everything when they call.

5. The single most important factor in selling major accounts is an understanding of how their organizations work. Bureaucracies may not seem important, but try fighting against them. There's no point in trying to sell a product to a department head who doesn't have the budget to buy it this year.

Calling on major accounts:
Finding decision-makers

Calling on major accounts can be compared to walking through a maze with endless blind alleys. It's difficult to find out just who makes the decisions on many products. Department heads hide behind their phone mail. No wonder! If they talked to every salesperson who called, they wouldn't have time to do their jobs. Purchasing, whose job it is to talk to salespeople, will claim to make the decisions, but frequently, they merely execute the requisitions of the actual product users. The major account salesperson must rely on logic and experience with other companies when deciding whom to target for calls. For example, the salesperson selling shelving might target the warehouse manager. Decision-making responsibility at a major account may not always be obvious to an outsider. The four levels of decision making at most major accounts are:

1. *The senior-level executives or strategists.* These are the people at the top responsible for long-range planning and plotting the company's course. They make very few product-buying decisions, except for those that have a major impact on the corporation. You can bet the people in the executive suite at Ford will decide whose steel they will be putting in their cars next year.

2. *The V.P.s and others just below the top level.* These managers are responsible for carrying out strategy. They don't make many product-buying decisions either, but they often review decisions made by those middle-level managers who report to them.

3. *The department heads and other third-level management people.* These are the major account salesperson's primary contacts because they make most of the decision on the countless products purchased by major corporations. They are responsible for the department's operating budgets. A good tactic for a major account salesperson is to concentrate on the manager who has the budgetary responsibility.

4. *The purchasing agents and buyers.* These people make purchasing decisions on most commodity items and they execute the requisitions of department heads on other products. They have no budgets, except for those funds which are necessary to operate their own department. Purchasing doesn't define which products are needed, but it is this department's responsibility to make sure that the corporation has bought at the best price.

SETTING UP A MAJOR-ACCOUNT SALES TEAM

Many companies establish a separate sales team to handle sales to big corporations and to government agencies. These teams often operate independently of the regular sales organization, though management may be the same for both groups. Separate major account sales teams are established because:

1. The sales cycle to these organizations is much longer than with middle- and small-sized companies. It may take up a year to romance and close a major account. It takes individuals used to the rhythms of major accounts to be successful.

2. The profit margins on major account sales are often much smaller because of the potential large-volume orders. On some government bid situations, there may be almost no profit at all. It makes sense to put salespeople working these accounts on different compensation plans. In some instances, these compensation plans are more heavily weighted toward salary rather than commission.

3. More than any other area of selling, the major account program requires seasoned sales pros. The stakes are too big, the potential contracts too lucrative, and the battleground too littered with minefields, to make major accounts a training ground for apprentices.

Responsibilities of a major-account sales team

The definition of what constitutes a major account varies from company to company, but for most organizations, the major account team will be charged with the following responsibilities:

1. Sales to very large corporations with multiple divisions or locations.
2. Sales to federal government agencies, including the military.
3. Sales to state and local government agencies.
4. Sales to institutions such as public school districts, colleges, and universities.

GETTING PAST THE RECEPTIONIST: FOUR STRATEGIES TO GET THAT IMPORTANT FIRST APPOINTMENT WITH A MAJOR ACCOUNT

Decision-makers at major accounts often, out of necessity, develop a defensive posture and make themselves unavailable to all but the most persistent and the most creative salespeople. Just getting past their phone mail is a chore in itself, and, once past that hurdle, the decision-maker is likely to deny an appointment by pleading an impossible work schedule. The following is a short list of approaches that major account salespeople often use to stimulate a major account prospect's interest:

1. They offer something absolutely brand spanking new that no one in the industry has. Many prospects will be curious to learn more about the new whizbang.

2. They recite a success story in a similar industry: "Big Green Corporation just installed this equipment and saved eight thousand dollars the first month. I can show you how they did it and provide some names at their shop for verification."

3. They display obvious expertise. Major accounts like to speak to those who are knowledgeable about the industry and who are willing to share that knowledge. If the salesperson's pitch indicates product and application knowledge, an appointment may be granted so the prospect can do a bit of brain picking.

4. They display insider industry information. This almost overlaps the expertise category, but they're really two different things. The industry insider is active in the trade association, is familiar with the names of the players, is prominent at the national convention, serves on panels and committees, and so forth. Appointments have been granted just so the prospect can learn the latest gossip. A tightrope must be walked here. The salesperson can't reveal proprietary information learned when working with other industry accounts.

AVOIDING CONFLICTS BETWEEN MAJOR-ACCOUNT SALESPEOPLE AND THE REGULAR SALES CREW

When companies do develop major-account sales teams, jealousies often develop between these individuals and members of the regular sales crew. This friction is only natural. When a major-account team is established, territory people are told their juiciest prospects are now off limits. It doesn't matter that the prospects haven't been sold, the possibility of selling them has suddenly been eliminated.

Conflict can be avoided if the territory salespeople are credited with any sales from major accounts within their area of responsibility. Even if the commission rate is much smaller, receiving sales credit changes attitudes from one of resistance to cooperation.

SIX THINGS TO CONSIDER WHEN SETTING UP A MAJOR-ACCOUNT PROGRAM

Setting up a major-account program is a way to build sales volume. There are, however, some hard questions that must be asked and answered before the program can be put into operation. These questions are:

1. How will the potential major accounts be contacted across the country? Will the company's regular sales staff be used, or will specialists be hired?

2. What special value-added programs can the company offer to major accounts? In other words, why should the big fish do business with the company?

3. Will special pricing be available to major accounts? If so, who will be responsible for preparing bids, quotations, and proposals?

4. How will accounts with multiple locations be serviced? Who will call on these locations and how will any installed equipment be maintained?

5. How will local salespeople, dealers, and distributors be compensated if a major account is sold within their territories?

6. How will inter-territorial deals be handled for compensation purposes when the decision is made in one location and the product shipped to another?

SWEATING THE DETAILS: WHAT COMPANIES MUST DO TO MAKE MAJOR ACCOUNTS FEEL COMFORTABLE

Large companies are always apprehensive about doing business with new vendors. Six steps to develop a "comfort index" for major accounts are:

1. Formulate a uniform major-account policy. The policy demonstrates that the company is serious about acquiring and keeping major-account business. (The cynic might suggest that the policy statement is merely a laundry list of the concessions the company is prepared to make to win major account business.)

2. Develop a special, uniform pricing policy. This policy should take into account the higher volumes that major accounts sometimes require. Hint: Good prices are important to major accounts. Rock bottom prices are not.

3. Demonstrate a national-service capability. Large companies want to know that the product can be serviced no matter where it is installed. If national service is beyond the scope of the company, make arrangements with one of the third-party service outfits.

4. Guarantee parts availability. Fortune 1000 customers want to be sure what they buy today can be repaired several years down the road. This is also true for sales to the federal government. To get a product on GSA schedule, parts availability must be guaranteed for seven years.

5. Provide record keeping. This service could include keeping track of the customer's product inventory levels, reordering schedules, and sales made to the account's other corporate divisions or branch locations.

6. Provide a single source of contact. The major account customer wants an ombudsman within the vendor company who will address complaints, expedite orders, and generally serve as an advocate for the customer's point of view.

7. Make it easy for the major account to do business. Don't let orders, invoices, returns for credits, repairs, and so forth get caught up in the company's bureaucracy. Some companies set up online order entry systems so the customer's purchasing office can enter orders directly into the company's computer system.

A SAMPLE EIGHT-POINT MAJOR-ACCOUNT POLICY STATEMENT

A major-account policy statement is a summary of the promises made by the company to its major-account customers. The following one is applicable to most industries.

We guarantee the following to our major account customers:

1. Prompt deliveries. Major accounts receive preferential delivery on back-ordered or scarce items.

2. Most current factory production schedules. Major accounts receive factory-fresh equipment. They will never be shipped obsolete models, unless these models have been specifically requested.

3. Deliveries by qualified installers. All installations will be made by company-trained personnel.

4. Prompt service by trained technicians. Any required service will be handled by company-trained technicians within twenty-four hours of notification.

5. Price protection. The company guarantees the price offered to major account customers will be the lowest available for the quantity ordered.

6. Service and availability on parts. The company will maintain an adequate parts inventory for all products purchased by the major account.

7. Single-source responsibility. The company will provide an account executive who will be responsible for maintaining contact and for the resolution of any problems that should arise.

8. Customer record keeping. The company shall furnish a quarterly record of all units purchased.

How major accounts are lost

When one company acquires a major account, another company has just lost an important customer. Careless! What factors cause companies to switch suppliers? The following are some common causes:

1. *Lack of service.* It's crazy, but some salespeople will sign up a major account and then just take the orders from that customer for granted. All customers want to feel that their business is appreciated. Major accounts are even more demanding. They want to feel they are treasured.

2. *An unwillingness to make things right.* One of the most frequent causes of major account switching is a squabble about product performance, a disagreement about service, or a stonewalling bureaucracy. Squabbles can escalate, egos become involved, and the letter of the contract invoked by both sides. Righteous indignation flares like sunspots. Both sides stand on principle, but only one side, the vendor, loses the business.

3. *Uneven dealing.* If a major account learns that another company is getting the benefit of a better price for the same product at the same quantity, look out.

4. *Changes.* When a vendor changes something, such as phases out a product the customer loved, moves production to a new plant, substitute one material for another, assigns a different person to the account, raises prices, reduces a discount, and so forth, the customer may decide it's time to reevaluate the relationship. Any change not anticipated by the customer is a risk for the supplier.

5. *Bureaucracy.* The more difficult it is to do business with the company, the more likely the major account will eventually find a more acquiescent supplier. Sure, the major account has its own rules and regulations which may be just as rigid, but they are the customer.

Rule to live by: Companies prefer to do business with those vendors with whom it is easy to do business.

BLANKET ORDERS

Prices to major accounts are sometimes based on the total quantity of the product they commit to purchase over a specified period of time. For example, the major account may issue a blanket order for one thousand units of a product to be taken over a twelve-month period. Releases are made against this order as the customer needs the product. The advantage to the vendor is that the blanket order commits the customer to take a large quantity, it keeps the competition at bay, and it allows lower pricing than would otherwise be possible. The advantage to the customer is that the price is guaranteed for a long period and no single big shipments are required that result in large invoices and tie up warehouse space.

The problems occur when the customer is too optimistic about requirements for the product and doesn't take the specified quantity within the order's time frame. The customer has, in essence, received a higher quantity discount than earned. Most blanket orders carry a provision for backbilling when this happens, but backbilling a customer for products already received and paid for is one way to sour a relationship fast. Most companies will simply ignore the shortfall and ask their customers to be more realistic when placing the next blanket order.

SELLING TO GOVERNMENT AGENCIES

Selling to government agencies is a quick way to build sales volume. The government uses just about everything. Uncle Sam is the largest purchaser of goods and services in the world. Local governments also consume large quantities of all types of products.

Unlike major account sales, being a small- or medium-sized company isn't necessarily a handicap to doing business with the government, and frequently it can be an advantage.

Five types of government agencies

Government agencies come in five distinct "species." They are:

1. *The federal government.* This category includes all the countless federal government offices, the military establishment, the Post Office, the Veteran's Administration, and much else. Federal contracts are awarded by the General Services Administration (GSA), but many purchases are also made on a local basis.

2. *State governments*. Every state government has a procurement agency, which is usually headquartered in the state capital. Some of these governments purchase more goods and services than medium-size countries. California, for example, has an economy which, if separated from the nation, would be the sixth largest in the world. Their annual purchases reflect this economic strength.

3. *County governments*. These agencies also maintain procurement offices which purchase goods and services, although some counties will "piggy-back" off state contracts.

4. *Municipal governments*. Big and small cities alike offer excellent selling opportunities for many different business and products.

5. *Schools*. Although not technically government agencies, educational institutions are frequently lumped in the same category because they are bureaucratic establishments and they often purchase products in the same manner (via competitive bid) as government agencies.

SELLING TO THE GENERAL SERVICES ADMINISTRATION (GSA)

The GSA is the primary purchasing agent for all federal government civilian agencies. Its purpose is to negotiate the lowest possible price for products and services used by these agencies. It does this by negotiating pricing schedules, called GSA schedules, with various suppliers.

It is very desirable for companies to have a product on GSA schedule because it means that any federal agency with money in its budget may purchase the product if there is a demonstrated need for it. There is no haggling over price.

To get a product on GSA schedule the company must meet the following two conditions:

1. Prove that the product has been commercially successful. The company must show that sales for the specific product offered have been made and that it has been accepted by the marketplace.

2. The company must offer the lowest possible price. The publicity about $2,000 coffeepots aside, the GSA is a tough negotiator. Don't expect to sell a product for one dollar to private industry and two dollars to the GSA.

The negotiation process may take several months. There are pages of forms to fill out, and the federal buyers will want detailed information on the company's costs and pricing offered to others.

Getting a product on GSA contract does not, in itself, guarantee the company any sales, but it does allow the company representatives to approach government agencies and offer the product. Without a GSA contract, there is simply no point. In effect, a GSA contract is a hunting license.

COMPETITIVE BIDDING

Competitive bidding is used by most government agencies, and many educational institutions, when the goods and services they require exceeds a certain dollar figure. The idea is to give every qualified company a chance at the business while ensuring that the agency gets the best possible price.

For the federal government, any purchase that exceeds $25,000 will trigger the bid process. For other agencies, the amount that triggers a bid varies.

One of the fascinating aspects of the bid process is that winners of lucrative contracts are decided in a single afternoon when the bids are opened. One day a company may be struggling to keep its doors open. The next day, they could be awarded a big contract that triples their sales volume.

LEARNING ABOUT BID OPPORTUNITIES

Outside the federal government, every state, every county, every city, and many schools use competitive bids to purchase products. The problem for small- and medium-size companies is learning about the many available bid opportunities. As with many things, the key is knowing where to look. There are many sources to access. They include:

1. *Daily newspapers.* Most government agencies are required by law to advertise their bid opportunities.

2. *The Commerce Business Daily.* The GSA advertises their procurement requirements above $25,000 in this daily publication. It's available in most libraries. Subscriptions can be obtained by writing the Superintendent of Documents at the Government Printing Office in Washington, D.C.

3. *The purchasing offices of government agencies.* The bulletin boards at government agencies will be posted with bid opportunities.

4. *Bidding information and bid registry services.* Bid-alert services, such as BidNet out of Rockville, Maryland, publish newsletters listing hundreds of new bid opportunities every month. Bid registry services, such as Information Handling Services out of Englewood, Colorado, will, for a fee, list a company's products in a directory on floppy disks, the Internet, and the World Wide Web. The directory is then made available to government procurement officers.

5. *From government solicitations.* Agencies will send out Requests for Quotations (RFQs) to companies on their approved vendors list. To get on such a list, write the appropriate agency and request it.

6. *From calling on government agencies and school buyers.* The best way to learn about pending bid opportunities is to make sales calls on those buyers within the agency responsible for purchasing the kind of products the company offers. The advantage to these calls is that the company will often receive advance knowledge of the bid, and conversations with the buyer may help shape the specifications.

THE FIVE STEPS IN THE BID PROCESS

Various agencies use different methods and they apply different standards when requesting competitive bids. The bid process itself, however, is remarkably similar. Here's how it usually works:

1. The agency requiring the product will draw up a list of specifications. These specs will detail the equipment required including acceptable models, size, weight, speed of operation, capacity, and so forth.

2. The agency's purchasing department will send out to qualified bidders a document called Request for Bid (RFB). In addition to specifications, the RFB will list the quantity of product required, delivery dates, installation, training, warranty, service support, and so forth.

3. The RFB will also contain a due date, including the time of day when all bids will be opened.

4. One minute after the due date and time, the bidding closes. Late bids are considered nonresponsive. One of the first things that new bidders must learn is that promptness is vital. No government agency—federal, state or local—will accept a late bid.

5. The agency opens all bids and reviews them for completeness. (Reviewing bids for completeness before submitting them is very important.) Many bids are rejected because they failed to meet a requirement listed in the specs, such as including a list of service locations. The contract is awarded to the company bidding the lowest price whose product meets all the specification requirements.

Companies who are not familiar to the agency may have to prove they are qualified to handle the job.

"Specmanship"—the key to winning bids

In competitive bidding, if the specifications favor the company's product, the chances for winning the bid are greatly enhanced. Major account reps can influence the specs by visiting with the buyers and actual product users, demonstrating the product, and offering suggestions on product features that make sense to the agency. If they like the feature, they'll put in the specs. This hand can be overplayed, however, by suggesting product features that no other vendor can meet. The procurement office wants a bidding situation that is open to multiple vendors.

Sole-source contracts versus multiple-award contracts

Contracts offered for bid by government agencies are generally of two types:

- Sole source.
- Multiple awards.

The sole-source contract is considered much more valuable to the vendor because the agency agrees to buy the entire quantity of the needed product from a single source, the winning bidder. The vendor has, in effect, a lock on a quantity or a period of time during which the agency will order his product exclusively.

Many state governments use multiple-award contracts. In these contracts several vendors may be selected to provide the product over a period of time. For example, the state may place four or five vendors on its annual facsimile machine contract. The price is negotiated, but the quantity is not. There are no guarantees by the state that even a single unit will be sold. Agencies within the state that have requirements for fax machines are allowed to choose from any vendor on the multiple award. That makes multiple-award contracts essentially a license to hunt for business. The companies which benefit the most are those that make the calls and show the product.

TELEPHONE BIDS

When the quantity required for a product is small, many local government agencies resort to a process called "telephone bidding." In this process, the buyer will call three vendors for the product, ask them for their best price, and give the order to the one that quotes the lowest number. The transaction is entirely verbal and takes but a few minutes. It is legal when the dollar volume for an order is under a certain figure. The exact amount that triggers a telephone bid varies from agency to agency. The way to get the opportunity for this kind of business is to become known to buyers at municipal and county governments.

DOING BUSINESS WITH THE GOVERNMENT VIA SUBCONTRACTING

Many companies with large government contracts are required, as a condition of the contract, to subcontract part of the work to small companies and women- or minority-owned firms. Outfits in this category include defense contractors. Their procurement officers actively seek qualified small companies they can place orders with to meet the conditions of their contracts. The procurement office at any defense contractor can provide details on specific opportunities in their organizations.

Pricing for competitive bids

Competitive bidding represents an opportunity to build sales volume quickly. The process is so competitive, however, that products must often be offered at very low margins. Companies that are successful at competitive bidding often strip any excess cost from the product before submitting their bottom-line numbers. They consider this business as the volume needed to help with the rent, pay the light bill, and keep the production line going.

What some companies do on very large contract opportunities is to subtract certain "burdens" normally attached to the product's costs when prices are determined. For example, the company may subtract advertising costs because government sales via competitive bidding really require no advertising.

Selling to the military

Many salespeople never approach military bases because they appear intimidating. They wouldn't know where to go once past the guards at the front gate. Yet, most military bases want to be good neighbors in the nearby community, and they have specific programs designed to purchase products from local merchants. The bases may even hold open houses in which local merchants are invited to display their products.

The way to approach a military base for the first time is to ask for the "small business officer." This person is designated by the base commander to work with vendors and help guide them toward sales opportunities.

Selling to schools

Most school districts use the competitive bid process for their major purchases. The bidding is done at the school-district level. Individual schools buy little, except for consumable supplies. For school districts such as Los Angeles Unified, the contracts awards can be for seven figures. The sales process is much the same as with government accounts:

- Get involved in specmanship.
- Learn about bid opportunities.
- Submit the lowest qualified bid and submit it on time.
- Make sure all the necessary paperwork is included.

Colleges and universities are not uniform in their purchasing habits. Individual departments normally decide which products they require. Their purchasing departments merely handle the paperwork. That means the selling to this market must be done department by department.

REQUEST FOR PROPOSAL

Some government agencies with special requirements, such as the Department of Defense, will write a request for proposal which will be sent to several qualified vendors. These proposals are often for complicated systems that require sophisticated engineering talent. The proposals are usually just the first step. After they have been submitted, the government agency will pit one vendor against another, picking and choosing the best parts of each proposal, request many changes, bully the vendors about pricing, and finally choose the one that has made the most concessions.

LIMITING BUSINESS FROM MAJOR ACCOUNTS AND GOVERNMENT AGENCIES

Both major accounts and government agencies can help a company build sales volume fast. The low-margin pricing and the special services they require, however, means that companies should not rely entirely on this kind of business. The business is also highly volatile. The volume can be lost as quickly as it was gained. That's why some companies don't want more than 20 percent of their total sales volume coming from these market segments. It's also a mistake to tie up a major portion of the company's production capacity in the orders provided by one or two very big customers. The company becomes the captive of these customers who demand ever more at each new contract. Companies in this position have few alternatives if the business is lost.

Chapter Eighteen

HOW TO SELL

WHY KNOWING HOW TO SELL IS USEFUL REGARDLESS OF YOUR JOB

Everybody sells, including those who believe sales is a contemptible profession. The truth is that, at one time or another, we all try to persuade others to take a certain course of action and that attempt at persuasion is selling.

The young man who "hits" on a girl for a date is selling himself.

The teacher who tries to convince students that her geometry class will impart useful knowledge is selling the need for attention and effort.

The manager who has an idea that will improve the department's performance must sell senior management on the payoff that will come from any required investment.

The tired, stay-at-home housewife with two kids will try to sell her husband on the benefits of dinner out tonight.

In the above examples, and countless others, all of us try to persuade others to take courses of action they may not have taken without our efforts. That's what selling is: attempting to move individuals or organizations to behave in certain ways that benefit us. The persuasion part is convincing the other party that the action we want them to take will also benefit them.

What the salesperson must defeat

The thing that works against every individual making every sales pitch is inertia. Inertia is a principle of physics that says a body will keep on moving in the direction it is moving unless some force comes along to make it move some other way. That physical law can be applied to individuals and organizations. They will keep on doing what they are used to doing unless some force comes along that makes them change. That force is the salesperson. The salesperson then is a prime mover, an instigator of events.

How the salesperson influences change

Even contemplating change requires energy. No one wants to spend energy unless they feel they will benefit. The salesperson as prime mover first finds the benefits of change and then describes them to the organization or individual he or she wants to influence. This description of the benefits of change is called persuasion.

How persuasion is used

Persuasion is not a black art. There is nothing magical, malevolent, or unethical about it. It doesn't hypnotize people into acting against their own self-interest. What it does do is to identify what their self-interest may be. People and companies alike can be persuaded to act in a certain way when they are convinced that action will benefit them. We're back to that all-important self-interest.

So here's the first rule of selling: Identify the prospect's (the person or company you're trying to persuade) self-interest, highlight how your proposition serves that self-interest, and the "sale" is made. This rule applies whether you're trying to persuade General Motors to use your company's steel in their cars, or whether you're trying to convince your wife that a weekly poker night with the boys will help her out because those guys are suckers and you'll come home with a pot full of money.

Here are a few examples of how persuasion is used in the workplace:

1. Persuasion is useful in convincing others of the organization of the brilliance of your ideas.

2. For managers, persuasion is necessary to fire up enthusiasm for the company's programs.
3. Persuasion helps motivate fellow employees or subordinates to excel.
4. Persuasive skills are handy when trying to convince the boss that you've done a darn good job.

How to find out what benefits the other side

The key to persuasion is finding out what will benefit the person or organization you're trying to persuade. In personal relationships this discovery process requires empathy, which means thinking and feeling like the other person. What would motivate you to take a certain action if you were in the other person's shoes? For those who find the answer, persuasion is duck soup.

Empathy also works when managers want to persuade their employees to behave in certain ways. That's one of the reason that managers who come up through the ranks often have an advantage over their counterparts who begin their careers in managerial positions. The bootstrappers know what is likely to motivate their workers.

When salespeople try to uncover what may benefit a company they are targeting, the discovery process is called probing. That's what surveys are all about. One of the things that makes this process easier is that what benefits one company in an industry is likely to benefit another. That's why success stories and referrals are important when selling. They testify to the benefits that others have received.

Benefits that companies find particularly attractive are sometimes called "hot buttons." The idea is to find the prospect's hot buttons and push them.

SALES TECHNIQUE

Sales technique is the entire process of finding the benefits of change and then communicating these benefits to the prospect. The key word here is communication:

1. Does the prospect understand the benefits of the proposition?
2. Does the prospect truly believe these benefits will occur?

There are an infinite variety of sales or communication techniques and they all are effective. They also all fail miserably. The trick is putting the right method together with the right personality. (As a sales attribute, glibness is much overrated.)

BELIEVABILITY AND HOW TO ACHIEVE IT

What creates believability is sincerity. The way to make people believe what you say is to first believe it yourself. Say what you know to be true and others will recognize that truth. It doesn't matter how well the message is delivered if the person receiving it doesn't believe what is said. Ever listen to some salesperson wax eloquently about a product or service, but fail to convince anyone to buy? What that "spellbinder" lacked was believability.

According to Queen Victoria's prime minister, Benjamin Disraeli, "There are three kinds of lies: lies, damned lies, and statistics." It isn't as simple as it sounds to always be truthful. It means:

- No half-truths.
- No evasions.
- No omissions.
- No disingenuous statements.
- No statistical claptrap.

HOW TO BEHAVE IN FRONT OF PROSPECTS AND CUSTOMERS

The impression a salesperson makes those first few minutes before a prospect or customer can affect the entire relationship. Indeed, those first few minutes often determine whether there is going to be a future relationship. The salesperson's work begins even before entering the prospect's office. He or she should be observing things such as:

1. If the office is ancient or modern.
2. The kind of office equipment used (this reflects their willingness to make investments in efficiency.).

3. The "tone" of the office and its workers (spirited, listless, frantic, extremely busy, sullen).
4. The amount of paperwork on employees' desks.
5. Any personal effects in the interviewer's office.

These "tells" may provide clues as to the personality of the prospect company and the individual contact.

When meeting a prospect for the first time, some salespeople like to begin the conversation by exchanging a pleasantry or observation to relax the situation. Do this if it is natural, but never adopt a style that is strained. Respect the prospect's time by quickly getting to the purpose of the call.

1. State your name and the name of your company.
2. Provide background information about the company if the prospect doesn't know it.
3. State the reason for the visit.
4. Talk about the product or service the company offers.
5. Ask questions to get the prospect talking about how his or her company uses that product. Listen carefully to the answers.
6. Try to establish your personal credentials as someone knowledgeable about the product, industry, or both.
7. Promise a future action that will move the prospect closer toward a decision (conduct a survey, provide an answer to the prospect's technical question, deliver a sample, or arrange a demo).
8. Leave, and deliver on the future action promise.

Learning how to listen

Of all of the above steps, questioning and listening are the most important. Uncovering the benefits that will influence people and organizations to change requires learning how to be a good listener. Just about everyone who has been in sales for any period of time has known salespeople who could make a brilliant sales pitch but never seemed able to land any deals. Perhaps they lacked the ability to listen. They knew what they wanted to sell, but they never bothered to learn what their prospects wanted to buy.

Many experts believe that the ratio of listening to talking should be four to one. That means for 80 percent of the time salespeople should be keeping their mouths shut and their ears open. (That ratio works in personal relationships too. Try listening four times as often as talking and people will flock to befriend you.)

Why is listening effective? Because it's the way to find out what the other person thinks is important. In business, and personal, relationships, people will tell you exactly what needs to be done to get the deal. They also learn what the problems are. The salesperson who only talks will never learn about the obstacles that stand in way of making the sale.

How to ask questions and what questions to ask

Attentive listening means more than merely propping up your elbows on the other person's desk and sitting there with an attentive expression on your face. Questions must be asked. The best questions are the open-ended kind that require exposition. Avoid questions that can be answered with yes or no. Show interest in the answers and let the answers lead to other questions. Don't interrupt, except to show that you have understood.

One way to demonstrate to the responder that you have listened and understood is to occasionally summarize what the other person has said. Summarizing also gives the other person the opportunity to correct any misunderstanding.

The trick is to ask the right number of questions. Too many and the questioning becomes an unpleasant interrogation, even a cross-examination. Too few indicates a lack of interest. Appearing judgmental ("I can't believe your company is still following that antiquated procedure!") is a quick way to get the other party to stop talking.

What happens when the questioning is over

Responding to questions should result in a payoff for the respondent so that he or she doesn't feel time has been wasted. This payoff comes in two forms:

1. The salesperson summarizes the entire conversation, emphasizing the highlight: "At last," the respondent thinks, "someone who understands my problems!"

2. The questioner promises a future action that will benefit the prospect: "I may have a solution for that bottleneck you have in order processing. I'll do a study and get back to you with the results next week."

These payoffs can be applied to any questioning or probing situation, even when selling internally, or in personal relationships.

MAKING PRESENTATIONS

Effective persuasion requires four times as much listening as talking, but there is a time when the salesperson must explain the benefits to an individual or group if there are going to be any changes. This explanation process is called "making a presentation." The presentation may be before a group or a single individual. (Keep in mind that the more people attending a presentation, the more objections to proposition the salesperson can expect.) The hope-for result is a decision to change—in other words, an order!

All the prior work of gaining an appointment, establishing credibility, asking questions, doing surveys, and so forth, leads to the presentation. There is so much riding on presentations they often make even experienced salespeople nervous. There are ways to reduce this nervousness.

1. *Be prepared*. Understand the benefits of the proposition to the customer. Know what you wish to say and the end result you hope to achieve.

2. *Practice*. Go over the presentation again and again. Use guinea pigs, such as the spouse or fellow workers, as a sample audience.

3. *Take along notes*. If you have a podium, the audience can't see them. If you're at a table, they can be placed in front of you. Even if the notes never get out of your pocket or purse, they are a comfort.

4. *Get to the presentation room early*. You'll have a chance to relax, check out the facilities, and go over those notes.

5. *Check out the props*. If slide projectors, videos, and so forth will be used, make sure they are on site and working properly.

6. *Make sure there are friends or coworkers in the audience who will be rooting for you.* Speak directly to one of them when making your presentation.

7. *Start by telling them what you're going to tell them.* Tell them. Summarize by telling them what you told them. Then give them a written copy of the presentation on their way out.

8. *"Bundle" questions from the audience.* Questions taken and answered at random can distract both the presenter and the audience. Promise to respond to questions at specific points in the presentation.

9. *Use a presentation style that comes naturally to you.* If you can't tell jokes, don't try for humor.

10. *Don't ramble.* You'll lose the audience. Keep the presentation brief and to the point.

11. *Know your audience.* Senior-level executives will want to know the bottom line. Engineers will want to know how the darn contraption works. Middle managers will want to know how much trouble it will be incorporating the changes into their current routine.

A simple tip that helps persuade others

Say what needs to be said several times. Never assume that the prospect completely understands what is being presented. Sometimes information, no matter how well presented, take time to sink in. After reflection, the prospect may be persuaded, but doesn't always acknowledge the "conversion." That's why good persuaders repeat the salient points in their presentations several times. They will list the benefits in the body of the presentation, go over them in a summary, and talk about them still a third time if the prospect appears undecided. This tactic of repetition is effective no matter what is being sold. To sell more, repeat the benefits more often.

VISUAL AIDS–INVOLVE THE SENSES

Any presentation is helped by the use of visual aids. If you're just talking about the proposition only one of the prospect's senses, hearing, is involved. Use charts and graphs and two senses are now engaged. Put a product out where prospects can touch and feel it, and a third sense has come into play. The more senses used to engaged the prospect, the better.

Charts and graphs, for example, help prospects understand relationships between numbers. It's more effective to show on a chart how a proposed maintenance program will increase the lifespan of a product than it is to simply quote the percentages. Typical props for visual aids include:

- Easels.
- Overhead projections.
- Videos.
- Computer generated graphics.
- Chalkboards.
- Slides.

WHY PROSPECTS MAKE OBJECTIONS

Most presentations don't result in a mad rush to sign the order pad. One reason is because people resist change. This resistance comes in the form of objections which are the reasons why changes should not be made; they are a cry for the status quo. Some of the reasons may be valid, others merely are reflections of fear.

You can expect to hear the following typical objections:

- It costs too much.
- I'd like to do it, but there's no money in the budget.
- We don't do things like that here.
- I haven't got the time or people to do that.
- It won't work.
- We've got other fish to fry right now.

These objections may seem varied, but they are really all the same reason in different disguises: The salesperson hasn't proven the value of the proposition. When the value is obvious, fear diminishes. Fear never completely disappears. That's why salespeople must continually reassure customers after agreement has been reached.

Proving the value of the proposition means going over the benefits. In a commercial proposition, the benefits typically promise the prospect that they will:

- Save time.
- Save money.
- Save people.
- Save aggravation.
- Add prestige.
- Give a secure feeling.

There are others, but these are the big ones. Prove one or more of these benefits, and the objections melt away.

How to handle objections: A seven-point program

1. One of the most difficult things for new salespeople to learn is that not all objections need be answered. If the prospect loves everything about the proposition, the sale has been made. It's the salesperson's job to repeat all the positive points about a product. If they outweigh the negative, chances are a sale will be made.

2. When an objection is made by a prospect, the salesperson should repeat it back in his or her own words. This shows the objection has been acknowledged and understood. Repeating it has a way of softening the objection, somehow making it seem frivolous.

3. Write every objection down on a pad. Ask the prospect if the list is complete. Add any others mentioned. Then answer the objections one by one, checking them off the pad as you do.

4. Refer to objections as "questions." This makes them appear less of a barrier to a sale.

5. Act pleased when an objection is raised. Treat it as an opportunity to clarify or review an issue.

6. Use the answering of objections as the launching pad for the prospect's commitment: "If I can satisfy you on this one issue, do we have a deal?"

7. The important thing to remember is that objections are selling opportunities. Without them, there would be no need for salespeople; order takers would suffice.

Objections will also occur when people are selling internally. There's always one department, one higher-level manager, who wants to retain the status quo. Treat these objections for what they are: resistance to change.

Body language

Smart salespeople learn to read the body language of their prospects. Physical movements are good indicators to what a person is thinking or feeling. The following are hints that body movements provide:

1. *Arms folded across the chest.* This is a very defensive posture. The person is determined not to be persuaded by anything the salesperson says. Rather than going into the sales pitch, the salesperson should try to relax the prospect.

2. *Leaning back, or eyes shifting to papers on a desk or across a room, or glancing at the telephone.* The salesperson is losing the prospect's interest. Set off some flares or rockets!

3. *Leaning forward, nodding in agreement. Smiling.* These are signs of interest or agreement. If the salesperson also leans forward at this point, some intimacy may be established.

4. *Big, big desk between salesperson and prospect.* The big desk serves two purposes. First, it is a barrier the prospect has placed in the salesperson's path. (You've gotten this far, but you won't come one step closer.) Second, the desk proves the prospect's importance.

This body language is used every day in every office and not just when salespeople are about. They can help you interpret the reaction to any proposition or proposal, both external and internal.

Asking for the order

Asking for the order is known as closing. It is the natural conclusion of everything that has gone on before in trying to convince a prospect to take a certain action. After the probing has been completed, the benefits found, the presentation made, the objections answered, it's time to ask the prospect to make a decision to go forward. Few prospects are so overwhelmingly convinced of the benefits of the proposition that they will make this decision on their own. They must be "nudged" into it.

Many salespeople hesitate at this point because they are afraid of rejection. If the prospect says no now, all the work that has gone on before is wasted. This hesitation drives sales managers crazy. Closing is the final step and it cannot be avoided by any salesperson who wants to be a success.

There are two ways to overcome the fear of asking for an order:

- Be genuinely convinced that the order has been earned by the amount of work done for the prospect in uncovering the benefits.
- Be genuinely convinced that the benefits of the proposition are real and will result in real advantages for the prospect.

Closing techniques

There are as many ways to close as there are leaves on trees. They all work when used by experienced salespeople. Many of these methods are called "disguised closes," in that the salesperson doesn't appear to be asking for the order, but asks the customer to make a decision on something else that results in an order. There is nothing wrong, however, with simply directly asking the prospect for a decision to move forward. If the answer is negative, repeat the benefits of the proposition. If the answer is still negative, repeat how the objections have all been resolved. If the answer is still negative, go over the proposition again from top to bottom.

Take all these steps and you've asked for the order four times. That's more times than most salespeople. Your closing ratio will certainly increase.

A LIST OF WINNING SALES CHARACTERISTICS

The cliché of the successful sales personality is that of a glad-handing, fast-talking extrovert who will say anything to get a customer's signature on the dotted line. Thank heaven it's just that, a cliché with no relation to reality. The truth is that many personality types succeed in sales. There is no standard, and business would suffer if there were.

There are, however, certain character traits that are invaluable to those who seek careers in sales. They are the same characteristics that make people successful in other business careers and personal relationships as well. The good news is that these traits are not necessarily inborn. They can be acquired.

1. *Reliability.* Successful salespeople build confidence and trust by doing what they say they're going to do.

2. *Empathy.* Sales winners genuinely like their customers and prospects. They're interested in solving their clients' problems. Guess what? People can't help liking those who like them. If nothing else, they admire their exquisite taste.

3. *Patience.* Sales winners understand that business must be earned. They don't try to rush things.

4. *Honesty.* Successful salespeople don't lie to their customers or to the managers of the company. They're not evasive. When asked, they give their opinions candidly.

5. *Industry.* Successful salespeople put in full days, every day. The value of just plain hard work can't be overemphasized.

6. *Persistence.* Winners don't give up and go on to something else when things look bleak. This may be the most valuable character trait of all.

7. *Grace under pressure.* Hemingway had it right. The ability, or fortitude, to maintain poise when things are falling apart is still the most admired trait.

All of these character traits are invaluable to any endeavor, including sales. They can be acquired by those who are convinced they are worth having.

Bonus Section

Start-Up Sales and Marketing: A Primer for Entrepreneurs

BONUS SECTION

How to get started:
What every entrepreneur should ask

You have this sensational idea for a business. As a creative breakthrough, this idea ranks right up there with the invention of the wheel or the silicon computer chip. This baby can't miss! It will make you a pile and, by Jove, you're actually going to take a crack at it. Before you mortgage the house, rent out the children, and ask your spouse if he or she would be inconvenienced by working two jobs, ask yourself one simple question about your terrific concept: Where will the customers come from?

This question is not an attempt to throw cold water on your brainchild—a dash of reality perhaps, but not cold water. The question is, however, the beginning of marketing. Marketing is nothing more than figuring out where your customers will come from and then making it attractive for them to come to you—Boy, is that second part hard.

Too many entrepreneurs with ingenious ideas, boundless energy, and excellent organizational skills have only a suspicion of who, exactly, will buy their products or services. This is plain silly: Why would anyone want to open a business with only a vague idea of who will support it? So ask yourself early on, who are these folks or organizations you hope will sustain your enterprise with their custom.

When thinking about the answer, it's important to be specific. The following section will tell what you need to know about your potential customers.

351

FOUR QUESTIONS TO HELP IDENTIFY POTENTIAL CUSTOMERS

1. What do the potential customers for your product or service look like? Form a mental image of their demographics: Are they affluent? Middle class? College educated? Married? Teens? DINKS (*Double Income, No Kids*)? If the product or service is aimed at commercial organizations, what are their profiles? Are they big or small companies? What industries will the product serve?

2. Where do the potential customers hide out? Are they located in major metropolitan areas? Small towns? The suburbs? Everywhere? People passing by on the way to the subway stop?

3. What do the potential customers want? If you're a dry cleaner, for example, are the customers you're targeting more interested in service, convenience, low price, or something else? Better find out before you open the doors for business.

4. What will encourage potential customers to buy your product or service instead of from someone else's? With this question we're getting into the value that your enterprise will be adding. More on this topic later.

Thinking through the answers to these questions is called identifying potential markets. It is an important exercise. Marketing research companies have some very sophisticated, and expensive, methods for identifying potential markets. Most budding entrepreneurs can't afford these kind of studies, but they must spend time researching this important subject.

If a profile of a likely customer (a prospect) can be developed before the business is officially opened, the chances of that business becoming a success are vastly improved. The answer to the question, where will the customers come from, also shapes and molds the business. It will help determine things such as:

- The product or service that will be provided.
- Where the company will be located.
- How the product will be distributed.
- How the product will be packaged. (A product aimed at teenagers will be packaged differently from a product aimed at retirees.)

WHERE MY CUSTOMERS WILL COME FROM WORKSHEET

My business is: _____

_____

_____

_____

_____

My customers will come from _____

_____

_____

_____

_____

These customers want the following: _____

_____

_____

_____

_____

This is a profile of a typical customer: _____

_____

_____

_____

_____

_____

These customers can be found:_____

_____

_____

_____

- How much money is needed to start and run the business.
- How the product will be priced and packaged.
- Just about everything else associated with the enterprise.

As a beginning marketing exercise—this is basic, basic stuff—prepare the sample worksheet (see p. 353) on just where you expect the customers for your enterprise will come from. Think about the answers carefully. This will be the most important marketing problem any entrepreneur can address. It is also the hardest. If you can't come up with logical answers, if you just have this deep, abiding faith that customers will suddenly materialize at the appropriate time, a gift from the gods, then your business idea is in trouble. Deep trouble.

Keep the worksheet close at hand as you make your business plans and decisions. Refer to it when you think about the product or service you plan to offer. Revise and update this worksheet as you learn from experience. It won't look the same one year, or even six months, from now, but it's a start.

STATEMENT OF PURPOSE

In the sample worksheet we tried to sneak something past you. Did you notice it? The worksheet asks you to define your business idea in a few lines. No extra paper or lines were allowed if you ran out of room. That limitation was a deliberate attempt to determine if you have a concise idea of what your enterprise is all about. That idea is described in the company's statement of purpose.

The statement of purpose is the foundation of any business marketing plan. Many experts feel it is the very first thing any entrepreneur should do. If developing such a statement is difficult, if you can't put your finger on the core idea behind your enterprise, then work on it until you can. Distill, limit, refine, and focus the concept until you can describe your business idea in the few lines allowed. Be precise. If you only have a vague idea of what your business is all about, so will your potential customers.

ADDING VALUE

Potential customers are out there, but what, specifically, is going to make them beat a path to your door? They managed to get along nicely before your enterprise existed. What will attract them to you? The answer is the value your company adds. Adding value is what makes any business special. It can involve an infinite variety of business activities. The following are a few examples:

1. The local greengrocer's added value is buying fresh fruits and vegetables in bulk, displaying them attractively in a retail setting, and making them accessible to customers in the neighborhood.
2. The steelmaker's added value is shipping in iron ore and converting it into finished steel in a variety of forms and selling the finished product to industry.
3. The temporary employment firm's added value is finding qualified workers and providing them to industry on a short-term basis.
4. A distributor's added value is buying products in large quantities, warehousing these products, and selling them in smaller quantities to dealers and end-users.
5. An assembler's added value is buying parts and subassemblies from various sources and putting them together in a finished product.

Each one of these companies did something to the product as it "passed through" to give it added value. The greengrocer displayed the fruit and vegetables to make them more attractive. The steelmaker converted the iron ore. The temporary employment agency maintained a database of qualified people so they could quickly respond to a client's labor problem.

What is your enterprise's added value? Describe it in a few words.

My company's added value is: _____

_____

_____

POSITIONING, OR GOING AFTER A MARKET SEGMENT

No matter what product or service you offer, you will not be the only company doing what you do. In fact, the bigger the market there is for your kind of product, the more competitors who will be out there, anxious to provide it also.

Small, new companies that wish to distinguish themselves from others in the same general category often try to cater to a particular market segment. That is, they deliberately limit what they do so they can better focus on one kind of customer. This focus allows them to better cater to the customers' needs.

The advantage of this approach is that the companies which specialize may eventually gain a reputation for their specialities. This reputation further enhances their market position. An example is Gerber's baby foods. They are food canners, just as Green Giant and Del Monte are food canners, but they are not direct competitors with them. They distinguish themselves by processing the food into a mush that is palatable to infants and packaging it in very small glass containers. Gerber's has several direct competitors, but it's fair to say they own the market segment. They have accomplished this by processing and packaging their product differently.

NICHE MARKETING

Niche marketing means going after a market segment that has been ignored, or is too small to attract the attention of the big boys. It is often an excellent strategy for new and small companies to follow. One of my associates who serves a niche market used to say, "I live on the soft underbelly of big business."

An example of niche marketing is the candy manufacturer who distributes the company's products through churches and schools. These institutions then sell the candy in their fund-raising campaigns. The candy is packaged by the manufacturer to make the fund-raising easier. The manufacturer won't enjoy the same sales volume as Hershey or Mars, but he also isn't fighting these giant competitors for shelf space at the grocery chains.

Marketing exercise: find a market that others have ignored and figure out how to go after it. Going after it means configuring the product or service to meet the market's needs. Many entrepreneurs have discovered niche markets because they needed or wanted something for themselves that wasn't readily available. When they learned that others wanted that same thing, their enterprise was born.

How to specialize

Specialization can take many different forms. Companies can choose to specialize or aim at a particular market segment through:

- The product itself.
- The service offered.
- The packaging. (Put a pretty plastic pink handle on a razor and it is transformed into a "woman's" razor suitable for legs and underarms.)
- The location.
- The advertising. (If you're selling leather belts you're going to reach a different kind of customer by advertising in *Guns and Ammo* as opposed to *GQ*.)
- The price.
- The distribution channels.

Any enterprise in any market can specialize to appeal to a particular market segment. As an example, let's return to our entrepreneur who wishes to start a dry-cleaning operation. For a dry cleaner, being different would appear to be a difficult challenge. Major metropolitan areas have dry cleaners on almost every street corner. There is nothing proprietary about the service they offer. No special skills are needed. Anyone who has the money to lease dry-cleaning equipment and a store location can get into the business. A new dry cleaner still has a variety of options to distinguish the service offered from others. The dry cleaner can focus on:

1. Value: inexpensive pricing.
2. Quality: providing hand-blocked pressing and handling delicate garments.
3. Environmental correctness: using nontoxic chemicals.
4. Service: providing one-hour turn-around on cleaning or home delivery.
5. One-stop shopping: locating the shop in a strip mall, close to a subway stop, or next to a popular grocery supermarket.
7. Minor tailoring: repairing tears, alterations, sewing buttons and hems.
8. Custom work: handling certain items such as heavy comforters and blankets, drapes, and curtains, not normally accommodated by average dry cleaners.
9. Some combination of the above.

Which of these services to provide depends on the entrepreneur's perception of what is most important to local clientele, which services offer the most potential for growth, and where the most profit can be made. By selecting certain services the dry cleaner is positioned against the other dry cleaners in the area.

As an exercise, decide how you will position your company against all the others out there. What will make your company different from every other company in the market?

POSITIONING WORKSHEET

I will go after the following market segment(s): _____

_____

_____

_____

I will do so by distinguishing my product or service in the following way: ___

_____

_____

_____

WHAT MAKES CUSTOMERS BUY

Why should customers buy from your enterprise instead of the one next door, or in the next county, or one that is half way across the world? In the tenuous form of prospects, customers are all about you; but they have managed quite nicely up to now, thank you, without the product or service you intend to offer. They're contented folk. What's going to make these blissful people plunk down their money for your company's goods or services?

When searching for an answer, there's a need to be specific because customers need a clear reason to make buying decisions. As a hint, here are the typical reasons why people buy:

1. *Price.* You can sell these hesitant darlings what they need cheaper than their current source. (Saving a few pennies is one of the least convincing reasons to impel change.)

2. *Service*. You can get the product to them faster, or you're there with advice and corrective action when things go wrong.

3. *Convenience*. You're located next store, or on the way home, or you take orders on the phone so you can provide faster delivery.

4. *Superior quality*. You use better parts, or superior engineering, or offer a longer warranty. The stuff you provide never breaks down.

5. *Easy credit*. You offer longer payment terms or little money down.

6. *Innovation*. You have developed a revolutionary product or service that is not available from other sources.

7. *Name recognition*. You've spent more on advertising than anyone else in the industry.

8. *Savings*. Your product costs less to operate over the long run.

9. *Emotion*. Your product makes customers feel good about themselves.

10. *Prestige*. Your product is exclusive and shows the buyer's good taste. (Both Rolex and Casio watches keep good time. The Rolex displayed on the wrist, however, shows that the wearer has "arrived.")

Make a list of the things your company can offer that will motivate people or organizations to buy.

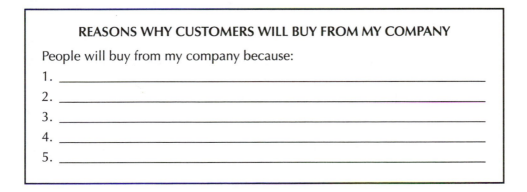

REASONS WHY CUSTOMERS WILL BUY FROM MY COMPANY

People will buy from my company because:

1. _____
2. _____
3. _____
4. _____
5. _____

We kept this exercise short on purpose. If you came up with more than five solid reasons, you're probably too optimistic. Marketing plans shouldn't be based on blue-sky scenarios.

With the completion of these exercises, your marketing plan is beginning to come together. You now know the following things about your budding business:

1. The purpose of your enterprise.
2. Who your potential customers are.
3. The value added the company will provide.
4. The market segment you plan to attack.
5. How you plan to shape the product or service to appeal to that market segment.
6. The salient reasons why prospects should buy from your company.

Congratulations. You've come a long way. Many entrepreneurs invest time and money into an enterprise and never acquire this basic knowledge. There is, however, still a lot of marketing distance to go before you are fully ready to open for business.

DISTRIBUTING THE PRODUCT

How do you plan to get the product into the hands of end-users? Will you sell it directly, using company personnel to call on end-users? Will you sell through dealers, retailers, or distributors? How the product or service will be distributed is a key decision, one that requires careful thought.

Some products almost dictate the distribution method that will be used. For example, fine china is primarily sold through upscale retail establishments. Some china is also sold via mail order, and every discounter carries "stoneware." But for really fine china go to Bloomingdales, Saks, or Neiman Marcus.

Women, who are the primary buyers of fine china, prefer to shop where they can see samples of the product and choose among different patterns. A manufacturer of fine china must develop sales and marketing plans that will convince upscale retailers that carrying the line of china will be profitable.

Some distribution methods require more marketing and sales expense than others. Selling the product directly to end-users requires a larger sales staff and that means more salaries. The advantage of direct selling is that it gives the company the most control.

Offering the product to large third-party distributors means the company need maintain only a small sales force, but the fate of the product is in the hands of a few companies who may not do a good job.

Selling directly to end-users through mail order is becoming increasingly popular. Dell Computer and Gateway Computer have both emerged as billion-dollar companies in the last ten years by using a telephone sales/mail-order strategy.

Typical distribution channels

When considering which distribution channels are most appropriate for your company's product or service, you may wish to choose from among the following:

- Through a sales force that directly contacts end-users. Many industrial and commercial products are sold in this manner.
- Through retailers. This category covers a wide range of establishments from upscale department stores to mass merchants such as Wal-Mart.
- Through dealers or distributors.
- Through independent third-party resellers, such as manufacturer's reps.
- Through mail order.
- Through telephone solicitation (telemarketing).
- Through the Internet and World Wide Web.

Check off the channels you wish to use, remembering that it isn't necessary to restrict distribution to a single channel. Many companies move their products through several channels, making minor alterations or cosmetic changes in the product to avoid conflicts.

There are trade-offs with any channel:

1. Distributors require heavy product demand before they will agree to carry it. They can't afford to allocate warehouse space to products that do not move out quickly.

2. Mass merchants may offer heavy volume, but their marketing muscle is such that they can extract very low prices from their suppliers. This means the suppliers to these organizations must operate at low profit margins.

3. Manufacturer's reps offer low initial sales expense, but the coverage is often indifferent.

4. Upscale retailers will often discontinue a product if it is also sold through discounters because they can't compete on price.

5. Retail grocery chains often demand shelf fees before agreeing to stock a product.

THE IMPORTANCE OF LOCATION

With the advent of FedEx and other one-day shipping services, maintaining a local presence is not as important as it once was in industrial sales. Products can be delivered from central warehouses the next day. Fax machines and online services provide instant communication.

It is still more efficient, however, to be as close as possible to potential customers. Being close to the customers they hope to serve is a good strategy for small and start-up companies. You'll sell more fertilizer in an Iowa farming community than you will in New York City.

Location is all-important in retail sales. Our dry cleaner attracts customers from the surrounding neighborhood. The kind of neighborhood it is determines the type of services the dry cleaner offers. In a lower- or middle-class neighborhood, the dry cleaner might opt for budget-type cleaning. In an upscale neighborhood the cleaner might specialize in handling evening clothes.

Sometimes the best location is next door to another enterprise offering the same product or service:

1. The mall with upscale stores attracts shoppers with large disposable incomes.
2. "Restaurant Row" attracts diners seeking an evening out.
3. A street with half a dozen jewelry stores will attract young men and women shopping for engagement rings.

In these instances, being close to the competition is an advantage.

Location doesn't matter in every business. When it makes no difference, site costs should be kept at a minimum. Prestige can come later.

The following simple worksheet can help you decide where your business should be located.

LOCATION WORKSHEET

In my type of business I need to be close to my customers:

Yes ___ No ___

My potential customers are located: _____

_____

_____

My competitors are located: _____

_____

_____

ADVERTISING

The new company must decide on how potential customers will learn about the product or service it offers. The answer almost always is through advertising, but advertising can be expensive and the results are often uncertain.

Still, every new enterprise should allocate a certain percentage of its marketing budget to advertising. The question is, How much is the right percentage?

1. For a retail dry cleaner, sufficient advertising might be a sign in the window and flyers handed out to passers-by.
2. For a company manufacturing a product aimed at a certain industry, advertising might be required in an industry publication.
3. A dealer in office equipment might send a direct-mail piece to surrounding businesses.
4. A grocery store might advertise weekly specials in a local newspaper.

Marketing exercise: Calculate what your company's advertising budget will be and determine how it will be spent. Research the rates and efficacy for various media choices.

Seven questions to ask before committing money to an advertising campaign

When making plans for advertising, the marketing manager should ask the following questions:

1. How much can I afford to spend?
2. What do I want the advertising to accomplish?
3. What markets/prospects am I trying to reach?
4. What media choices are most appropriate for reaching these markets?
5. What message do I want to deliver to these markets?
6. How do I determine if the advertising is successful? How do I define success?
7. Should I use an advertising agency? (In almost all instances the answer is Yes! Yes! Yes!)

NEW PRODUCT ANNOUNCEMENTS: A VEHICLE FOR FREE ADVERTISING

Want some free publicity? Most industry trade publications include a section that carries information about new products that have applications for organizations within that industry. It is a service the magazine offers its subscribers to keep them current with industry developments. Companies with new products, or new companies entering the marketplace, can get free space in these sections by sending the magazine a press kit with the following information:

1. A press release form containing the product announcement. This release should include all pertinent information about the product; its applications, specifications, and features; when it will be available; and how it applies to the industry.
2. A picture of the product or a product brochure.
3. The name of someone in the company the magazine editor can contact for further information.

The magazine will usually carry the story in its new product review section. In essence, the company has just received a free advertising plug. Any inquiries about the product will be forwarded to the company because the magazine is looking for new advertisers and each inquiry proves just how effective that magazine is. Expect a call from a space salesperson for the magazine when the release is run.

Marketing exercise: This one is easy and it's practically cost free. Find the trade publications for the industries that use the company's products. Put together a press kit and send it off to the editors. (Obviously, this won't work if the product has been around for twenty years.)

TEST MARKETING: A CAUTIONARY TALE

Some ideas seem wonderful when being discussed, but fail miserably in the marketplace. That's why products, advertising, and sales strategies should be test marketed whenever possible. Don't manufacture large quantities of the product until there's evidence that the marketplace accepts it. Don't send a million direct-mail pieces until there's proof that the letters produce a sufficient return. Direct-mail professionals tinker with the cover letter, with the offer, with the enclosures, with selected market segments, sending out small batches of mail until they find a successful formula.

Start-ups and small companies don't have a lot of money to spend on test marketing. They can, however, solicit the opinions of impartial observers, potential customers, and industry experts.

Test marketing gives marketing managers the opportunity to fine tune products, ideas, advertising, and marketing campaigns. It is not a guarantee of success, but it improves the chances for success.

Marketing exercise: Determine how your company's product or service can be market tested before committing large sums to manufacturing or distribution.

USING OUTSIDE SERVICES TO JUMP-START MARKETING

New companies usually have limited internal resources. The entrepreneur may have a great idea for a product, or be knowledgeable in production, but unless the company was started by a marketing type, there may be no one on board who is an experienced marketer. These companies should consider the use of outside services to help develop marketing campaigns. Some obvious avenues for these kinds of services are:

1. Small advertising agencies who can help with logo design, promotions, brochures, and putting a limited advertising budget to best use.

2. Direct-mail companies who maintain large databases and can zero in on your company's potential markets. These companies design, conduct, and monitor direct-mail campaigns.

3. The Small Business Administration which offers the services of retired business executives to counsel new companies in all aspects of business, including marketing.

4. State-run agencies which help small businesses get started.

5. Local colleges and universities which often offer low-cost business consulting services.

6. Industry associations which offer seminars on marketing topics relevant to the industry.

7. The local library which has many books on monthly publications on marketing.

POACHING FOR CUSTOMERS

Are the kids out of the room? We're going to discuss the facts of life now: Almost all new businesses begin as poachers. The customers they bag were grazing in some other company's game preserve. The super discount chain drives mom-and-pop stores out of business. The door-to-door Bible salesman takes sales from the local bookstore.

This phenomenon is true even with breakthrough products. When Thomas Edison began installing electric lighting in large cities, he took customers away from the gas company. When Henry Ford starting selling automobiles, he put the buggy manufacturers out to pasture.

Even though the benefits of these products are obvious to us now, they weren't all that apparent to people at the time. The appearance of early automobiles, on the streets were inevitably greeted with cries, of "Get a horse." Many people felt that electricity "in the air" could be harmful to humans. These lessons of the past are useful to the marketer. Anything really innovative is likely to be greeted with derision, or fear, or both.

As proprietor of a new enterprise, you're going to have to be a poacher too. The customers you hope to acquire are currently doing business elsewhere. If you feel this practice is distasteful or unethical, then a business venture is not for you. The question is not whether customers should be lured away, but rather how.

Defining the specific reasons why customers should stop doing business with what they consider a reliable source and now buy from you adds a new factor to the marketing problem. It is competition. The companies your potential customers are buying from now are those nasty folk: your competitors. The first thing you need to know to successfully compete is who they are.

When armies go to war, their military intelligence services compile dossiers on the opposing forces. Here's what they want to know about the other side:

- Who are they?
- Where are they?
- What are their strengths?
- What are their weaknesses?
- How have they fought past battles?
- What are they likely to do in this battle?

All of these questions, plus a few others, can be modified to apply to business competition:

- What service or product do they provide?
- How do they market this product or service?
- How do they price their products?
- What, exactly, makes them successful?
- What are their perceived weak points?

Determining the answers to questions such as these is called competitive analysis or competitive intelligence. It is a sophisticated marketing technique, and here you are about to take a crack at it.

Begin by filling out the following worksheet for every potential competitor you can think of:

COMPETITIVE ANALYSIS WORKSHEET

Name of Competitor _____

Location _____

Products or services sold _____

_____

_____

_____

Marketing Method: ___ Direct ___ Dealers ___ Retailers ___ Wholesalers
___ Catalogs ___ Direct mail ___ Radio & TV ads ___ Internet
___ Other channels _____

List of their best customers _____

_____

_____

_____

Pricing policy _____

_____

Competitor's strong points_____

_____

_____

Competitor's weak points:* _____

_____

_____

What competitor is likely to do next:** _____

_____

_____

_____

*You're far better off worrying about competitors' strong points than developing a false sense of optimism over perceived chinks in their armor.

**When hunting ducks the hunter doesn't aim directly at the flying bird, but rather at a position in the sky where he thinks the duck will be when the shot arrives. It is the same with competitive analysis. The marketer doesn't set sights on what competitors are doing now, but rather what they will be doing in the foreseeable future.

Eight ethical ways to gather information about the competition

How do you obtain the kind of information needed to complete this worksheet? Observation and a little honest digging will be your best assistants.

1. If the product you hope to provide is sold through retailers, go to a store and see how competitive products are priced through this channel.

2. If feasible, buy a competitive product and take it apart to see how it is made.

3. Send for competitive literature.

4. Attend trade shows and stop at your competitors' booths.

5. If the competition has a toll-free HELP line, call it and ask questions.

6. If the competition are public companies, obtain copies of their annual reports.

7. Talk to their customers. What do these customers like about your competitors' products or services? What don't they like? You won't always get a candid response, but you may obtain useful information.

8. Talk to competing salespeople whenever possible. You'll be surprised at how much information they will reveal.

None of these activities are unethical if you don't misrepresent yourself. Always identify who you are and the company you work for.

Completing the worksheet is the first step in becoming a successful poacher, in taking business away from competitors. Pay particular attention to competitors' customer lists. These are the accounts you covet for your company. Now, put yourself in the minds of these customers. How strong are their loyalties to your competitors? Why should they change? Remember what we said earlier: Change is always perceived as risky. What do you have to offer that is worth the risk? Also, heed the strong points that makes your competitors successful. What are they doing that is worth copying? What are they doing that you could do better? What are they not doing for their customers that should be done?

WHEN THE OWNER OF THE COMPANY IS ALSO
THE DIRECTOR OF MARKETING AND THE SALES MANAGER

In many small outfits and start-up operations the owner of the company is also the chief marketer and sales manager. This is particularly true of the more than three million home-based businesses that open up every year. Being both marketing manager and boss has distinct advantages because decisions can be made on the spot: "You say we can have the contract if I cut the price by five percent? You got a deal!"

The obvious problem with this approach is that marketing and sales are just two of the many responsibilities of a business owner. The owner pays attention to these activities when there is time available. They become lost entirely when there are fires to put out. Then, sales disappear and the business goes down the tubes.

What is required of the owner/marketer/sales manager is discipline. Marketing is the single most important activity of any enterprise because without customers there are no company to manage and no problems to solve. The following list will help owner/marketers make sure they have paid enough attention to selling the product:

1. No matter the size of the enterprise, a marketing plan should be developed. Knowing what to do next is easier when there's a blueprint to follow.

2. The owner must put on the marketing/sales manager's hat every day. Every day! If other activities continue to interrupt the time spent on marketing, set aside certain hours of the day for marketing and selling and nothing else. Problems not related to marketing or sales are put aside during this period.

3. Use outside services such as advertising agencies, small business consultants, local agencies, and so forth to extend your marketing reach and to become more familiar with modern marketing techniques.

4. Don't cancel sales calls to solve other problems. Instead, defer problems to make sales calls.

5. When finances get tight, cut other expenditures but keep the marketing budget. There's no better way to spend scarce resources.

A marketing tip for small business owners: Being the owner, even of a small company, is impressive to other organizations. Use your title to marketing advantage when making sales calls. Your title will get you more appointments, and that will result in more sales.

THE TWELVE BIG REASONS WHY BUSINESSES FAIL

Start-up operations have a very high failure rate. This statement is not offered for discouragement, but rather as one of caution. The failure rate can be reduced by observing the common mistakes other entrepreneurs have made. The following are the "dirty dozen." They don't all directly relate to marketing, but most of them do.

1. They began their businesses with insufficient capital. This is the number-one reason for failure. (Rule of thumb: You'll need twice as much money as you thought you would.)

2. They expected to take money out of the business much too soon. This puts an added burden on any enterprise because it must become a quick success. When beginning an enterprise, set money aside for living expenses. Don't draw a salary from the business until profits can support that salary.

3. They had no specific marketing plan. Every enterprise needs one.

4. They had no specific budget for marketing.

5. They had no specific idea of who their potential customers might be, where they might be located, or what they might want.

6. They didn't spend enough time on selling.

7. They didn't test market the concept.

8. They failed to use outside services who had the necessary expertise.

9. They didn't value advertising.

10. They spent too much money on frills before the business generated enough money to support those expenditures.

11. They didn't generate enough cash flow. This is vital to keep a business going.

12. They underestimated their costs and didn't price the product or service to produce a profit.

HIT THE GROUND RUNNING:
SIXTEEN FAST AND EASY MARKETING TIPS

Now you know where your customers will come from, you know the market segment you will go after, you know the value you will add to the product or service, you know why customers should change what they're doing now, you've done a simple competitive analysis, and you've completed the marketing exercises and worksheets in this chapter. What you have is a basic marketing plan.

You're now anxious to get started. Here are sixteen quick, inexpensive steps you can can make, even before a more formal marketing plan is completed, that will help get you off the blocks fast:

1. Don't hide your light under a bushel. Let all your friends, neighbors, and business acquaintances know that you're going into business. Tell them about the product or service you intend to offer and when it will be available. You may get some business through word-of-mouth.

2. You'll need an identity for your enterprise. Select a company name and have a logo designed. (Use an ad agency or graphic artist for this.)

3. Get a business phone installed, preferably a fax phone, and buy a small Yellow Pages listing. The listings are usually inexpensive. You can decide about a big display ad later.

4. Get stationery and business cards printed. Hand out cards to anyone who will take them.

5. Join the appropriate trade association for your product or service. This move gives your enterprise immediate credibility. Use the association's services. In addition to promoting conventions and trade shows, many associations offer statistical information and marketing assistance.

6. Join the local chamber of commerce or merchant association. Attend meetings. Participate!

7. Visit the local Small Business Administration (SBA) office in your city. Many offices employ retired business people who offer marketing advice to small companies. While you're at the SBA, ask them about sales opportunities with federal agencies in the area.

8. Send an announcement about your company's formation to the local newspaper. They may give you free publicity.

9. Send product release bulletins to appropriate trade magazines. Most of these magazines will print news about new products or new companies free of charge. They'll even pass along leads that result in the hope that you'll advertise in their publication.

10. Visit local government agencies, schools, and military bases to get on their competitive bid lists. Competitive bidding is a quick way to build sales volume if you don't mind working on low margins.

11. If you're a retail merchant, visit the other retail merchants in the vicinity. Discuss joint marketing efforts such as sidewalk sales. Discuss promoting one another's merchandise or service. Discuss the possibility of displaying signs and advertising in one another's windows.

12. Participate in local business shows, particularly if the entry costs are low.

13. Print flyers illustrating your product or service and distribute them to local companies, or on the street. Flyers are an inexpensive way to get your company's name before potential customers fast.

14. Have brochures printed that describe your product or service. If you can't afford an advertising agency, many printing companies offer design services. Distribute these brochures to target markets. Get all your printing done quickly. More elaborate or thoughtful design work can come later. To hit the ground running you want your enterprise to look as professional as fast as possible.

15. Devote several hours each day to marketing. Devote twenty-four hours a day to thinking about it. Nothing else you are doing will be as important.

16. Don't become easily discouraged. All new businesses go through rough patches. The successful business owners are the ones who persevere.

INDEX

X

Xerox, 93–94, 201

Y

Yellow Pages advertising, 47–48
   pros/cons of, 47
   purpose of, 48
   responding to sales prospects, 48

Z

Zero-based budgets, 17